MW00987114

THE
GOLDEN
NUGGET
AN ENTREPRENEUR SPEAKS

WILLIAM R. JONES, FASM
with **HEATHER IDELL**

The Golden Nugget: An Entrepreneur Speaks

Cover photo featuring a Ford Fiesta inside the hot zone of a VFS furnace, showcasing capacity of the furnace. *Photo courtesy of Heat Treating Magazine.*
Book design by Breanna Fong
Edited by Michelle Hubele Rubin

Authored by William R. Jones, Solar Atmospheres, wrj@solaratm.com and Heather L. Idell, hidellcreative@gmail.com

Printed in the United States of America
First Printing: September 2017
ISBN: 978-0-692-93657-3
Library of Congress Control Number: 2017952642

Dedication

The writings of this book are dedicated to the love of my life, friend, and life long partner, my wife Myrtle E. Jones (Myrt). Our marriage has been continuous and without argument or abuse for over 60 years. Myrt from the beginning of our marriage has maintained our home, raised our two children, and attended to all our personal family finances. Since the start of our first business Vacuum Furnace Systems, VFS, she also was co owner, backing all of our business decisions, banking, and liabilities with her personal signature, without which our companies could not have been maintained or expanded.

Besides Myrtle, my development and learning was dramatically influenced by my mother and father, Elmer S. and Agnes E. Jones, by Mr. Slaybaugh my high school science teacher, and later Penn State University. My first employer Dr. G. Bergson, my second employer Don Hall and Dr. George Bentley, IDL my third employer Charlie Hill and Vern Gooderham, and Dr. Alfred Martin, ABAR, all contributed greatly, as well. As for the start up of Vacuum Furnace Systems (VFS), this would not have happened without the influence of Charlie Hoeflich, Union National Bank, and Al Pritchard my financial advisor. It also wouldn't have been possible without all the employees of VFS and Solar Atmospheres, including my son Roger and daughter Holly Craven and her husband, Bruce. There are many others too numerous to mention such as Jim Williams of Metal Treating, Cincinnati, and Abe Willan of P&W Hartford, Conn. and still others from G.E. Evandale, Ohio. The list is almost endless, and to all of you, I'm grateful.

—William R. Jones

Bill, with wife Myrt Jones, after receiving the ASM Fellow Award.

During the interview process for this book, my good friend and former advertising agent, Ron Zorn, gave us a quote to reflect upon. He said it had always hung in his office, to remind him of the importance of staying true to your word and God's word. He gave it to us because he said he thought it rather beautifully summed up my business and life practice of honesty and integrity at all times; it made him think of me. Since he so generously shared it with us, I thought I'd share it with those who read this book. Thank you, Ron.

Aside from the strictly moral standpoint, honesty is— not only the best policy—but the only possible policy from the standpoint of business relations. The fulfillment of the pledged word is of equal necessity to the conduct of all business. If we expect and demand virtue and honor in others, the flame of both must burn brightly within ourselves and shed their light to illuminate the erstwhile dark corners of distrust and dishonesty...The truthful answer rests for the most part within ourselves, for like begets like. Honesty begets honesty; trust, trust; and so on through the whole category of desirable practices that must govern and control the world's affairs.

—James F. Bell (1879-1961), a Philadelphia-born business leader and philanthropist. Served as President and later Chairman of the Board of General Mills, Inc.

Therefore, all things whatsoever ye would that men should do to you, do ye even so to them: for this is the law and the prophets. —Matthew 7:12

Contents

BOOK 3: INNOVATIONS

BOOK 4: A REFLECTIVE LENS

TRIBUTE TO WILLIAM R. JONES

APPENDIX

Foreword

You are holding a book about the life of Bill Jones in your hands. Why was it written? Many people accomplish much more than Bill has in their lifetimes, so what makes his story particularly interesting to anyone other than his close friends and family? In fact, it may not interest many outside of the vacuum furnace or heat treating industry, however, Bill's history in this industry is only part of the story. Yes, he's had many impressive achievements throughout his career. But a book about those achievements alone might be pretty boring to most people. That's not the whole story, either.

Bill Jones wanted to leave a legacy, to his family and the industry which has served him so well. His career has been an interesting one, and in the past several years, many have asked Bill to tell the tale of how he came to be the successful businessman he is today. That's what set him on his journey, but he quickly realized…he didn't just want to tell a tale of getting from point A to point B. In addition to learning about Bill's role in the world of vacuum furnaces and heat treating, he wanted readers to understand the "why" of the story, too. And for Bill, that "why" is the essential part of the story.

The real story—the "why"—is about that ethereal element which drives all entrepreneurs; how to recognize it and how to foster it. Try describing what "makes" an entrepreneur. It's pretty hard to put into words. Anyone can be ambitious, anyone can take risks. Lots of people pursue their passion but fizzle out before they've reached their goal, whatever that may be. But true entrepreneurs possess a spark of something exceptional, something special which drives them, and, in Bill's experience, you either have it or you don't. Bill has had it all his life. This is a story of recognizing that spark, then fanning it into a flame which has burned consistently and constantly.

From quite a young age, Bill worked hard for his successes. Nothing was handed to him. For every successful entrepreneur, there's someone thinking "that guy has all the luck." Opportunities present themselves, or, a good entrepreneur can see an opportunity where others don't. You either take them or you don't.

Bill told me about a conversation he had with a man by the name of Bill Leighton, from FJ Stokes, *the* industrial vacuum pump manufacturer in Philadelphia. After Bill and his wife, Myrt, started their first company, Leighton said to Jones, "Bill, you're one of these people that, if you fell into a cesspool, you'd find a golden nugget." He said it with a mix of incredulity and humor, admiration and respect. "You lucky so and so," is what he meant. Bill remembers thinking, "It's not luck, Bill. I dug through that cesspool when others dismissed it. And you know that."

Bill's point is this: even in a difficult environment, where there's seemingly nothing much except difficulties and mess, a little searching and a little ingenuity may yield the golden nugget hidden among the muck. You find the opportunity, when others might mistake it for something considerably less appealing. That's at the heart of entrepreneurialism. The entrepreneur can see the value and opportunity where everyone else sees a worthless pit. In other words—vision.

This, then, is Bill's tale of finding and polishing golden nuggets.

—Heather Idell, co-author

The Golden Goose that begot the hot zone, depicting the start of VFS and Solar Atmospheres, from whence our funding comes.

Introduction

DAN HERRING
author of *The Heat Treat Doctor*

I have had the privilege of knowing, working for, and learning from, a number of outstanding people. While they have all helped shape me as a professional and, to a great extent, as a person, only my father—and Bill Jones—have transformed me.

Bill has left, and continues to leave, an indelible impression on my soul—as an entrepreneur, and as a creative genius. He is a humanitarian role model; a person with a true spiritual belief that our many talents come from God. He is a mentor. He is, most definitely, a "character" (perhaps his most enduring trait). He will take the time to help you succeed in life, and he is the type of human being you wouldn't mind your children striving to emulate.

Anyone who knows Bill or hears his story may wonder, what drives this man? What motivates him? What inspires him to contribute to society as he does, both personally and professionally? How has he succeeded in the face of sometime seemingly insurmountable odds?

In his book, *The Golden Nugget: An Entrepreneur Speaks,*

Bill offers unique insight into his entrepreneurial spirit, his thought processes, his hopes, dreams, fears, and the passion that drives him. He reveals the unwavering support of his wife and partner, Myrt, just as critical to his success as any financial backing. He tells of the unconditional support of family and friends, as well as stories of the many individuals he's encountered on his incredible journey in the vacuum and heat treat industries; business connections that resulted in life-long friendships. Finally, Bill provides the reader a glimpse into his faith, firmly rooted in his belief in God almighty.

But in my humble opinion, this is only part of the story. What makes Bill Jones the successful entrepreneur can't be found in business textbooks? It's in his DNA. He is the sum total of all who have come before him. Almost mythically, it would seem Bill was born under the right providence of God, an occasion that often skips multiple generations and only seldom manifests itself in a single person. The result—an indefatigable army of one. But as Bill explains, if one has passion, drive, and vision, nearly anyone can achieve unlimited potential, just as he has.

Leaders such as Bill Jones, have great vision, are driven to inspire others, are doers and not just thinkers, are bold when necessary, and are resilient and persistent at all times. Bill embodies the qualities and traits shared by great entrepreneurs and leaders. He is:

- A tireless worker
- Relentless, refusing to offer anything less than his best
- Filled with creative energy
- Curious
- A person who sees opportunity in every venture
- A person who embraces learning and shares what he has learned
- A person who leverages his life lessons to achieve his goals
- Self-confident
- A visionary

- Honest and ethical
- A motivator
- A game changer

While Bill is a certified wellspring of entrepreneurial wisdom and experience, he is, also, simply my friend. My life has been enriched by his friendship. Without a doubt, the heat treatment and vacuum furnace industries are richer for his involvement as a thought leader and influential member of their societies.

ROGER FABIAN
A Word About Bill Jones, as delivered to the 26th ASM Honorary Symposium (2011)

I t is not every day that this opportunity comes along: the opportunity to honor a man who in our industry is truly a legend in his own time.

Why the honorary symposium? It is easy just to look at what he has done for vacuum technology, and let us not forget the heat treating industry. I purchased my first 54" diameter x 48" high bottom-loading vacuum furnace from Bill when I was a neophyte in the business. I believe it was in the early 1970's. That furnace was an outstanding design, with patented moly heating elements, and has only recently been retired from active duty. That was when Bill was just a furnace builder. Bill and ABAR built many bottom-loaders, including at least one about 100" in diameter, which are still active today. I think that says something about how Bill approached that task.

So I can say in part that to honor him is to pay tribute to his furnace building career. Yes, but this symposium is really to honor a man who has been an innovator and a risk taker; a guy who learned how to be a heat treater and a brazing expert. You become an expert by using your engineering talents to look at the problem and then find a solution. That is exactly what Bill has done at Solar Atmospheres. Solar Atmospheres has vacuum heat treating and brazing shops across North America that are the envy of our industry.

You need a big vacuum furnace? Just call Bill. Solar Manufacturing builds them up to 36 feet long (now, in 2016, up to 48 feet long): just the size you need for components on the new Boeing 787 Dreamliner. I do not know anyone in our business who would have taken on the challenge of designing such large furnaces, and then actually built them. But what amazes me is Bill's ability to focus on the problem, and bring his own, and the resources of his companies, to bear on the problem. Another example: high-pressure gas quenching. Bill's companies are leaders in promoting this technology, with the use of helium and hydrogen to obtain outstanding results. This technology is game changing for our industry.

Bill has been honored for his frankness, his straightforward approach to problem-solving, his honesty, and his contribution to our industry. As I was preparing for retirement, Bill was the first person I called to ask for advice on how to approach this new time in life. His advice was sound and correct, and is being followed. I would like to personally honor Bill for all of the above, and for being my friend.

Honorably submitted,
Roger J Fabian
Past President, ASM Heat Treating Society
Past President, ASM International

BOOK 1

THE FORMATIVE YEARS

Twins "Billy and Dicky" playing with Tinkertoys.

Growing Up Experimenting

I don't believe in hiding your light under a basket. What you know, share with others as much as possible and practical. —WRJ

I had an inauspicious start in life, as most people do. I was born at home, in the middle of the Great Depression, on a steely cold day, January 30, 1935. My parents owned a small, brown, cedar shake house with two bedrooms, in a little suburb 20 miles north of Philadelphia, called Bethayres. At the time, Bethayres was a small town surrounded by farms. Ours was probably the smallest house in town. It did have indoor plumbing, though, which was a bonus, since some houses in the neighborhood still had outhouses. It was a fine little house, but it lacked insulation and storm windows, so in winter months, the inside of the glass windows would be covered in ice, and condensation would drip water on the sills. It was icy inside and out when my twin brother Dick and I were born.

These were the days before ultrasounds, so my parents

were unaware that I was not alone, and that they were about to receive twin boys. I was born first and my brother, Dick, arrived 15 minutes after. As you can imagine, this was cause for endless discussion between my brother and I, as I asserted my dominance as the elder twin. I wasn't the eldest son, though. That distinction went to my brother, Elmer, who was five years older than Dick and I.

While my start in life may have been uninspiring, my growing up years were truly interesting. For starters, every winter until we were about 12 or so, Dick and I were sick with every possible childhood disease. Back then, as was the common practice, the house would be quarantined, and a big red poster would be tacked up on the front of the house to alert our neighbors.

Things were direct and simple back then. My mother was a high school graduate, with business training, and she worked as a secretary and bookkeeper. My father worked for the Philadelphia Electric Company (PECO) for 45 years. Before World War II, he was a meter reader. Back in the 1930's, stable employment was essential, and my father worked for a very stable company, with consistent pay—it wasn't good, but it was consistent. It offered good benefits and stability, and that was something to hold onto. We didn't have much, but we were grateful for what we did have. When Dick and I were about seven or eight years old, we each received a brand new flashlight as a birthday present. This single gift was a prized possession.

My parents were absolutely devoted to each other, and provided my brothers and me with a solid family foundation. They were wonderful parents. Mother was a Christian, an Episcopalian. My father was an agnostic. At my mother's insistence, we boys attended a small Presbyterian church in town. We attended Sunday School and summer Bible school until the confirmation years. My parents didn't attend, but we boys were sent faithfully. Occasionally I would stay past Sunday School for the church service, and sometimes the communion element. The Pastor always issued a stern warning that, if you weren't a practicing Christian, you were in deep trouble. In truth, that put me off, and I didn't want to attend. Around age 14, both Dick and I decided we were done with church.

With three boys out in the country, there was much to do and we made good use of it. Three blocks away, there was a little brook that ran into the Pennypack Creek. This was known as the Buttonball Creek, which started at a spring at the Philmont Country Club. It was about five miles long, and along the way, it was fed by many springs, which made the water extremely cold. However, it's a wonderful thing for boys! We had a tree house that we built and had great fun exploring the creek and surrounding countryside. It was a good childhood.

My father had a good electrical background. Even though he only attended school up to the 7th grade, he took every course offered by PECO. He possessed an outstanding knowledge of things technical and electrical, and he was well versed in some technology which was not easily understood by most people, like three phase power and power factor (power efficiency rating). These were always a bit of a mystery, but he knew them well.

As a PECO technician, Dad was "on call" and because of this, we had one of the only private telephone lines in our neighborhood. Everyone else had a shared, or party, line. When Dad would be called out because of a bad storm, I often went along. Here I was, a young boy, with thunder booming and lightning flashing, watching transformers buzzing and snapping at the local substation. It was exciting and a little scary.

I recall watching my father repair things in a way that not many others could do, or would have thought to do. He was adept at taking something apart and understanding the mechanics, but perhaps not having the specific parts, he would use what he had on hand. He was a sort of early MacGyver. When I was about five years old, he repaired our refrigerator. Perhaps not too unusual, but it was the way he did it that was remarkable. Our refrigerator used ammonia gas, and he needed to recharge it and put ammonia gas back into it. Instead of calling a repair man, my father brought in a small gas tank of ammonia, put it in a bucket of hot water to drive the pressure up, and then charged the refrigerator with ammonia. I was just amazed at that. Growing up watching this sort of ingenious problem solving, I learned to look at mechanical processes and challenges in a unique way. This was natural to me, the normal way of repairing things. My father was not a genius but he worked hard and figured out what needed to be done. Over time, after watching Dad tackle issue after issue, I believed there was nothing I, too, couldn't fix or build if given enough time.

Father also had a side business in the early days, repairing radios. He had a workbench in the basement where he would work on these radios. I spent hours down with him in the basement, watching him work. He showed me as he went along and taught me little by little about it. He was also somewhat of a scavenger. Back then, the electric company had stand-by lights, like emergency lights, used in their substations, with lantern batteries. About 3" in diameter and 8" tall, it was like a big dry cell, 1.5 volts. However, they can develop a considerable amount of current, and you could get a little more than 10 amps out of one of them. The electric company would change these batteries out about every six months, though their life wasn't completely gone. They would be thrown out. My father brought them home for me, and I learned to sort out the bad from the good.

You could series them, or connect them, and develop some reasonably high voltage, like 30-45 volts. He also brought home all kinds of little electrical devices, like little motors and clocks, which he gave to me. At this time, I was about 5 years old. I wired these little motors in series or parallel and I would take them apart, rewind them, and so on. I had a curious mind that enjoyed finding a result.

Duplication of an early electrical project by great grandson, Cole Jones.

When I went to school, which was small and contained all grades up to 12th, I had a difficult time writing, and would have been diagnosed today with dyslexia. I wrote upside down and backwards. My young first grade teacher was confounded by this, and sought help from the principal, an older woman, who offered a common sense solution: I was given a mirror. I would use the mirror to help me write the correct way, by looking into it as I wrote. Soon I became more proficient, the mirror was taken away and I wrote correctly. This didn't bother me or frustrate me; it was simply another problem to solve.

Back in the 1920's and 30's, Philadelphia was the center of the world of radio. My dad had one of the first radio amateur licenses in Philadelphia, by around 1910. He built a spark-generator transformer/receiver for code, something not easily done. My father subscribed to several electronics magazines, and in second grade, I came across one hugely popular among electronics "tinkerers," devoted to radio amateurs ("ham radios"). I stumbled across an article on one tube radios. Using the instructions and circuit diagram included in the article, I used the discarded PECO batteries to build a one tube regenerative radio. I was seven years old. I wound the main coil on an oatmeal box—a "Mother Oats" oatmeal box, per the instructions in the magazine. It worked! I made any number of those over the next couple of years. Radios, amplifiers, those types of things. I had my own little work area in the basement, next to my father's. I was learning the basics of electronics and achieving desired outcomes at the age of seven, but I didn't find this unusual or worthy of any fanfare. My methodical approach and matter-of-fact view of myself helped instill a sense of confidence which would grow with each small success.

In the early thirties, all the old farm houses had battery radios, particularly interesting because they weren't wired in the "normal" way of today. They were all wired with heavy-gauge wire and were not soldered together. Instead, they were put together with hundreds of screws and nuts, very mechanically intricate, but you could buy them at auction for a quarter in the late thirties. My father would buy them for the parts; more equipment with which I experimented.

Around the fifth grade, my father gave me a Christmas present—a Heath Kit, vacuum tube volt meter, a highly sensitive multi-meter. It will measure electrical voltages under no load. A normal multi-meter loads the circuit, but you don't get as accurate a reading that way. A vacuum tube volt meter at that time was relatively unknown. Not many people had them. Costing only around $20, it consisted of a whole box of parts, with a circuit diagram and instructions on how to build it. I worked about a day straight through building that thing, and I loved it.

Now, I was active as a boy in all the normal pursuits, playing with my brothers and my friends, but I enjoyed experimenting. I was very interested in technical things. I enjoyed the challenge—I wanted to build something that would work and become a tool. I was exceedingly interested in the ever-changing world of electronics—radio technology then eventually television technology.

The architect whose radio I'd fixed when I was 10 or so, called to say he wanted to buy a television set, but he didn't want an antenna. In those days, your antenna was outside on your roof, and this gentleman thought it was unsightly. He wanted me to build an indoor antenna. He asked if I could. "Of course," I said. And I did. Although I'd built prototypes and had tinkered with building antenna, I'd never custom-built one for a paying customer. It was quite a contraption, but it worked. It was one antenna for each channel, at that time—3, 6, and 10. I built it up in his attic and he was tickled to death with it. Each time I was presented with a new opportunity to build or discover a better "thing," I jumped at it.

I had this technical drive that just propelled me forward, and now I'm in high school and my reputation was growing. Unfortunately, because of all my other activities, I was not a good student, but I still enjoyed school. I never failed any of my courses. I was well-liked and respected by my teachers, and I helped them with most of their television sets. They knew I was unique, and I was given some leeway because of this. I was given the enviable responsibility of running the projector, so I got to go from room to room, showing movies to the other students instead of staying in class. For a Valentine's Day dance, another student and I built a huge heart, but it wasn't just an ordinary decoration—it had a motor that I built and it slowly rotated. There were no Audio/Visual clubs or technical groups in school, and I was pretty much on my own. I had many friends and got along well with just about everyone, but I suppose I was considered quirky because of my abilities. This didn't bother me; I was comfortable with it. Eventually, I met a pretty girl named Myrt, and for some reason, she took a liking to me and invited me to her 16th birthday party. She was my first and best girl from the moment we became a couple.

In school, I was interested in anything scientific, but other subjects were not as intriguing to me, and in fact, I was quite challenged in some areas. Our science teacher, Mr. Slaybaugh, taught all three sciences for each grade in the small high school. I learned more of my science from him than anyone else, and he was a good teacher. We had fairly extensive lab courses, which I particularly liked because of the hands-on experience.

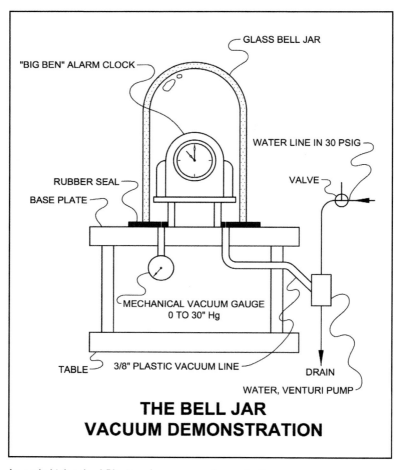

THE BELL JAR
VACUUM DEMONSTRATION

An early high school Physics class vacuum demonstration.

In my senior year, I entered the school's science fair. I wanted to do something different than the typically presented projects. I built a Geiger counter. I found a diagram and a set of instructions and I told my father what I wanted to do. As usual, he was supportive and helped me find the surplus Gei-

board boxes that contained our belongings, and two aluminum lawn chairs, which we set up in our living room. Stability, steady pay, and benefits, such as MEECO offered, were crucial to a young couple like us. We benefitted from my experience at MEECO and Dr. Bergson's respect for me, as well as from the bonuses he provided. It was a good living for us.

Myrt was a housewife and an exceptional one at that. She cared for our money and controlled our budget. Under her careful eye, within two years of starting our life together, we'd saved up enough money—$1,000—to buy our first house, a new, small, $10,000 home.

Now out of college, a homeowner, and a father with a degree and five years invested in MEECO, my professional career was about to begin. And it began with Dr. Bergson.

Bergson was an interesting man. He wasn't social—more of one to sit alone and think. The many years with Dr. Bergson and his tiny staff of about 20 employees would help to shape my early opinions on how a business should work and be run. He molded my management style based on what I saw and how he treated his employees: while he always treated me well and with respect, he was often unrelenting with other employees, and I didn't like that. He kept his business to himself, he was closed off to everyone else and kept the day-to-day business—all the business results, financials, etc.—very close to his chest. As a result, we employees didn't know what the company was really doing, why we were doing it, or where we were going. We weren't as invested as we could have been. We had no idea whether the company was solvent or not—were we even making money? That began to bother me and it frustrated me. Though I had been given many large responsibilities and knew Bergson trusted me, I knew I'd gone as far as I could with the company. Still, I wasn't sure if I should leave. Where would I go and what would I do?

I applied to several companies after college, but almost all of them required a four-year degree for any engineering position. I didn't have too many options, so I decided to talk to Dr. Bergson and continue with MEECO. He agreed to keep me on, but I had a couple of requirements. I wanted to become a salaried employee, and I wanted to earn $75 a week, which at that time was quite good. I knew there was a certain prestige that came with being a salaried employee, as opposed to an hourly one, and how I was perceived by others was becoming more and more important to me. I knew from my early days mowing lawns and fixing televisions that if you do what you say you're going to do, and do it well, you make a good impression. That impression stays with people, and you can use that to your advantage. I knew being salaried would improve my image. Although it wasn't the most economical move for me, it was an important one.

I worked quite hard and for many, many long hours, for which, as a salaried employee, I wasn't paid. But I knew it would pay off, and Myrt trusted me. In fact, her faith in me never wavered, despite the twists and turns I would take in my career. In that first salaried year at MEECO, I would be given opportunities to flourish in ways I hadn't imagined. Later, of course, something would happen to change that, as it always does.

It was around 1955, and Bergson had a relationship with the DuPont Experimental Station in Delaware, where they were developing all kinds of advanced things. He began building advanced electronic measuring instruments for DuPont. He told me something very important, something that I've never forgotten. He said, "Bill, don't ever get involved with making things where you're in competition with other people, particularly the North Jersey types, as part of a production process. It's important in the manufacturing process to be a critical point nearest to the end of the production line." In other words, you want to do things that are critical to the manufacturer, things that are nearest to the end product. You don't want to be the one building the supply of a product when someone else finishes it and potentially earns the credit for the entire body of work.

The DuPont Company had designed an instrument known as the Tri-Stimulus Colorimeter, a form of a modified spectrophotometer. It was made primarily for the measurement of color—for paints, plastic, textiles, etc. It was a quality control instrument based on the tri-stimulus equations, and it had a unique design, which was all DuPont. Bergson was awarded the contract to build a few of these Colorimeters, but there

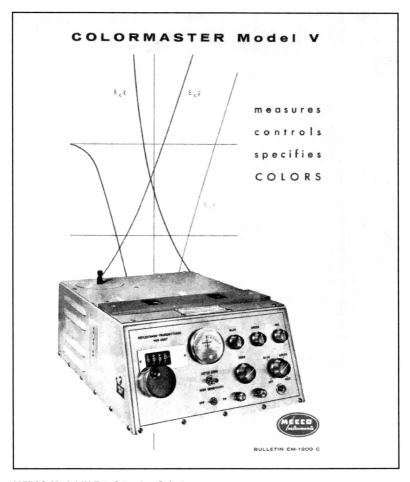

MEECO Model IV Tri- Stimulus Colorimeter.

were some deficiencies in the instrument. He and the DuPont engineers redesigned it to work the bugs out, and by the time I worked on it, the colorimeter was in its fourth product generation, the Model IV.

Bergson had orders to build about 30 of these instruments, but he couldn't make them work. The inherent flaws in the design remained. So I worked in this little test center, a small room in the kitchen of a house where MEECO was headquartered. An assistant—a young girl by the name of Mickey—and I worked on the redesign night and day to work out the problems while Bergson also worked hard to get the units to work. At one point, after working all morning on one unit, Dr. Bergson slammed his notebook on his table and declared the instruments completely useless, a total disaster. He could not get it to balance, no matter what he tried. He did everything he could think of and nothing worked. We'd have to redesign it.

Knowing Bergson was at his limit, I suggested he go to lunch, take a break, and let me work with it. He was so disgusted and frustrated, he agreed and went off to eat and then work on other business. I stayed through lunch and took it completely apart. When I did, I found a simple wiring error. It was immediately obvious to me what was wrong, and I fixed it quickly. I put it all back together, put the two test panels on it, and, snap! It balanced perfectly. When Bergson returned to check on my progress, I told him about the reversed wiring. Though he was probably delighted I'd found the error, the Harvard Ph.D. was nonetheless a bit ruffled at the ease at which I'd found and corrected the problem. He shuffled out of the test area with no more than a grunt of appreciation.

After that, Bergson never set foot in the lab again. He turned it completely over to me. He never said a word about it, but he turned over the testing of the instruments. I straightened all the kinks out of the units, and we tested everything to make sure all were calibrated, etc. We set up all kinds of test standards in the shop to make assembly and testing more efficient. When we'd shipped all but three or four of them, I sat down with Bergson and reminded him that, after we shipped these last few units, we wouldn't have any more instruments to build. After a pause, he decided we needed to start selling them. He put me in charge of selling the instruments, too, and with that, he and I went out in the field to sell.

The units we shipped needed to be set up at their new locations, and I was also assigned that task. Many customers were laboratories, so I met with the chief chemists, set them up with their new instruments, and taught them how to use the tool. I was introduced to some pretty sophisticated people in this way. The whole world of color science was extremely interesting, and it always satisfied my technical curiosity. In some ways, I wish I'd stayed with it, but other paths beckoned me.

Dr. Bergson also worked with DuPont on another instrument, this one a secret. We didn't even know what it did, but we were building it for DuPont. The tool was an "electrolytic water analyzer," the Model W. We were building it, but we didn't understand it—DuPont had applied for a patent for it, and they didn't want anyone knowing details about the instrument. So, we built the Model W, but we only tested the components because we couldn't test the whole thing—we had no clue what the end product was.

Bergson later bought the license from DuPont for $10,000 to build and sell the Model W to other companies. Only then did we find out what the instrument did: It was a very low level dew point analyzer—it would measure water in gases down to one part per million. DuPont had the basic design, but they didn't have the techniques to build it particularly well. We had to develop those. The core of the instrument, the cell, was ingenious, but they had not perfected it, and it had a few design defects. One of the stipulations of the purchase from DuPont was that they had to come teach us how to build the core. Joe Janis, the head of our mechanical shop, and I met with a man from DuPont, and he taught us how to build the core. When he'd finished, Joe and I looked at it and thought, "This is really difficult. It's too difficult." So, between Bergson, Joe, and I, we redesigned the core so it was easier to make. But the final making of these cells, the core, fell to me.

Now I had the colorimeter department and the cell department. I hired several technicians, and slowly, we worked the bugs out of the Model W. We were ready to sell it.

Bergson understood the gas dynamics very, very well and developed different applications for the instrument. He was

MEECO Model W, Electrolytic Water (dew point) Analyzer.

extremely astute and developed ways of marketing the Model W that were ingenious. I worked closely with him on these plans. I gave lectures on the Model W, gave demonstrations, and made a trip to England, flying on one of the first jets to England—a Qantas airlines 707. I stayed for about a month, meeting with numerous companies about the unit. It was a bit of an adventure to me, and the people I interacted with were all high-level professionals, all heads of their departments. That appealed to me.

The work I did on the Model W was one of the ways in which I was introduced to the furnace industry. Companies using high temperature furnaces, vacuum furnaces, whatever they may be, were measuring the gases that went into their furnaces. They wanted only pure gases. I picked up that technology from the Model W and continued to build the skills and technological know-how needed to excel in the furnace industry. Still, I did not see that on the horizon for myself.

Now, during this period, I was approached a few times by other organizations wanting me to leave MEECO and join their teams. I was happy enough where I was—I enjoyed the work and the freedom Bergson allowed me. He sort of gave me my head, so to speak, and it was an invaluable experience.

But then, something occurred to me while I was working with Bergson.

Bergson was a character, and management-wise, he taught me more about what not to do than how to manage effectively and successfully. He just mistreated people. I was never a recipient of his fickle temperament, but I couldn't stand seeing how he treated others. Though we all worked hard and were dedicated to the business, we never knew where we stood or how the business was operating. Not knowing if what we were doing was successful or not outside the company's walls was very frustrating. I began to feel like I wanted to know more about the real business world, and I knew I would never get that at MEECO. In short, I was dissatisfied.

Bergson was a genius, absolutely, but he kept everything to himself. I knew I'd gone as far as I could. If Bergson had opened up and run the company more efficiently, he could have flourished. But he was strictly a one-man show. As it is, MEECO is the same size today as when I left it.

IDL—INSTRUMENT DEVELOPMENT LABORATORIES

As my dissatisfaction with MEECO grew, I found myself looking at want ads and trying to sort out where I might go next. I knew it was time to leave Dr. Bergson and company, and Myrt supported my decision. I came across an advertisement in the Philadelphia Evening Bulletin want ads for a Regional Applications Engineer at a company in Attleboro, Massachusetts called Instrumental Development Laboratories. I had heard of IDL and knew a little about them from working with color technology. They were building a competitive instrument to MEECO's ColorMaster as well as a two-color optical pyrometer called the Color-Eye, which was a way of measuring temperature optically since temperature is related to color. I had heard about this technology while at MEECO and saw the move to IDL as an opportunity to get in on the ground floor of some new technology. I also wanted to be a part of a more sophisticated company.

At MEECO, my title had been that of a Project Engineer. A Project Engineer is an engineer fresh out of college with a little bit of experience, assigned a particular project or endeavor. Of course, I was doing a lot more than that, including taking trips out into the field, teaching people how to use our instruments, selling, and developing new projects. I had been the equivalent of Bergson's direct understudy, more a Chief Engineer than Project Engineer. Though I was only about 25 years old, I had already amassed quite a bit of experience and technical abilities.

At that time, MEECO, IDL, and Hunter Labs were the forerunners in color technology, and IDL was looking to branch

almost endless. It was very exciting technology, and I really felt I was getting in on the ground floor.

The first instrument to be sent out in the field came to me, which was an indication of how much Dr. Bentley respected me and what he thought of me. I took this instrument around to various places, and it was well-received. I became deeply involved in some of these applications, including furnace technology, as this was an instrument that could look at exceptionally high temperatures. That technology didn't immediately excite me, exactly. Nonetheless, the world of furnaces would become a regular part of my visits to customers as I became more involved in the applications and potential for this instrument.

As this time was the beginning of the rocket age, measuring rocket-engine temperatures was most interesting, and a lot of people were excited about instruments with such applications. However, the Pyro-Eye had a distinct flaw that IDL did not see during development: it suffered from spectral emissivity—it didn't always measure temperatures the same, depending on the material. If you were looking at a piece of copper, it would measure one way. If you looked at iron, it measured another way. Sometimes the temperature variance between materials was so great, it was an impossibility. At one point, at Bell Labs, I looked at a piece of silicone and then a piece of graphite, all in the same hot zone, and the temperature difference was 500 degrees. Impossible. That emissivity problem became quite significant.

After I'd worked with this flaw and the Pyro-Eye for two years, I went to Don Hall with my disappointment in the inadequacies I knew wouldn't be overcome. I said, "Don, this thing has been presented to the market as doing something it can't do. It's going to be awhile before all the bugs are worked out, if ever. I think I'm going to leave."

I left over the inadequacies of the Pyro-Eye, and the frustration that it could only provide a partial solution to customers. Though I never sold it as a perfect solution, the fact that it was only near-perfect bothered me. I never stretched the truth about the Pyro-Eye, but I did feel strongly that customers weren't getting all they paid for—it would never work at 100%, and I knew I couldn't repair it, no matter how hard I tried. That was my primary reason for leaving. This equipment had an inherent disease, and it wouldn't be resolved. I had no desire to continue working with such a limited technology. The Color-Eye was ok, but it wasn't new or different, and I was looking for something that would change industries and the way people would think about and do things. That wasn't going to happen at IDL. Incidentally, the spectral emissivity was never resolved, and the product was eventually taken off the market, well after I'd left.

When I gave my notice, Don Hall talked to Dr. Bentley about my resignation. He was hoping Bentley would talk me out of leaving. Don recalls, "I said, George, you have to meet with Bill and talk to him. Tell him we can work it out."

I was called to Boston to meet with Dr. Bentley. I made the then-eight-hour drive up north, wondering what he would say. To Don's surprise and mine, Dr. Bentley had no desire to persuade me to stay with IDL. The conversation didn't last too long, only about 15 minutes, but it was one I'll never forget. We talked about why I wanted to leave and what I wanted to do. Dr. Bentley assured me that, while he valued my contributions and my abilities, he understood my need to move on. Then, he told me something I'd never heard before, and wouldn't fully understand for many years. He said I'd never truly be happy unless I ran my own business.

Over the years, I've thought about that statement. Dr. Bentley only knew me for a couple of years, and most of that time, only distantly. He knew of my work, certainly, and of my dedication, but I wasn't in constant contact with him. He respected me and appreciated my contributions. He admired me, he really did, although he was an order of magnitude above me, technically.

But he didn't really know me. At that young age, I barely knew what I wanted to do myself, so hearing such a declaration from him was a bit startling. I never considered running my own business, though I had done so during my childhood. But that was lawn mowers and television sets, not a career to support a family. I asked Don Hall what he thought of Dr. Bentley's statement:

"

I think he saw himself in Bill—the drive and the determination to solve a problem. I think Bentley could see it and related to it. And he was right. Bill was always challenged by new information. You could see his "ears go up" when he was learning something new. It was almost as if Bill looked at whatever you were presenting and thought to himself, "I know some way to do that better," and most of the time he did. It was almost detrimental to him later. We would develop a product and he would take it into the field, and then adjust it or change it to suit each person's needs. We needed to sell what we made, not make unique units. It created tension from time to time, but that's what made Bill, Bill. He never stopped looking for the solution to a problem. He never said to a customer, "I'm sorry, our product doesn't do that." Instead, he'd say, "Let me see what I can do," and then adapt it. Great for the customer, not always great for a sales manager. In that way, too, George Bentley was right: Bill wouldn't be truly happy unless he was in business for himself and doing it his own way.

IDL was a well-organized company. It was clean. It was neat. Employees worked functionally. The company started on time, went to lunch on time, came back on time. Everything was done orderly. The files were in order; the finances were in order. Such a contrast to MEECO, which felt like a run-down barracks and was run like a lab at Harvard. I recognized the difference and admired it. It showed me exactly what I liked in an organization, just as MEECO showed me what I didn't like. It ran so well, but unfortunately, the product was deficient. The marketing plans for the Pyro-Eye, developed by the Marketing Manager, Ed Connor, were built on a house of cards. He didn't know the limits of the product, of course, but he had these grandiose marketing plans that were fictional and not going to fly. I knew that, and Don Hall knew that, and Don left not too long after me. He was Vice President of Sales and high up in the company, but he left for more or less the same reasons as I did. We also did not particularly like Ed Connor, an ex-G.E. marketing engineer.

So, I left IDL. And where did I go? Back to MEECO. It was what I knew, it was comfortable, and I wasn't really sure what I wanted to do. I had some contact with Dr. Bergson while I was at IDL, and we had continued to talk about industry matters. It was a respectful relationship. I'm not sure whether I thought it would be different or not, but I knew it was a safety net. I did not want to enter the general marketplace. I knew I was limited, because of my two-year degree. Everyone wanted a four-year degreed candidate. The world was much more technical, with Sputniks flying around. I had read resumes of some of the people applying for jobs at that time, and I didn't understand a lot of what I read. Most of it was highly specific, high technology jargon, and I couldn't make sense of it. So returning to MEECO was an easy move while I worked out where to go next.

But nothing had changed, except Dr. Bergson became intrigued by the IDL pyrometer and asked me to tell him more about it. He was an astute character, and he said, "I think there is a real need for that instrument." He wanted to take what they were doing at MEECO and the pyrometer technology and develop something. At the same time, I was queried by the people at DuPont about it. They knew about it, too, and one of their engineers came up to see me and quizzed me at length about it. But I told Bergson, "Look, there's this flaw in this thing, and I explained to him the emissivity problem. I told him I did *not* want to become involved with such a problem again. I had worked hard on it, and I didn't want to go down that road again. He pursued me on it and talked to me several times about it, but when he saw I was resolute, he dropped it.

But I saw the same problems at MEECO as before. And now, Bergson's daughter, Lisa, even though she was only about 12 years old at the time, was a sure candidate for a major position in her father's company. Where would that leave me? I'd be in the same situation, just under a different boss. So, shortly after I returned to MEECO, I left again. But this time, I would enter a new industry.

Charlie Hill with his ABAR Series 90 Vacuum Furnace.

Taking on Leadership, the ABAR Years

Wherever possible, hire people smarter than yourself, and those you know are willing to work. Check all personnel records carefully and do background checks. We like to hire people we know personally, and who are highly recommended. A bad employee or a poor employee is worse than no employee. —WRJ

I t was 1962, and while I was wondering where I would go next, I received a call from my old friend and former boss, Don Hall. He told me of a little company in Willow Grove, PA, a client of his—at this time, Don was a manufacturer's representative. He told me this company, ABAR, was building a high temperature vacuum furnace. "The man who runs the business," Don said, "his name is Charlie Hill. I've told him about you. I think you ought to consider going to work for him." I told Don I'd think about it.

Then Charlie called me himself and asked me to come see him. So, I did.

ABAR was this tiny company, a start-up with only seven people. But it would grow, and I would spend 17 years growing it, putting everything I had into it, almost literally. There were many events and moments at ABAR that changed the course of my career. Some were seemingly insignificant at the time, but I would later realize just how important they were to me. Just as my time at MEECO and IDL showed me the right and wrong ways to run a business, working at ABAR would put all of that into practical application. I had many successes, but I also had many failures. My work there and the company's development would also begin to underscore Dr. George Bentley's words to me so many years before. As he predicted, I would eventually recognize the need to work for myself and do exactly what I wanted to do, the way I wanted to do it.

When I joined him, Charlie Hill had only one furnace model—a Series 90 Vacuum Furnace. He was building it in direct competition with a company in New Hampshire, called BREW, where he had once been Chief Engineer. Charlie didn't get along well with BREW's owner, Dick Brew, so he'd left them and moved to Eastern Pennsylvania to form ABAR with some other people from a company called Pressure Products Inc.—PPI.

Brew had several vacuum furnace models, but the principle model—the one with which Charlie was competing—had the vacuum chamber built into a cabinet, purely for aesthetics, with all the electrical and plumbing inside the cabinet as well. Though it looked tidy and appealing, it was a real mess and a nightmare to work on or service. Charlie took the vacuum chamber outside the cabinet and mounted in front on a heavy-duty frame, making the furnace easy to assemble and service, top and bottom, where required. In the Brew furnace, work was loaded into the furnace through a removable port at the top—a large sight glass. So, the furnace internals were not easily accessible, either. Charlie removed the entire top head of the furnace with a simple lift mechanism, which exposed the entire top of the hot zone to make loading and servicing the hot zone easier. There were other innovations, but these are the main points.

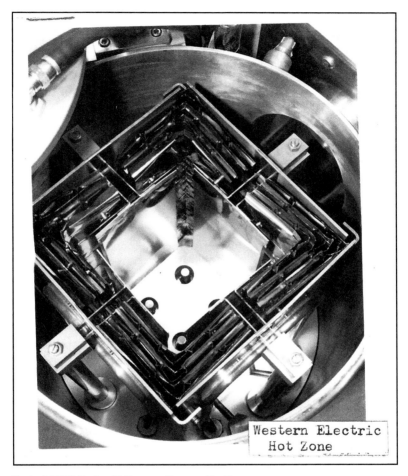

Typical ABAR Series 90 Vacuum Furnace Hot Zone.

The Pressure Products Inc. people were interesting; they built things that operated at very high pressure. They were a well-established company, and they had represented Brew in Pennsylvania. Once committed to Charlie and a new venture, three of the men who'd run PPI severed their relationship with

Brew to start ABAR with Charlie, who became president. They all put in the same amount of money, though Charlie wasn't the principal stockholder.

When I first met Charlie, I thought, "Oh my gosh, I don't want to get involved with this little company." I didn't really understand the industry. I knew vacuum technology to some extent, but I did not know high vacuum technology, and I didn't know really high temperature technology or how to generate it and so forth. There was an awful lot I didn't know. But I talked to Charlie, and we talked over a period of several months. He pursued me. He would not let up. Finally, I decided I would go to work for him, as his Technical Sales Manager. I even took a pay cut to join ABAR. He was that convincing. This was to change the whole course of my life, and within a year, I became one of the three principal owners.

By the time I joined ABAR, my reputation as a businessman and technical guru had grown by leaps and bounds. Others in the industry knew my word was my reputation, and when I said I would do something, I did it. ABAR would offer me the opportunity to hone my business skills and technical abilities, and to discover my true purpose. And it all began in a small, 3,000 square-foot, single-bay rented work space with seven other people.

During the interview process, I was introduced to Tom Gibb, an ABAR employee. While in a discussion with Tom and Art Couillard, ABAR's Plant Manager and one of the first ABAR employees, they alluded to some technical problem they were having at the time. Tom remembers:

Art had mentioned to me that they were interviewing some guy named Bill. During the interview, a problem was mentioned, and, though not yet an employee, Bill dug right in and ended up solving the problem. After a few days, Bill

arrived at the plant. He'd been hired. I was starting to test a new vacuum furnace that was being made ready to ship from Willow Grove when Bill came in, fully dressed in a suit. He sat down on the floor next to me and started to work. Not a word was spoken.

It took me awhile to get assimilated to what was going on. It was such a small company—I was the eighth employee—and there was so much I didn't know. From understanding everything that went into vacuum furnaces and the technology of how it all worked together to running a small company, the transition was quite a challenge, but it was also terribly exciting. We were designing and building small, and at the time, expensive vacuum furnaces for the heat treatment of special metals for the electronic and defense industries. Although I struggled a bit with being the inexperienced new guy, my zeal for understanding all things electrical and mechanical soon overtook any anxiety I may have felt. As with just about anything I put my hands on, I knew given enough time, I'd figure it out. And there was so much potential. I could easily see that, even if I didn't immediately recognize what it was.

After I'd been there a few months and felt I understood the basics pretty well, I went to talk to Charlie. I told him ABAR's problem wasn't with sales—we had more sales than we knew what to do with. The real problem was how to engineer, test, and develop—how to produce these orders that we had. Harkening back to my days at MEECO, testing and helping Dr. Bergson with development, and my time at IDL, developing applications for the Pyro-Eye, I knew where my true talents lie. I told him I would be more valuable to the company as the Chief Engineer.

Charlie agreed with me. At the time, he was doing everything—he was an absolute workaholic: sales manager, chief engineer, and everything else. But he couldn't do it all. As happens with a start-up, we were all working 12-14 hour days in the beginning, six days a week, trying to keep up with orders, selling, getting orders to the engineers to prepare the furnace per the customer's specifications. Then, once we built the furnace, we had to make it work. We were entertaining customers, developing new technology, getting the products into the field, teaching the customers how to use it, and so on. In those days, the work never stopped.

That would change.

During those early days with ABAR—around 1962—though the work was steady and, at times, relentless, the business climate for these vacuum furnaces was rapidly changing. These were the Kennedy years, and between 1961 and 1963, he took a knife to a lot of development money. There was a fairly big cutback within the atomic energy commission and other high technology defense industries, which was where our business was centered at the time. After a boom and plenty of sales, we suddenly found ourselves in a situation where the market for these high temperature furnaces was drying up.

Fortunately, there was another part of the market from which we drew business—the sintering of tantalum electrolytic capacitors. That phrase sounds like science fiction, but it's part of the whole technology of solid state technology, part of the power supply. The process for making these capacitors involved using a high temperature vacuum furnace. Unfortunately, because the defense market was going down, the market for these capacitors was also going down. We were losing another piece of the pie. The solid-state stuff and the public's general use of it had not yet come on, so the market for the furnaces used to make the capacitors was drying up. The nuclear market was drying up, and so on. We suddenly found ourselves with no business. This was an anxious time for all of us at ABAR, as we had been enjoying a prosperous beginning, and it had looked as though our success had no end. But changes in government have a major impact on business.

As we reviewed the industry, we could see where the money

was still flowing. As I've always done and would continue to do, I looked for the opportunities. We decided we needed to get more into the industrial market. Jet engines were the next logical step, because jet engines had materials and components that operate at high temperatures.

There were three places these engines were being built in the US: General Electric in Lynn, Massachusetts, the GE plant in Cincinnati/Evandale, and Pratt & Whitney in East Hartford. As it happened, my friend Don Hall came into the picture for me again. He was still a manufacturer's representative, and he represented ABAR. He took me to the GE plant in Lynn. He got me in to GE.

In this industry, all of the metals at the time were being heat treated in hydrogen atmosphere furnaces. Hydrogen is a very strong reducing atmosphere, operated at high temperatures. But the furnaces they were using at that time were temperature limited: they could not run much above 1700 or 1800 Fahrenheit without having deteriorations of the hot zones within the furnace, which led to contaminations and other things happening. But the vacuum furnace is an exceptionally pure environment. So, we went after that market. Charlie sold the first furnace at GE Lynn, with Don Hall, and then later, I received an order from GE Evandale for a huge furnace. And there was another company in Indianapolis called Allison. Allison was part of General Motors, but they were also making jet engines for turbo prop planes—small engines for driving propellers. Business just went on from there. Where we saw one industry fade, another emerged, and we were at the forefront of it.

We enjoyed success in this new market for several reasons. We were driven, we knew the product, and we provided technical expertise above and beyond our competitors. The same work ethic that propelled me at MEECO and IDL continued at ABAR, and Charlie Hill and Art Couillard worked just as hard.

There was competition, of course. Ipsen, a direct competitor, was on the top of the heap. But they built a somewhat different type of furnace. Our furnace had good vacuum technology. Charlie Hill, while he was in New England, had worked for National Research Corporation, NRC, who built high vacuum diffusion pumps that would pump down into extremely deep vacuum, into what we call "outer space vacuum." With these diffusion pumps, we could duplicate the atmosphere on the surface of the moon, which is very, very sparse. So, we could offer these remarkably pure atmospheres. Ipsen didn't do that very well—the materials used in their furnaces would decompose at high temperatures, whereas ours operated at a wider range of temperatures. So, they had homemade vacuum pumps and leaking vacuum chambers, which contrasted with our furnaces.

At ABAR, we specialized in a furnace that we called an "all metal hot zone;" we used metal heatshields to insulate the furnace. We were starting to carve out our niche with this hot zone, and we were in a war with Ipsen, with their rather crude technology going up against our more sophisticated, purer atmosphere technology. Ipsen made some attempts at keeping up with us in these sophistications, too, but they were not successful, whereas we had had years to work at it. They did have other advantages that ABAR didn't have, but we were still able to build, and keep, a solid niche in the industrial market. We were able to compete with them quite well, regardless of their lower prices.

In the first couple of years at ABAR, I convinced Charlie Hill and Art Couillard that we should have an operating Series 90 vacuum furnace sitting available to use as a demonstrator. Being a sales-oriented person, I wanted this to show how vacuum furnaces work and the capabilities of our furnace. But I also wanted it for R&D work. So, we built it, with our own money.

Well, we would have phone calls from customers who would say they were thinking about a vacuum furnace but were not sure whether it was going to work; they wondered if ABAR could run a test for them. And so, they would come down to the plant, and we would run their tests. Usually, they were relatively small components, and our example furnace was not very big. It had a hot zone similar to a lab furnace—about six inches by six inches by 12 inches high, like a shoe box. So, we would take samples—or in some cases, a whole part—and I ran the furnace. I was really the only one devoted to that task. I ran it, and I gained a lot of experience from working with this furnace. The tests also opened my eyes to the things we couldn't do, and that led to other developments. When someone works with a furnace in the same way a customer will, an operator or engineer can see the limitations of the equipment or the "bugs." This led, for me, to "light bulb" moments, which would be incorporated into later furnace designs. Having this operational furnace turned out to be a key factor in ABAR's success. Again, as in so many other circumstances before, I saw an opportunity that was seemingly obvious, but no one else was really capitalizing on it. I took the chance, and it worked.

When I think back on those opportunities—all the way back to that very first radio that I built when I was seven years old, winding coil onto an oatmeal box—I see some golden nuggets. Yes, the oatmeal-box radio came with instructions. But considering the size of the oatmeal box, and the many turns of this ultra fine wire that needed to be laid in very carefully, I realize others could also have done it, but they didn't. Many people built those things, but I didn't personally know anyone who had. You needed to have the patience to do that and the will to try—and possibly fail. By the time I was seven, I understood, on some level, that I had a desire to attempt and a willingness to fail, and that not everyone does. This realization stayed with me.

I extrapolated from each experience the understanding that I took risks when others did not. I tried something—making a homemade radio, repairing a faulty switch, taking something apart to understand how it works—instead of passing up the chance to learn something new. It seemed to me that too many people overlooked these opportunities. Were they afraid of failure? Did they prefer to leave the work to someone else? I took each success or failure and saw that I could build on each trial, success, or mistake, to develop myself further and learn more about whatever I held in my hands at the time. That's the innovator in me. The entrepreneur sees an opportunity, thinks "I can really do something with that," and then has the courage to take it a little bit further.

As time went on, there came an occasion when I was able to impress Charlie with my electronic technical abilities. There was a certain type of vacuum gauge we were using simply because Charlie had used it at Brew and was familiar with it. It was used throughout our industry, but they were not made particularly well, and they were not terribly well engineered— about every other one that came in the door didn't work, and we had to ship them back. It was immensely frustrating. One day, we had an order we were working on and had this faulty gauge, and we really had to get this thing online. We were too far along and pressed for time to ship it back for another. So, I pulled this gauge out of the cabinet, took it apart and I fixed it. I put it back in and, of course, it worked. Charlie and Art were with me as I did this, and they were dumbfounded. They both looked at me and asked, "How'd you do that?" So, I told them what the problem was, and I told them it wasn't a problem for me to take it apart, see what was wrong with it, and then easily fix it. That "wow" moment for them sort of set the stage for me, and from then on, I took over all the testing, the design, and also the selling. Being a small company, any one employee had to be able to do everything.

The beginnings of ABAR were really troubled. We were in this really tiny building, which we rented. The landlord was in the HVAC business, which was doing poorly. As the landlord was slowly going out of business, we took over his unused space in this building. We ended up taking over the entire building. He eventually declared bankruptcy, and we came to work one day to find yellow tape around everything and the doors locked. The government had sealed the building. We explained to the government official that we were a separate entity from our landlord's business, and we were free to take over the building. As we grew, we needed additional space and moved the offices next door, turning the original building over to manufacturing space. Eventually, we needed to expand again. This time, we moved our offices down the street, to an office building on top of a bar. "ABAR on top of a bar, ugh." You couldn't work past about 6:30pm or so, because it became too noisy downstairs and the smoke would filter up through the floor. It was really unpleasant.

The original ownership of ABAR was between Charlie and Pressure Products Principles. After I'd been there about a year, the gentlemen from Pressure Products Principles came to us and said we were requiring so much financial capital, we were hurting their company. They wanted out. They wanted us to buy the business from them. So, Charlie Hill, Art Couillard, and I all mortgaged our homes. At that time, my home was only worth around $12,000, and I mortgaged it for $5000. Each of us put up $7500, and using that and other borrowings, we paid off the Pressure Products people. The total was about $50,000. Now, we three owned the business.

Because Charlie had been president, we thought it was only right that he continue. I'm not sure if he put any money into ABAR originally, but because he was the founder, we decided to give him 66% of the company, and Art and I each shared the remaining third of the business. I never thought this was too risky or too much to take on. I knew I wanted to be at ABAR, and I never questioned we could do it. Myrt was just as steadfast in her faith in me as always. We were stable, our marriage was a happy one, and although she knew I was working too hard and she didn't like it, she wasn't worried. We were financially stable. She knew if I was going to do it, it was going to happen.

We were banking with a local bank in Hatboro, at the time, which was bought by a big Philadelphia bank, PNB. Shortly after this merger, the bank called us and said they no longer wanted our business. We were too risky. They gave us 60 days to find a new bank, so Charlie set out to find it. He met with Charles Hoeflich, then President at Union National in Souderton. Hoeflich came to interview the three of us at the office, and, after talking with us and seeing what we were doing, he agreed to take on our accounts.

What's amazing is, we were not good businessmen. We knew how to design and manufacture vacuum furnaces; we knew how to sell them; we knew how to answer our customers' questions and offer solutions. Technically, we knew what we were doing. But the day-to-day operations of a business—managing paperwork and finances—we weren't adept at that. We had an accountant on staff, but he was more like a bookkeeper. We were in an industry that relied primarily on U.S. government agencies for work, and if you weren't the lowest bidder, you didn't get the job. It was a hard business, and we weren't very sophisticated. We really had a lot of financial issues. Charlie had started ABAR in 1960, and now the three of us were running it in 1963. Charlie had had three years of absolute burn-out work, and, quite frankly, he was coming to the end of his rope. This is a side-effect of startup businesses, and you have to be mentally prepared for that.

We needed to learn the next step.

ABAR & THE VRT

Despite Charlie's fatigue, the early days of ABAR were interesting, and Charlie, Art, and I were excited to be a part of it. You never knew what was going to come your way or who was going to knock on your door. In those days, we were in our facility on Wyandotte Road in Willow Grove. It was an area of primarily commercial properties, and the back of the plant faced the Pennsylvania Turnpike.

One day, in early 1964, Art Couillard called me. He said there was a man named Bud Brock, from the Hunterton Transformer Company, who'd come calling, and he wanted to talk to us about the electrical power supply design of the furnaces. He thought I should be the one to talk with him. So, he sent Bud to my office. This very tall, lean man of about 50 met me. He was skinny as a rail and a chain smoker, with hands and teeth discolored from tobacco. He presented his idea to me for a new transformer for vacuum furnaces that he had designed. He'd just been to Stokes to discuss it with them, but they weren't interested. They referred him instead to ABAR, so he drove immediately over to see us and just sort of fell in our door. What I didn't realize when I met with him was that he'd left his wife waiting patiently in the car while he talked with me for several hours.

Bud took out a yellow pad and explained to me how what he called a "transformer reactor" was going to work. Previously, the industry used a saturable core reactor transformer and a separate step-down transformer. These were really big and bulky. We had to have a step-down transformer because we had to operate the heating elements in the furnace at a relatively low voltage. Keep in mind that the normal power line voltage is 460 volts. We didn't want to run our heating elements over 60 volts, because if you get over 60 volts, you start to get arcing and corona in the hot zone, under vacuum conditions. You can run at higher voltage at atmospheric pressure, but not in vacuum. So, a step-down transformer.

Additionally, we had to have something that could control the power into the transformer. In our type of furnace, you couldn't just plug it into the wall and have it come screaming up to full power. That puts too much stress on the heating elements. Besides, we want to have controlled heating. At ABAR, we used one or two of these reactor/transformer combinations, but they were big, and they were ugly, and they did not have complete power range of control. They could go up to high power range without too much difficulty, but you could not shut down below about 5% of max power. In other words, you always had a leakage into the power supply. What did that mean? Well, that leakage gave you minimum operating temperatures—you couldn't cool the furnace below about 300 degrees or so. Now, there were ways around it, but that just added complications.

ABAR had used some of these reactor/transformer combinations, but when Bud Brock showed up at our door, our favorite control system was a big variable transformer, something like a variac. A variac is a small transformer with a little carbon brush that slides up and down through multiple turns, similar to a rheostat. A competitor, Superior Electric, made something called a Powerstat, by taking six of these units and connecting them together, but that would only put out 54kw. We couldn't get any more power out of it than that. Plus, it wasn't conducive to automatic control. It was a manual thing—motor-driven— and we had to use a little switch on the control cabinet to run the power up and down. So, we would have the power down to zero when we started the furnace, and then we would bring the power up slowly by bringing this set of contacts up. We had to have someone standing there, and at certain intervals turn it a bit more, then a bit more, and so on. Though the furnace operators were experts at reading the controls and adjusting accordingly, this process was tedious and time-consuming. Most of our furnaces were that way, everything manual. All our vacuum valves were all manual, the way we backfilled with gas, again—manual. This power control was no different. Working with it over time, it was apparent to many an operator or engineer, myself included, this power control was inefficient.

So, Bud showed me his new thinking, and I could see the advantages of it right off. He claimed that his device would have an excellent power shut down. Most attractive, though, was that the transformer and reactor were all built as *one* unit, and it would be all vacuum encapsulated. The only visible part was this round reactor, filled with epoxy, completely smooth and actually, a good-looking unit. Bud's design used a special kind of transformer. They were four toroidal transformers stacked up in one unit. They were all water cooled, and since the furnace was water cooled to begin with, that didn't present a problem to me.

Surprisingly, Bud hadn't built the transformer reactor yet. He had this idea in his head, but had no way of knowing if anyone would buy it. So, he shopped his idea around, and until he came to ABAR, no one had been interested. Bud had designed something new, something no one else had come up with, and he was presenting it to me, wondering if I might find it useful. I knew right away that it was an incredible piece of new technology, and I told him I'd buy it on the spot and give him a purchase order for a small 25kw unit. I told him to go build it, and when it was completed, I'd come up and take a look at it. They were in Flemington, NJ, working out of Bud's plant, the size of a four-car garage.

A couple of months went by and Bud called me to say the reactor was done and ready for inspection. So Myrt and I went up to Flemington and sure enough, there it was. He had it all connected, with a temporary load on it, and it worked! The transformer reactor was set up on a test bench, and it did all the things Bud promised. Following the testing, Bud's wife, Irma, who had so patiently waited in the car when Bud presented this idea to me, served us lunch at their kitchen table. The house was a stone's throw away from Bud's plant site. Pleased with everything Bud showed me, I bought his product, put it in the trunk of the car, and brought it back to ABAR. When I showed Charlie and Art, I said, "Well, here it is—it's real!" And they looked it over, slightly bewildered, and said, "what are you going to do with it?" I replied that I didn't know. I suggested the next furnace that we quote would include Bud's reactors. Prior to this, we could only get the 54kw from the Power Stats we used before, but now I could buy three of Bud's reactors, each one at 50kw or more, and we could have whatever we wanted. More power equaled more production, and more production equaled more sales, and so on.

Now, as exciting as all this was, I really made a mistake. Bud and I shook hands on a deal. I asked him for an exclusive agreement, building his new reactors only for us, since I gave him his first order. He agreed. After all, he mused, who else would he sell them to? I told Bud we needed to name his product, since we needed to let people know we had this new technology at ABAR, and he gave me the privilege of naming it. I called it the Variable Reactance Transformer, or VRT.

We started adding the VRT's to our specs, and as a result, we started receiving orders simply because of it. No one else had that power supply but us. Another first for ABAR. It put us in a prime position, and it unquestionably helped build our business. We were selling these exclusively in our furnace for about five years, when Bud Brock came to see me again.

Bud introduced me to his new sales manager, and explained their current predicament to me. They were being inundated by ABAR's competitors with requests to buy the VRT. I had no agreement with Bud, other than a handshake. Even though I knew it would eat into our market share, I couldn't, in good conscience, hold Bud to our handshake arrangement. I should have drawn up a formal contract, but I didn't see the need, and clearly, neither did Bud. But five years later, he came to me as a gentleman, asking to be released from our agreement. I told Bud he had to do what he had to do. And he did. I completely understood his situation, and I knew it had been difficult for him to ask me to release him from our arrangement. Financially, it was a mistake to enter into such an agreement with Bud Brock, without a binding contract. I learned a lesson there. My conscience, however, tells me I did the right thing. Today, that transformer is the standard in the industry the world over. It made their company. Others have tried to copy it but, because it is so difficult to make, they all gave up.

ABAR & KING FIFTH WHEEL

Around the time that we met Bud Brock, in 1964, Charlie decided he'd had enough, and he wanted to sell the company. I really did not want to do this, but I wasn't smart enough to buy out my partners. We sold ABAR to King Fifth Wheel, a solid company owned by Dr. Al Martin. The company had enough money to back us, and they were looking to diversify. KFW paid $250,000 cash for ABAR in 1964. We three previous owners of ABAR were, in effect, paid off. The monies we had put in to purchasing ABAR from Pressure Products were paid back to us, plus a bit more. Charlie, of course, received the most. The payout in cash to Art and I was about $25,000, while Charlie received about $75,000. At the time, that was all the money in the world to him.

We were in these three buildings, scattered all around, and we really didn't have the right facilities. So, KFW built a plant for us as well as their Philadelphia operation, and they put us into this one building in Feasterville, PA. It was a good facility: we had good offices across the front, a nice engineering office, a pretty, nice plant. We also had a high bay area with a crane so that we could build our bigger furnaces, which is what we wanted to do. Around six or eight months after we sold to KFW, Charlie decided to leave the company. He was completely burned out. He left everything behind and moved to Florida and basically left the high vacuum furnace business.

After Charlie left, Dr. Martin at King Fifth Wheel brought in Vern Gooderham to run the company, and he became the next President of ABAR. Vern brought the ABAR/King Fifth Wheel companies together in the first place. He was sort of the sales agent, and he was a strong businessman, a pretty shrewd individual. I liked Vern. He was a good man. But he was not an engineer.

Vern invested in the stock market, and used to tell me that he had won and lost several million dollars while playing around in the market and with little startup companies. He had recently purchased a major interest in a small electronics company based in New Jersey, called Winslow Electronics. They were building electronic test and communications gear for the Army. This was now the beginning of the Vietnam War, and Winslow Electronics was flooded with orders. Vern began to slowly sell his stock and ended up with several million dollars in cash.

One day he came into work and said to me, "Bill, to be honest, I don't want to continue working here. I want to go work for myself. I've been working hard, but I want to do that for myself, not for someone else. So, I'm going to leave."

I said, "But you're the president. What's going to happen to the company?"

By that time, I'd gone from Chief Engineer to Operations Vice President. Technically, I was running the business, and I felt quite comfortable with that role. Well, Vern went to Dr. Martin and told him he was leaving. As for new leadership, Vern told him that I was there, I knew the business, and I should continue to run it. So, I did, though I was not made president of the company. I was still Operations Vice President. Dr. Martin stepped in as President of ABAR, but he was president in title only. He was a figurehead; he didn't work at it. Let's face it, he was the owner. But he was more interested in his own business. His limited interest in ABAR allowed me to continue to grow as a leader and assume greater responsibility, all of which I enjoyed.

In the early 1970's, we were selling furnaces for building jet engines to General Electric, but we weren't able to crack Pratt & Whitney. They exclusively used hydrogen gas furnaces. Abe Willan, a chemical engineer educated in Brooklyn, was the sole individual in charge of all their metallurgical furnace acquisitions. He believed in hydrogen furnaces and only hydrogen furnaces. In fact, he and I presented papers on vacuum heat treating at an American Vacuum Society meeting, with his presentation in the morning and our presentation later that afternoon. I presented a paper, along with Jack Graham, an ex-GE man who was a representative for us, on the benefits of vacuum heat treating metals; Abe presented on the reasons why vacuum was never going to work. We were diametrically opposed to one another, but we needed to convince Pratt & Whitney and other naysayers otherwise.

Besides his love of hydrogen and belief that vacuum furnaces were useless, Abe was a tough guy and a tough guy to get to know. But at this meeting where we had just presented strong conflicting opinions, Jack insisted we get to know Abe as well as Pratt & Whitney's Chief Metallurgist, who was also there. Jack was a pretty forward person, much more so than I was, so he invited the Pratt & Whitney duo to dinner that night. Surprisingly, they agreed. We went to dinner, talked a little about industry and our differences, but we kept it light. Then we went to a magic show afterwards. And that's how I met Abe Willan. That evening of light-hearted entertainment and conversation allowed me later to follow-up with him and to get the first toe of our foot in the door at Pratt & Whitney.

I made a call to see Abe, but he didn't want to give me five minutes. He let me in, but told me pointedly that Pratt & Whitney didn't want any part of high vacuum furnaces. He said, "We have all of these hydrogen roller hearth furnaces, and they're doing what we need to do. As a matter of fact, we once bought a vacuum furnace from Stokes out of Philadelphia, and that furnace never worked right. We had to scrap it, and I don't want to go down that road again. We are hydrogen, and it's going to be hydrogen, hydrogen, *hydrogen*, Bill. Do you understand?" I respectfully said that I did. I thought that was the end of the conversation, but he completely surprised me and kept talking.

He went on to say that Pratt & Whitney had another plant, the Canal Pratt & Whitney plant in Southeastern Connecticut, which was in the process of developing an atomic engine for use in outer space. Abe told me, "We have a bunch of nuts over there. They're all Ph.D.'s, Bill, and they're working on all this crazy stuff. They always want to buy these way-out furnaces like you make. I don't want to do it. I think they're all crazy. But I'll tell you what. You know this technology, and I want you to look at the bids they send me, and I want you to tell me why we shouldn't buy it. Let's see what happens. You're not going to get any orders out of this; I just want to use you to beat these people down." Abe was very direct and up-front with me, that's how he was, always. But I thought, "I need to get myself into this company somehow," so I said ok.

So, about once a month, he would send me one of these "way out" things, and I'd look it over and tell him, by return letter, what was good or bad about it. We never bid on any of those, and I don't know if he had anyone else bid on them, or if any were ever bought.

One day, he called me and said, "Bill, I've got something that's real. We have to buy a vacuum furnace here at East Hartford. We have some titanium jet engine parts that need to be out-gassed. Others are doing it, and we aren't. We have to do it. I'm going to send you specifications of what we are thinking about." What he sent me was really an outline of specifications, but I looked at it and produced a proposal. They had also asked Ipsen and some other companies to bid on this. It was a big furnace, and when Willan reviewed my proposal, he called me. He said, "I want you to come up here, Bill, and meet with our Chief Metallurgist and a couple of our other engineers. They have some questions." So, I went and met with them.

Now, this was a big moment for me and for ABAR. We had been unsuccessful in breaking into Pratt & Whitney thus far, and this could be our moment. There was a lot of pressure on me to make the presentation. I was also dealing with some really high-level professionals. But I'd learned early on that confidence was key, and I always came prepared. I always brought my proposal, the relevant paperwork, and my slide rule. Always. The paperwork showed my professionalism. The slide rule revealed my true nature as an engineer and my technical knowledge. I always told myself going into a meeting like this that while these people may know a lot, I'm the only one in this room who is an expert on *this* furnace. That mindset has always worked for me.

The meeting went well, as I knew it would. A couple of weeks went by, and Willan finally called me to tell me they were placing the order with ABAR. "You're the only one we can trust," he said. The fact that I knew the technology and I had willingly worked with them for about a year without expectations won Willan over.

So, boom, bang, down from the purchasing department comes this order from Pratt & Whitney for this huge $500,000 vacuum furnace. We built it, put it into operation, did what we said we were going to do, and it ran as it should. A successful transaction by all accounts.

About six months later, Willan called me again with another application. He sent me his specs, which were highly irregular, and we sent our bid, and ended up with that order, too. He must have purchased 12 or 14 vacuum furnaces from us. We were basically their sole source. He froze everyone else out. Even though he had other vendors bid, they couldn't get past the front desk. He let them quote, but wouldn't award the job to anyone but ABAR, I think simply because I had passed his test. Abe was maybe 15 years older than I was, and he treated me somewhat like a son. We developed a firm friendship. But at the plant, there could be no fraternization. I couldn't even take him to dinner as a client, though he took me to lunch at the company's cafeteria a few times. Later, Abe Willan's dedication to ABAR would be questioned.

Now we were gaining momentum and building a name for ourselves, carving out our niche in the jet age. But Ipsen was still a major competitor, having broken into the industrial vacuum market around 1956 or 1957. But they didn't go into the high vacuum part of the business—they stuck with tool and die manufacturing, and with a cheaply built furnace, they weren't keeping up with us. We were in the same business, but we had a very different animal. Ipsen was selling their furnaces, but their furnaces weren't doing the job. Their furnaces lacked the vacuum integrity ours had—our furnaces were built tight and had good vacuum-pumping technology. Essentially, Ipsen failed to innovate—they continued producing furnaces that fit the needs of their customers from ten or more years ago, though their customers' needs had been evolving and faced greater metallurgical challenges. Additionally, Ipsen's customer service was sorely lacking. At ABAR, if anyone from Pratt & Whitney or GE called, they went right to the top. We were highly attuned to their needs and very responsive, and they knew it. The switchboard operators knew to interrupt me or the next in command if Pratt & Whitney or GE called. Ipsen relied heavily on salesmanship and pricing, letting their sales staff do the job, but falling down on service and maintenance once the sale was closed.

Around 1972, after establishing a solid relationship with Abe Willan, a curious thing happened. I was invited to meet the upper echelon of Pratt & Whitney. In all my years building furnaces for Abe, I dealt with him, the Chief Engineer, and so on, but never the upper strata. They had plans to build an automatic casting facility for casting engine blades. At the heart of it was a special vacuum casting unit with a loading degassing furnace—a vacuum furnace. We quoted on this. A German company also quoted on the project. Coincidentally, a big wheel in the Pratt & Whitney machine, their Operations Vice President, was married to a German woman. This competing German company put pressure on this man, through his wife, to secure the order for them. But Willan wanted to place the order with ABAR. So, Willan called me and told me to make a presentation to this executive, since the decision was going to come to his desk. Willan needed me to report to the Pratt & Whitney office by 6 a.m. the following morning.

Though I had virtually no time to prepare a presentation, I knew the material inside and out. I set off for the meeting.

Upon arriving at Pratt & Whitney, I sat first with Abe Willan. Willan proceeded to tell me that my upcoming meeting with this P&W executive was the most important meeting of my life. He told me, "Bill, whatever you say, you must be very, very careful. The wrong word and maybe 10 people could be fired. Be very, very careful." Well, that set the stage.

From there, we went to his boss's office, who told me exactly the same thing: I must, must be very careful. With that warning, we went up to the next level. Now, I'm left with a new executive, who issues the same edict: be very, very careful. He told me I'd meet with yet another Pratt & Whitney executive, and said, "I don't know you, but you have to be very careful about what you say. This man has 10,000 people reporting to him. You could do unheard of damage to the company and our employees if you say the wrong thing."

This was pressure. I couldn't imagine the magnitude of it. I was only around 36 or 37 at the time and still earning my stripes, and these top executives are warning me to watch what I say or people will be fired. It was ABAR versus the Germans, Abe Willan's recommendation against the Operations Vice President's, and people's jobs were at stake. All I could do was make my recommendation based on the technology I knew would suit their needs and leave the politics, and what other factors were at play, outside of it.

Still, I was not worried. I knew how to present these furnaces and how to answer questions. I was confident in what I knew. I always approached meetings such as this as an engineer, not a salesman. Again, I knew more than anyone else in the room about the technical aspects of this furnace. So, after a morning of tense meetings with nervous executives, the magic hour came. A secretary ushered me in to the top office. I wasn't sure what I would encounter, but he caught me completely off guard when he spoke. He said simply, "Bill, would you like a cup of coffee?" I replied that I would.

Now, there was an unwritten and well-known rule at Pratt & Whitney: nobody drank coffee. I knew of this rule, and I was interested to note that this rule did not apply to this man. Employees, vendors, guests, etc. could not drink coffee in that plant, except in the cafeteria. But this gentleman had his own coffee machine. I was clearly at the top, and if this man wanted to offer me coffee, I would accept. At that point, I had the confidence to see myself at his level, and I was unflustered. A less-confident person would perhaps politely decline, but I saw no reason to do so. In a way, this levelled the playing field and now we were both simply businessmen having a discussion. With this formality dispensed with, he had his secretary come in with a tray and served us coffee and a couple of cookies, decidedly polite and hospitable. And we got down to business.

He started to talk to me about this furnace. He said, "You know, there's a real argument going on about whether we should buy this thing from Germany, or whether we should buy it here in the United States. If we buy it here, we're going to buy it from you." He asked me my opinion on the matter. Why should they buy from us? I gave him my honest and classic answer of customer service, proximity to Pratt & Whitney and speed of support, and so on. Never once did he bring up a specific person or persons, never did he hint at any influence on a particular party, and I, of course, didn't mention it, either. After a bit more discussion, he thanked me for coming up to see him, we shook hands, and I left.

I went back down to see Willan and his boss, who wanted to know word-for-word the conversation I had had with the top brass. They debriefed me, and I told them what I'd said. They were nervous and a bit skeptical. "We'll see, Bill," they hesitantly told me.

By the end of the week, the executive had made his decision, and we had the order. All of the tension and hand-wringing finished with a brief discussion. It was done. It was a great experience for me. I had been thrown into an extremely contentious situation and could have cracked under the pressure. But I didn't. Why? Not because I have a cast iron constitution or because I'm arrogant. No, I knew my product and the technology. I knew I was the most knowledgeable person in the room where that was concerned. I had the answers to his questions, and that was all this executive wanted to know.

Abe Willan was a constant presence in those days. Around 1974, he called me, quite concerned. He had learned that OSHA intended to write a policy on vacuum furnace safety, and he admitted, "We're scared to death of that." He went on to tell me about the NFPA—National Fire Protective Association—a committee responsible for writing standards for an industry, and about a book called the NFPA 86 Standard. It seems there was no standard for a vacuum furnace. Abe decided he and I would join this committee and that I would write the standard.

I said, "Abe, I don't want to go on this crazy committee and write a standard!"

But Abe pressed. He told me, "You're going to have to. Because if you don't write it, OSHA is going to write it for you." And with that explanation, Willan dragged me along and I, too, joined the committee and wrote the first standard for the vacuum furnace on the 86-D Committee.

Now, this was a large committee, comprised of about 20 men from all kinds of groups—Pratt & Whitney, GE, Honeywell, Ipsen, all the insurance companies—and everyone had their own agenda. But despite the breadth of experience on that committee, there was no one else who really knew and understood vacuum. That book was written directly around the ABAR furnace, though there was a small section about the Ipsen furnace. The spec was written around the ABAR furnace completely. It went through the committee but no one challenged it, because no one knew enough about it. If I spoke at that committee, it was a done deal, because I was at the top of the heap at that time. Though it was a conflict of interest, and there were a few updates throughout the years, it remains an honest, accurate standard.

BECOMING PRESIDENT OF ABAR—1975

As the years went on and we'd built a significant number of furnaces for Pratt & Whitney, Abe and I had cemented our respectful relationship. Sometime in 1975, he called me out of the blue with a question. In his inimitable way, Abe blurted out without preamble, "Bill, why aren't you president of ABAR?" I reminded him that there was a board of directors, and they appoint the president. I only have a small ownership. "Doesn't make any difference, Bill. I'm going to call Martin and tell him you should be president."

He called Dr. Martin, just as he said he would, and suggested my promotion to president of ABAR. King Fifth Wheel was also selling to Pratt & Whitney at this time, and even though Willan wasn't the buyer for those components, he was still a top client for both companies and commanded attention. We all understood if Willan had something to say, we had to listen.

A few weeks went by, and Dr. Martin came to my office, relaying that phone conversation with Willan and wondering if I'd put him up to it. I replied that I certainly had not, but right or wrong, Willan thought I should be president of the company. Martin declared, because of Willan's high praise and recommendation, I should be president. And so, I was promoted and became president of ABAR. I was not yet 40 years old.

When I'd first joined ABAR, and King Fifth Wheel bought us out, they believed we would be prosperous and make a good deal of money. They didn't want to freeze us out, the three original owners, so they offered Charlie, Art, and I an opportunity to buy back 6% of the company, after one year, for whatever the new value was at that time. We did not blossom as KFW thought we would. In fact, we lost money, and ABAR was worth zero when we were eligible to purchase the shares. Charlie and Art declined, but I bought my 6% share for $500, despite their protestations. They reminded me that ABAR was virtually worthless, and I was effectively throwing money away. I disagreed with them. I had a good feeling about where we might go, if we could get ourselves straightened out. At the time, however, Dr. Martin was not pleased. He didn't want to sell to me, but we had this legal buy/sell agreement, and he had to stick to it. So, I owned 6% of ABAR, and Martin owned 94%. What I didn't realize at the time was the power and value of being a single minority ownership. I could have caused all sorts of trouble, if I'd wanted to, in various business dealings, and so forth. I didn't, though. In fact, I was acquiescent about the whole thing. I didn't know the power I had. I was only interested in the technology, not the business aspect of ABAR, except I wanted the company to grow and become profitable.

We knew Martin wanted to sell all his company interest and retire eventually. And here I was with 6% of the company. As time went on, Martin became aloof to me. He would come to the plant every week or so, and invite various management team members to lunch with him. Soon, I was no longer invited to lunch. I was held at arm's length.

There was a man who worked for KFW, Jack Gibbons. His title was Vice President of Sales. He and Martin became personal friends when Jack, a Captain, served under Martin, a Colonel, in the Second World War. After the war, Jack came to work for Martin as his sales manager. He had previously been a salesman for a firm selling dynamite to construction sites. Well, Jack was an alcoholic. He had done a great deal to build the sales of KFW, but not all of it in the most legitimate way. I knew of many escapades, some ending in a jail cell. The executives at KFW grew weary of bailing him out, so they pulled Jack from the field and bound him to the office. He ended up with no assignment. For his last five years at KFW, he came to work and was paid to read the paper. They gave him the "assignment" of being ABAR's Executive Vice President. Martin was CEO, I was President, and Jack was Executive Vice President.

Jack would come to my office nearly every day around 10 a.m., and just sit. He was privy to my phone conversations and the daily goings-on in my office, but he only listened. He never interfered or said anything to me about my decisions, conversations, anything. He did, however, report back to Dr. Martin.

I didn't mind, I knew what he was doing. I had sort of become accustomed to being under the watchful eye of the boss when I worked at MEECO. I worked right next to Dr. Bergson, and this was a similar situation. When Bergson came in to work, he was consumed with heady things and left me alone, but all my work was basically done in front of him. Gibbons was much the same way, except Bergson produced work. Jack did not, and for that, I resented him a bit. But slowly, I came to take him into my confidence and slowly, he did the same. Jack and I became quite good friends. Every now and again, he might make a suggestion or advise me in business matters or personal matters involving ABAR. This was a unique situation.

One day, I approached Jack about my strained relationship with Dr. Martin, hoping he'd have some insight. I told him about Martin's obvious disdain for me. He agreed with me, and I admitted I didn't quite know what to do about it. I suggested it might be because of my 6% ownership, and Jack confirmed my suspicion. He said plainly that Martin wanted my 6% and was willing to buy it. I explained to Jack that I really didn't want to sell it, that it was my key to staying at ABAR.

With the sale of ABAR to KFW, we were asked to sign a non-compete agreement, which I did. It was an iron-clad, attorney authored agreement in which I agreed to remain loyal to the KFW organization. By the time I had this conversation with Jack over my 6% ownership, I was the only one in the company who had this agreement. I discussed with Jack my willingness to sell my ABAR ownership back to Dr. Martin for ABAR's current market value, provided this agreement ended. I was not going to stay employed under those circumstances when I didn't have any ownership of the company.

Jack took this information back to Martin, as I knew he would, and Martin eventually invited me to come talk to him about it. Martin didn't care about the agreement, he only wanted the stock. The accountants got to work and arrived at the value of the stock, based on the market value of ABAR at that time. My investment of $500 in only 6% share of ABAR, at a time when it was just about worthless, earned me $50,000.

When Martin learned this value, he was absolutely infuriated. But that figure represented 17 years of hard work, dedication, and vision. I didn't do it alone, of course, but I turned that company around. I had a lot of good people working for me, but my leadership and technical drive propelled the company from near-failure to profitability. Martin agreed to the sale, for $50,000 and dropped the agreement. The money was paid out over the next three years, which was fine with me, as I intended to stay with ABAR. With this transaction completed, Martin was free to sell ABAR with his KFW company whenever he wished, as we knew he would do. The fact is, within the next few years my 6% ownership would have tripled in value. So Martin, in fact, made a very good deal. At least financially. Later, it would not turn out to be so valuable.

After the buyout was complete, ABAR's patent attorney, Zach Wobensmith, came in to my office unannounced one day, closed the door, and sat down. He said, out of the blue, "Bill, you're going to need a patent attorney. I can't represent you, of course, but you'll need someone." I had no clue why he said this, as I had no intentions of leaving ABAR at the time. He gave me Bill Cleaver's business card. Wobensmith recommended Cleaver to me based on his previous dealings with him and his respect for a worthy opponent. I didn't think much of this, just accepted the card and filed it. With that efficiently handled within ten minutes, he left my office. I wasn't nervous that it meant more than it was, and I honestly didn't give it another thought until Wobensmith's prediction proved true. I would need my own patent attorney.

At the time, as with many such conversations or meetings, I had no idea those few minutes with Wobensmith would be so crucial to my success. Those moments were, I believe, providential. They happened to me almost without my understanding, and certainly without my orchestration, but they were nonetheless stepping stones to my future path. Dr. Bentley's prediction of my yet-to-be solo ventures; Abe Willan calling me out of the blue to declare my promotion to president; Wobensmith's seemingly inspired belief that I would need a patent attorney. Did they see something I couldn't?

Despite all of these changes and providential meetings, it was still business as usual. Ipsen was our principal competitor. They were the vacuum furnace manufacturer to the general industry. But as the years went on, ABAR was able to significantly narrow the gap, and by around 1976, we had Ipsen on the ropes. With our metal hot zone, they didn't have a product to compete with us. In the beginning, when we first went into the commercial business, Ipsen beat us every time. Eventually we found our niche and owned it.

But as ABAR was growing, troubles were brewing through a series of small, seemingly unrelated, decisions. Although I didn't immediately see them, these small issues would grow and ultimately lead to my departure from the company I'd helped to build.

Before ABAR found our niche, Ipsen had kept us on our toes, and we had decided we needed a sales manager. Bill Hoke had been hired to do the job. The interview was a bit tumultuous and was a portent of things to come. As my employee, I felt Bill and I got along just fine, but he was rather difficult to work for and with. I interviewed Bill, along with ABAR president Vern Gooderham. Ipsen was the industry leader, and we really needed to cut into their market share. There was a particular customer in Connecticut who wouldn't let us in the door, because their local sales rep for Ipsen, Don Frompkin, dominated the place. Later, we would hire him, on Bill Hoke's and

Abe Willan's recommendations. But at first, we needed Hoke to break apart Ipsen's stronghold.

During the interview, I asked Bill to tell us how he would handle this situation and how he felt we could get our foot in the door with this company in Connecticut. Bill, an experienced salesman, was really offended. He felt there was no way he could answer those questions, since he knew so little about our product, our company, or indeed, our business. He felt it was wrong of me to have asked such a question and put him on the spot. As a salesperson seeking a high-level position within our organization, I thought he should have the ability to examine the problem and tell me how he would have set about it. But he was visibly annoyed with that question. Despite this rocky start, we hired Bill as our Vice President of Sales.

With Bill Hoke at the helm of a good sales team, we started edging our way closer to Ipsen. We were making changes to our sales policies and allowing more generous warranties that Ipsen refused to consider. We were, of course, making technological advances, as well. Ipsen's vacuum chamber design remained the same, as did our competitors, while ABAR was taking risks and making great strides in technology. Ipsen's heating elements were very thick graphite elements. ABAR built thin, pliable moly elements. Even though Ipsen's elements were rugged, they had a few flaws. ABAR's skinny shields allowed our furnaces to cool quickly and evenly, but our competition scoffed at them, calling them "flimsy."

Bill Hoke hit upon the idea to produce a sales video, a brilliant solution to the problem of how to engage the customer and touch on the relevant points in a short amount of time. It was a short video, only about 13 minutes, but it had a major impact. It contained quite a bit of technical information a sales person might not be able to impart in the typical sales call. It also compared the ABAR hot zone to the Ipsen hot zone, and it directly answered the criticism of the so-called "flimsy" moly elements. We also offered a full, one-year warranty, something unheard of in the industry. All our competitors only offered a 30-, or at the most 90-day, warranty. All of this was in the video. Completely overseen by Hoke, the video was just technical enough and our customers responded.

Hoke and I also worked with Bob Drake, the president of KFW, to institute a new accounting method. Traditionally, engineering and sales butted heads frequently, because salespeople sell an idea and engineering has to make it real. Essentially, engineers have to keep the promises made to customers by the sales department. That can be tricky when engineering is only allotted so many hours to a project, due to budgets. Sure, you can make a product to exacting and sometimes unique specifications, but it will take time. Our profit margins left little wiggle room for that, and so sales, engineering, and accounting were often at loggerheads.

Hoke had heard of a new accounting method, called the contribution margin method, which would allow for that wiggle room and give the sales team a bit of leeway to close a deal. He went to see Bob Drake, who was proficient in this method, and came back excited about implementing it. He sold me on the idea, and I sold King Fifth Wheel on it, and that allowed us to create an even greater advantage over Ipsen. A dedicated sales team, good pricing, flexibility, and a good product. We were narrowing the gap.

As the company was growing and sales were increasing, I was approached by my chief engineer, Ben Kreider. He was insistent that he receive a raise so that he would earn more than our sales manager, Bill Hoke. Ben believed engineering was the most important aspect of the company, because without an engineer, you had no product to sell. Wanting to be fair and impartial, and because I was slightly perplexed by this problem, I hired someone from Manufacturer's Association (MADV) to conduct a wage comparison. Quite frankly, I wasn't sure who the higher contributor to the company was. After an audit of both positions, the gentleman wrote me a nice 10- or

12-page report. The net result was simply this: that without an order, you don't have an engineer. Bill Hoke trumped Ben Kreider, and I had to recognize that. Now, I didn't give Bill a tremendous increase but that infuriated Ben to no end.

Later, still furious about the decision, Ben talked to me about the assessment. Turns out, he had investigated the person I had hired to conduct the comparison. The person was, at that time, the general manager of MADV and, so as far as I was concerned, they had vetted him, and he was solid. Turned out: he had been a bartender. Ben said, "You know, Bill…Do you know who this guy is that you've hired? You've hired a bartender to evaluate us." Didn't matter. The assessment was accurate and professionally done, and helped clarify some issues in my mind. I was satisfied. Done.

THE ROUND HOT ZONE

The ABAR days, especially the early years, were truly an exciting time for me. It was the era of Sputnik, the Space Race, satellites, and commercial jet engines. It was a time when new technologies were emerging daily. There were many highs and lows during my 17 years there; that's the nature with business, of course. Throughout my career, I was privileged to be a part of a number of "firsts" in the industry; some I developed, some as part of a team. At ABAR, I experienced a significant number of "firsts" that would have an impact on me and start me on my journey towards self-employment. Those I felt were the most significant have been grouped together in their own chapter with other "firsts" from my other companies. But the Round Hot Zone…that deserves special mention.

Of all the ABAR "firsts," this was one changed the company and my career. Truthfully, it changed the industry. This new development in ABAR's early days would set us apart from all our competitors and would launch a new way of thinking about vacuum furnace hot zones. Everything changed because of this one particular event. The secret: thinking about something differently to achieve a new outcome.

What was the development? The first round hot zone.

When Charlie Hill was still with us, ABAR received an order from Union Carbide out in Oak Ridge, Tennessee. With the order, they provided a single line sketch depicting their furnace needs. There was the hot zone—with hearth bars coming up out of the bottom of the cold wall chamber that then supported the work grid—and typical internal heating elements. But the main point of it was the round hot zone, with a hearth support that enabled you to get under the grid with a forklift truck. With this feature, you could back in, pick the grid up, pull it out, put your part on the grid, put the grid back in the furnace, close the furnace up, pump the chamber down, and heat everything up. Then, the user could backfill the chamber with inert gas and cool it off.

Union Carbide didn't specify a cooling system, though it was obvious that the hot zone was not internally water-cooled. Prior to that, we were building furnaces with water-traced copper heat sinks—using copper plates—and the entire system was all water cooled. It was an absolute nightmare to build, and expensive. But the way furnaces were built in those days, you could not get anything of any real size or weight in them.

Well, we received this order, and Charlie Hill put two new engineers on the project, and they designed and built it. When it was all assembled on the floor, I looked it over. It was so unlike what we were used to building, and I was struck by the thought that the round metal rings, the integral part of the round hot zone, were just hanging from two supports at the top. What was to stop it from sagging from the high temperatures? We had no idea how hot the hot-zone ring was going to run. We didn't even have an estimate of it. We built it and really had no way of knowing if it would work or not.

By this point, I was used to examining a design or product and determining its potential or flaws, and I must admit, I was really concerned about the design—particularly, the ring. The way it looked to me, I could see the potential for it going egg-shaped. The only way to be sure was to test it.

The hot zone had three rings inside it. I asked for two of the rings to be removed, leaving only the center ring. I wanted to take that center ring up to full power and temperature and watch what happened. The two outer rings were removed, and that night, I went back to the plant alone. I don't know why I went alone, but I did. This was a defining moment for me.

I cranked that thing up. I started up the vacuum furnace and then put full power on that ring, and I observed it. I watched it with an L&N disappearing filament optical pyrometer—if not for my previous experience at IDL, I wouldn't have known how to do that. I watched as the internal hot zone and ring rapidly came up to temperature.

And it was like a sunrise. A brilliant, beautiful sunrise.

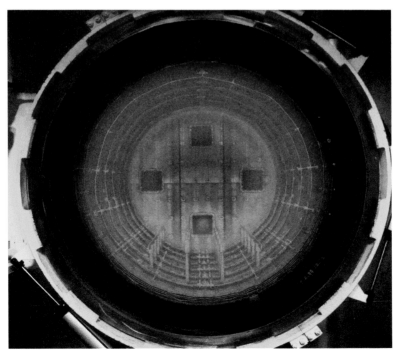

First test firing of the ring hot zone (simulated).

This may sound silly, but it was an emotional moment. It was a glorious sight.

I finally took it up to full temperature, and I measured the temperature of everything, including that ring. It was stable as a rock—no sagging, no movement whatsoever. It was the most exciting thing I ever saw in my life—like watching a glowing sunrise. Spectacular. I was thrilled to death to be able to test that and see how well it worked.

The next day, I shared the successful test results with everyone. I declared it an absolutely wonderful design. I was just delighted with it. I asked that the furnace be completely put back together for further testing. It was a complete success.

After it was all over, and shipped, I received a special "Q" clearance in order to go to Oak Ridge and put the furnace into operation. And I discovered what it was meant for: heat treating a half-sphere shaped piece of tantalum alloy. Given the time in our nation's history, you can imagine what these spheres were meant for. The magnitude of what we'd contributed to was not lost on me. It was a significant furnace.

Now, since we didn't have the copper heat sinks in this furnace, it was a vast improvement over our competitors' and our own previous models. The round hot zone allowed for oddly shaped or larger loads to be heat treated, vertically or horizontally. Additionally, one of the most significant features of the design was the ability to get under the load to pick it up with a forklift. Why? Because up until we designed this model, the typical furnace used rollers in a conveyor fashion to place a load into the hot zone, aided by another set of rollers, this time ceramic. You couldn't put anything too heavy in it, because you couldn't move it. Also, every time you cooled that furnace, you broke a ceramic roller due to heat shock. You were constantly replacing rollers.

With this furnace, all of that was eliminated. However, we didn't realize how valuable that was at first, beyond the convenience of not using ceramic rollers. We originally saw this space below the hot zone as wasted space, and it took us about a year before we realized how truly game-changing it was. Now you didn't have all the labor from the copper heat sinks, making it less expensive to build, and the round hot zone and the ability to load and unload with a forklift completely changed the game. There were so many applications. Best of all, no one was doing it. We were the first, and we changed the industry.

First ABAR round, all metal hot zone.

At the time, we were a small, struggling company. We didn't patent this industry-changing design. We didn't have the time or resources to do it. Also, we really didn't know what we had until after it was well established. Since we didn't know how unique this design was or how far-reaching the possibilities, we fired the two engineers who designed it. When they presented their hours for the project, we thought they killed us on engineering time. They presented about 2500 hours to us, and we thought it was obscene. Looking back, it was a reasonable amount of time for what was accomplished.

The round hot zone changed everything. It changed how the industry looked at furnaces.

Today, there's still a roaring controversy on whether you should heat treat inside of a round circle like we have or whether it ought to be in a square box. It's an argument about heat transfer. Here's the argument: you have a square hot zone, and your work is sitting in the middle of it. Those in favor of the square hot zone will say you have the most uniform heating in a square because you're heating from all sides and uniformly. But what about the corners? The corners are being overheated because they are being heated from the top, the sides, and the bottom. Comparably, with our round hot zone, the work load is in the middle. Now your load truly is being heated from all directions, and it's uniform because the heating elements are all the way around, encircling the work load.

Ipsen has always stayed true to their square hot zone. But I had long been a proponent for change in design; there's always a better way to do something. There's no sense in reinventing the wheel, unless you can make a better one.

After years of struggling with constraints at MEECO and IDL, this departure from the tried and true was refreshing. The round hot zone upped the ante and made people consider new possibilities. This is what I was happiest doing—how can we make it better? Our innovation was immensely satisfying.

Let's talk about Ipsen for a moment. Ipsen was really ahead of ABAR in the commercial world. Not so much in the more scientific world or in the high temperature world, or even in high vacuum—there were others who were in that field and dominated Ipsen. But here's what Ipsen did: Around 1950, Harold Ipsen went to Germany and found a man, a PhD, who had designed a horizontal vacuum furnace, and he hired this gentleman and brought him over to the U.S. The vacuum chamber was round but inside was a square steel box. It was heavily insulated with about six inches or so of high temperature insulation, called Kaowool®. Then, inside the insulation, the furnace had tubular graphite heating elements. Now, Ipsen had ceramic tubes that came from the sides of the steel box, and using these ceramic tubes, you could open the door and push a basket full of work over the ceramic tubes. They acted as rollers. Unfortunately, every run over those rollers was tricky. Ceramic is very sensitive to heat, and if you heat it and cool it too fast, those tubes would break. Coincidentally, he actually made these tubes as well, which was quite handy to his business model.

Typical Ipsen Vacuum Furnace with ceramic hearth roller.

Up in the top of the hot zone, Ipsen's furnaces had a shutter, called a bung; it was a cylinder with a fan at the top. Underneath this was a simple baffle, also on a cylinder. So, when you were under heat with everything closed up, no radiation escaped out of the hot zone. When you went to cool it down, you could simply backfill the chamber with nitrogen gas and open this, open that, and turn the fan on so you were pulling gas through the work to cool it.

Well, there were also these graphite heater tubes that would break, which was a problem. The graphite tubes were not screwed together—they were like Tinker Toys—so they tended to loosen up and arc. Then, there was this bung. It was like a door of a chest of drawers. This thing would warp, which meant it would open and jam, but nobody knew because you couldn't exactly see it. So, when the user turned the hot zone power back on again, all this radiant heat would come up, cooking the fan, distorting it, which would also burn up the motor. So, the furnace had those problems.

Then there were seals that were not too well designed, so you didn't get a very good vacuum. Or when you did backfill, you had some air leaking inside, and you wouldn't get clean work. Additionally, this Kaowool® insulation all around the hot zone would never go to deep vacuum. They did some tricky things with their vacuum gauges to make it look like it was a lot better than it really was.

But the thing about Ipsen furnaces was that they worked, were accepted, and had become sort of the standard, particularly for the commercial heat treating business because no one much cared if things came out a little discolored. It was also cheap: Ipsen built this furnace for 25 to 30% less than we could. Nobody could touch that price. Ipsen built hundreds, if not thousands, of these furnaces. They did make some improvements over time, but the basic structure remained the same.

I've always felt that if I had been at Ipsen, I could have done it—I could have worked those problems out of the furnace. But that was not Ipsen's way. Ipsen's philosophy was to build it, put it together like a pair of shoes, and ship it.

Despite the many problems, Ipsen stayed faithful to their model and design, and were leaders in the industry for quite a long time. When Charlie Hill, Art Couillard, and I started making changes at ABAR, sometimes we were surprised that no one had thought of these changes before, like the round hot zone. Once we saw it, it made perfect sense. But, for one reason or another, change and innovation were not widely practiced in our industry. That made it a perfect proving ground for me.

My reputation benefitted from the round hot zone's ground-breaking design, too. Certainly, I'd made a name for myself by then. But now we were the forerunners. We were the go-to guys for cutting-edge technology. As we took more risks and pushed the boundaries of accepted technologies, I was enjoying the freedom to expand on who I was as a member of an organization, too. I enjoyed leading. The limitations I felt from prior positions were being released with each successful project I directed. Though I had no inkling yet of running my own business, the feeling of being released to do things "my way" at ABAR was one I savored.

Additionally, as our reputation grew, I was learning it was better to be a big fish in a little pond, rather than a little fish in a big pond. I was getting bigger and bigger in our little pond, and I was careful to cultivate that—partly to benefit ABAR, but mostly to benefit myself. Call it ego, call it a drive to be successful, reputation was important to me. Innovations like the round hot zone would soon become synonymous with Bill Jones. And the idea that my name stood for innovation, knowledge, quality, honesty, and integrity became a major factor in who I would become as an entrepreneur.

ABAR & HEAT TREATING

Now, all this time, ABAR was all about furnaces—making them, selling them, supporting them. Well, we had a customer, Bennett Heat Treating, up in Newark, New Jersey, who purchased two furnaces from me for their heat treating business. From this relationship and a visit to their plant, I knew just how profitable the heat treating business could be. The two owners, Dave Mazer and Tony Quaglia, were making an unbelievable amount of money: One drove a Cadillac and the other a Lincoln, and their top company managers all had top-of-the-line company cars. All of them lived out in the suburbs of Northwestern New Jersey, in an area where Jackie Kennedy had one of her summer homes. Dave and Tony always took customers to lunch—to a good restaurant—and they always paid. They were well-dressed, smart, hard-working men, and, clearly, they were doing quite well.

The first time I went up to the plant—around 1965—I noticed the activity; they had a fair-sized plant, and they were overwhelmed with work. You had to park three or four blocks away due to all the cars crowded around the plant. There was product stacked up all over the sidewalk waiting to come in to be heat treated, and there were boxes waiting to be loaded and shipped out to customers. Trucks were coming and going, and you could barely get in the door. Once inside, the receptionist sat before a P.B.X. console lit up like a Christmas tree, with the telephone cords plugged in everywhere, and she was kept so busy by the constant ringing phone that she barely had time to look up and take my information. All this while she was typing invoices.

I could see inside the main office, and it was crammed with desks and people. Everyone had a great sense of urgency. People were everywhere, darting in and out of offices. Customers were on the phone with requests. Plant and office staff were having heated discussions (as only North Jersey people can conduct) about schedules, processing requirements, and specifications. Dave took me to the office he shared with his partner, Tony Quaglia, their desks facing each other. The two men never stopped. While one was on the phone, another was receiving someone from the shop, who stopped in for a question, and they spoke with me in between. The pace was relentless and dizzying. It was a mad house.

And I saw, quite clearly, they were making money hand over fist, like they were minting it.

From my experience with Bennett, my mind jumped to two conclusions pretty quickly: first, ABAR could also go into the heat treating business—quite easily—and secondly, we could build better vacuum furnaces if we became more knowledgeable about the users' processing needs. In other words, I realized that if we did what they did, we'd know better how to build exactly what they needed.

However, we weren't able to jump into heat treating until a bit later.

A number of months passed after that meeting at Bennett. I had a phone call come in from Kelsey-Hayes, a division of Heintz in Philadelphia, just a few miles away from us. One of their engineers had the front stator section for a jet engine they had fabricated. The stator was about four feet in diameter, with radial arms, and needed post-welding stress relieving, in vacuum.

We just happened to have a brand new vacuum furnace built for General Electric, with a 6' x 6' hot zone, ready to ship on the floor, and it was all connected. The engineer at Kelsey-Hayes wanted to know if we could run the cycle *that* day and how much it would cost. I thought about the time involved and if it would delay shipping this furnace to the customer, and decided we could do it. I came up with a figure—$1,000— and said yes, we could do it that day. He quickly agreed, and in came the part, a real beauty. I ran it myself, that night, for delivery in the morning, and it was successful. Then, we dismantled the furnace and shipped it to G.E. with hardly a delay. It was the easiest thousand I ever made for the company.

That experience became our entry into the heat treating business. It led to the formation of the ABAR Ivyland plant, now ironically owned by Bennett Heat Treating.

It wasn't unusual to build a furnace on spec during a production lag, whenever we were a little slow in between orders. We based these models on what we thought the industry would support, and at one time, we had three ready to go. We sold two, but one model remained unsold. We decided we would use that model to provide heat treating services for some local companies. It was our slow but successful start into the commercial heat treat business.

While we were still fairly new to the heat treating business, we were approached by TRW to heat treat a number of special titanium blades—parts for jet engines. In the heat treatment of these blades, the top temperature is highly critical. In metallurgy, there is something called incipient melting, which is when you are near the melting point—and most melting points are quite sharp, so melting will happen at precisely this temperature. This particular product had an incipient melting point that was a rather narrow band, and if you didn't come to just right under the incipient melting point and then cool it immediately, you would overshoot the temperature and ruin the part. These parts were quite expensive for the time—worth about $100,000 back then. We were willing to heat treat them for about $7,000, but the parts were worth so much more.

So, I went to KFW about this project and their accountants declared the need for insurance. They found a company willing to insure us, but for a steep price. Lloyd's of London would be happy to insure the parts, for half of their value. We couldn't afford that. I went back to KFW, explained my predicament to Dr. Martin, and he agreed that ABAR couldn't afford the insurance. However, he agreed to let me accept this job, if I alone ran the furnace and completed the order. No one but me. He would allow me to do it, but he wanted to make absolutely sure it was done right, and that meant I took on the responsibility alone.

I did it, and it turned out fine. And as a result, we received more orders for TRW. If I didn't run the job myself, I watched it very closely. And so the business grew.

We set it up as a separate division, with separate accounting for it. Because it did so well, we built another furnace and had it set up in the center of the main assembly area. Just like Bennett Heat Treating, this new little division of ours was doing nothing but making money. We decided to build a completely separate plant for the heat treating division and move it from our Feasterville location to Ivyland, PA.

One of our design engineers, Skip Martindale, was everyone's go-to guy. He was a mechanical draftsman, but because we had a need for electric design, he learned how to do it. He was extremely adaptable. If anything came along, we went to Skip, and he would get it done. I made the decision to put Skip in charge of that start-up plant. Now, though, we had overhead for this division, and that was a learning experience. Then, we desperately needed to develop sales for that division. Unfortunately, as this business started taking off, Skip began a decline into alcoholism that we could not help him through or continue to overlook. Eventually, we had to let him go, but before that happened, I'd hired his replacement, a man by the name of George Carter. He was a graduate metallurgist from Drexel. Carter had once before interviewed with Bill Hoke for a sales position with ABAR and was turned down. But I saw something in George Carter that Bill hadn't. I knew he could run that plant, and I also felt he could build the business. He did, and from there, the heat treating side of the business took off.

DON FROMPKIN

Once again, out of the blue, Abe Willan called with a commandment, this time suggesting I hire a salesman called Don Frompkin. It was 1975, and Don Frompkin was sales manager at Ipsen. I thought Abe was a little misguided, but he assured me that Frompkin "could sell ice to the Eskimos." By the time Willan called me about it, he'd already spoken to Frompkin and gave him my contact information. Willan urged me to take his call and interview him. Once again, when Willan had a suggestion, it carried some weight. I interviewed Frompkin and found him to be an exceptionally suave character. Although somewhat reserved and soft-spoken, I really didn't know if he would be good or bad for us. So, I asked Bill Hoke to interview Frompkin. Bill, of course, knew of Frompkin, and after interviewing him, Bill reported back to me. He was completely confident that Don would be able to bring in a million dollars in sales per year right off—"We have to hire him." At that time, we were a five-million dollar company, so a million in sales wasn't a minor claim.

Once again, though, I wasn't sure about it. Frompkin came off as a slick and divisive character, the smoothest talker you could meet. Since I was unsure, despite Hoke's recommendation, I asked the president of King Fifth Wheel, Bob Drake, to interview Don Frompkin. He interviewed Don and said, without equivocation, he thought I should hire him. He believed Frompkin could do what he claimed, and it would make a big change in the company. Bob Drake was a respected individual with good business sense and his opinion mattered greatly. So, now Bill Hoke wanted him, and Bob Drake had given his approval. I didn't have a good feeling about Frompkin, and although I didn't particularly want to, I hired him. That was the biggest mistake I ever made at ABAR and one of the biggest mistakes of my life.

Frompkin turned out to be a controlling character, and even though he worked for Bill Hoke and me, he did not follow orders or directions whatsoever. As soon as he joined the organization, the atmosphere changed. He needed to be a Big Deal with ABAR, because he'd been a Big Man at Ipsen. He needed an office instead of a cubicle. He convinced me that we needed to change our logo and our signature furnace colors. Bill Hoke went along with this, as well. Frompkin was definitely a force to be reckoned with. He had an agenda, and he was a highly competent individual.

There was a certain kind of furnace I never wanted to build. I had quite specific reasons for not wanting to build it: for one, it was somewhat dangerous, and two, we'd never done it before. It was built to go down into a pit. I told Don explicitly, I absolutely would not build that furnace, and he could not sell that furnace. Well, didn't he go out and sell one of those things, put the purchase order on my desk, and when confronted, simply said, "These people want it, they want it from us, and there's the order. What are you going to do about it? Are you going to mail the order back?" So, we built the furnace at a big loss, but by then he was on to bigger adventures (as is typical for salesmen in our business). He forced my hand and was pushing us into things we just could not do. At the time, the economy was just roaring, and there was a lot of business to be had. He was just taking advantage of it, but this type of situation just grew and grew.

He went on to outsell the company's ability to produce by about a factor of five. Our deliveries went out two or three years. He was a very successful salesman, but we couldn't support him. And this drove me to my wit's end. He committed us to a lot of things that were particularly difficult, and we really struggled because of it. Frompkin coming to the company, as much as anything, caused me to leave ABAR. He completely undermined Bill Hoke and caused so much trouble within the sales department that I ended up firing Bill Hoke. Bill's favor towards Frompkin disappeared pretty quickly, and the two were always at odds. Bill was a pretty opinionated character, but we could still get along together, and we respected each other. But Frompkin was a loose cannon, and he turned the whole sales department against Bill. Not surprisingly, Bill became adamant and stiff. Neither was repentant about their behavior, and there was a lot of animosity. I was caught in the middle and eventually I had to turn one of them out. Even though he was a very good friend, I chose to fire Bill Hoke, and that was another mistake. I should have fired Frompkin, and I kept the memory of this experience clear in my head when I eventually started my own business. Hiring the right people, aligning yourself and your company with employees who hold the same values as you do, is critical. Frompkin was a valuable, though painful, lesson learned.

But I must admit, Don Frompkin wasn't all bad. No employee is one hundred percent good or one hundred percent bad, and one learns to make allowances for people's shortcomings. A good manager will take care to place a person in the proper position, where he or she can flourish. I learned that through experience. As much as I criticize Frompkin and myself for this unhappy period of my history, I do want to acknowledge that his audacious nature, though it caused many headaches, also served us well at times. Especially in a pinch. He was cool and quick on his feet.

For example, one time we were working for several years on an ion-nitriding furnace—a development project of mine. Allison, a division of GM based in Indiana, came to us with a nitriding gear production application. They were nitriding the parts themselves, but were having difficulty achieving uniform quality. They sent us a small gear production work load, and we were able to nitride them beautifully. The people at Allison were elated. Since they needed to process a significant number of parts, Don sold them on the idea of purchasing two furnaces from us. This, we assured them, would allow Allison to keep up with production. They placed the order, and we thought we were all set. Unfortunately, to our horror, we realized that, in order to achieve a full production run, the job would actually require *three* furnaces, not two, as we had originally quoted. (I should note these furnaces each cost around $400,000 at the time.)

Well, Don and I flew to Indianapolis to break the news, and I didn't know how we were going to handle this. I admit I was worried we were going to have a difficult discussion with these men after we'd soundly convinced them that two furnaces would do the trick. I made notes on the flight and tried to work out our strategy. But when we arrived and were all assembled, without a word to me about it first, Don simply said, "Gentlemen, I'm sorry. You're going to have to add a third furnace." No preamble or excuses about miscalculations. I was stunned and waited in silence. And, surprisingly, once Don elaborated, they agreed. I was impressed.

No question, faults aside, Frompkin had a lot of moxie.

STEPPING DOWN

With the added pressure of the Frompkin selling machine, in 1978—just three years after I'd assumed the role of President of ABAR—I was at the breaking point.

In part, this strain was because, at this time, KFW suddenly demanded that I document, document, document. Well, I was not big on setting sales goals when I didn't know where in the world the sales were going to come from, and my management style did not jive with KFW. I knew what I expected each department to produce or provide, and each department, in turn, knew what I expected of them. We all held each other accountable for doing our parts, because if we fell down, orders wouldn't be filled. For the most part, though, I explained my expectations and let each department more or less figure out how they were going to fulfill that.

That was fine until Dr. Martin began looking to retire. Suddenly, my lack of paperwork and projections did not sit well with the two men hired to sell off ABAR and King Fifth Wheel's other companies.

Dr. Martin had recently hired Bob Drake and John Henry, both MBA's—Bob Drake had a manufacturing background, and John Henry's background was in finance, primarily as an analyst; he worked for the accounting firm retained by KFW. So, Bob Drake became president of KFW, and John Henry was hired as the vice president of acquisitions. Their assignment was to pretty-up the five operating companies held by KFW, including ABAR, and prepare them for sale.

Bob Drake and John Henry visited the senior executives at each company and said they needed a five-year sales projection to look like *this* and an operating profit to look like *that*. They told us, in no uncertain terms, where our companies needed to be financially. So, now we had to generate these sales and these operating profits to their specifications, something I hadn't been required to do before. Additionally, we needed to produce a quarterly report on this projection. We were told,

"You're going to tell us how you *intend* to do it, and then tell us how you are *actually* doing it, and we want it backed up with written reports." Those are tough demands. Worse, Bob Drake and John Henry needed certain percentages to show a history of success that would be attractive to a buyer. They forced each one of us in the manufacturing operations to generate these reports each quarter, and we had to continually show this five-year projection. It took a lot of time, and if you didn't make your numbers, you had to explain why.

This experience became quite distasteful to me and weighed heavily on me. I disliked this part of management, and I found it difficult to comply without resentment. The time and the energy to produce the reports and to make them look decent on paper took its toll on me. After nearly a year of this constant drum-beating, I rebelled against it.

I went to Bob Drake at King Fifth Wheel, my boss at the time, and told him I just couldn't take it any longer. I couldn't do it. I had come to the end of my rope, and I wanted to step down as president of ABAR. My health was suffering, as was my home life to some degree. Myrt and I soon realized I couldn't keep pace with the company's demands, and I needed a break. But I wasn't ready to leave ABAR. I suggested to Bob Drake that I step down and become head of the R & D department (not unlike Lee Iacocca had done at Chrysler). I told him I needed to step away from the combined pressures from manufacturing as well as running the sales and engineering departments.

Though not perfect, this solution would be an improvement for me. Because I was feeling a desperate amount of stress, I just wanted a way out of the boiling kettle in which I found myself immersed. Bill Hoke no longer worked at ABAR, and the sales department was completely in charge of the company because of Don Frompkin. I wasn't able to control him, and he and Ben Kreider, our Chief Engineer, were at complete odds with each other, which I couldn't control, either.

Even with all of our advancements and the memory of how far I'd come since joining the company in its heyday, the situation now seemed to be getting out of hand for me. Stepping down and into a new department would allow me to breathe a bit and find some space.

Bob Drake was neither surprised nor expectant about my request. He simply asked who I thought should take my place. I gave him my recommendation: John Henry, who was a really personable fellow with a lot of business, analytical, and financial insight. Henry was a financial analyst, not an engineer, but I knew he'd be the right man for the job. Of course, the powers that be at KFW made the final decision: I went to R & D, and John Henry took over as President.

John Henry took over when I resigned as president in August, and just like that, I became persona non grata. No one consulted me in the least. I was still respected for my technical abilities, but I was left behind. Don Frompkin had John Henry's ear completely. Frompkin knew the business; Henry didn't, so Henry listened to whatever Frompkin had to say. It was an ideal situation for Don, who didn't trust me from that moment on. I think Don was suspicious that I might start my own company and compete with ABAR. (I didn't know it at the time, but he was correct.) So, they were careful not to share too much with me. Once I stepped aside, the sales office door was kept locked. I went from president of the company to restricted access. Although such a change did impact me, I understood it, and it didn't particularly bother me. I was self-sustaining, and I had much experimental work to occupy my mind. I took the opportunity to focus on development projects and, ultimately, my next move.

It has to be said that although I expected ABAR to fold like a house of cards after my departure, it didn't. Quite the opposite, actually. Though Henry's underlings were fighting amongst themselves, and many people were either fired or left shortly after I did, ABAR flourished. John Henry was an astute business man, and after getting his house in order, he eventually bought up most of the competition—including Ipsen, which he bought for $12.5 million around 1992. In short, he built a monopoly. He put together the largest consortium of vacuum furnace builders in the country. So much so that at one point, many years later when I'd started my own vacuum furnace company, I was contacted by the Department of Commerce asking if I was at all concerned about this monopoly. My new venture, Vacuum Furnace Systems, was in full swing, and I truthfully replied, "No. No concerns."

However, John's purchase of Ipsen was a bit like the tail wagging the dog. I have always compared it to AOL buying Time Warner. How could a little fish take on a sick whale and work out a cure? Ipsen's problems couldn't be controlled, so the story ended in the demise of ABAR.

But before it all unraveled, John Henry did inevitably fire Don Frompkin. I imagine Henry learned—as I had—that despite his many strengths as a salesman, no employee should be bigger than the company he supports.

BOOK
2
ENTREPRENEURIAL
HISTORY

A Plan Reveals Itself, VFS Beginnings

Establish solid banking relationships. Don't bounce around for the highest possible return or lowest investment rate. In other words, don't be greedy. Keep the bank informed honestly, so they can trust you implicitly. This is necessary, as you need friends in times of difficulty.

Likewise, establish a good relationship with your accounting auditors, and do not jump around. —WRJ

A round 1978, while I was feeling despondent at ABAR, Myrt and I met independently with two couples, George Bodeen and his wife, and Sam Whalen and his wife. George was the CEO and owner of the Lindbergh Corporation, the largest commercial heat treating business in the United States at that time; Sam had founded his own company back in 1955, Aerobraze Corporation, which specialized in heat treating jet-engine components. I'd had the pleasure of meeting these men during my career, and their opinions mattered a good deal to me. They were well versed in the heat treating and furnace industry.

Myrt and I met with them to discuss my thoughts about leaving ABAR and starting a heat treating business, something we had been discussing as my next move. They both strongly encouraged Myrt and I not to pursue this path. Philadelphia was noted as a shrinking metallurgical market; there was also strong competition from at least a dozen well-established companies in and around Philadelphia. They felt going into heat treating at the time would be a very poor decision, because we lacked a few essentials for this business—the know-how, customer recognition, and a great deal of capital. These sobering conversations took the wind out of my sails and slowed me down a bit. I was left to carry out my work at ABAR as best I could, but the idea was still in the back of my mind.

Around the middle of October of that same year, after I'd stepped down as ABAR's president and was working in the R & D department, I received a phone call from a customer, Jim Williams, of Metal Treating, Inc in Cincinnati, Ohio. This phone call, though at first a seemingly innocent call from a customer, turned the tide for me.

Because of Frompkin, when Jim called me in mid-October, the backlog at ABAR was a least a year and a half out. Jim said he had an order for me, for a new ABAR furnace, but when I told him how long he'd have to wait, he was incredulous. He said he absolutely couldn't wait a year and a half for his furnace; he needed it within six months. He said he had a quote from one of our competitors—Surface Combustion, Inc.—for this furnace, and he asked me to review the specs with him. Well, it was nowhere near what the ABAR furnace was, although he could get it within his six-month timeframe. I told him the unfortunate but true fact that the furnace quoted by our competitor wouldn't do what he wanted it to do. He was disappointed, but admitted that I'd just confirmed what he already suspected. He was really over a barrel. He needed the ABAR furnace, but he needed it quickly. And just like that, I knew what I would do. I said, "Jim, how about a Bill Jones furnace." Jim paused for just a moment then said, "Well, Bill, I bought the first two from you, why wouldn't I buy another from you?" He wasn't the least bit surprised or questioning. Without missing a beat, I asked him to give me a day or two to think it over and get back to him. He agreed. Jim recalls:

All aspects of our business were booming at that time, and I needed bigger facilities. As soon as I got the next plant ready, I needed a big vacuum furnace right away. I went to Bill at ABAR and told him my needs, and explained I needed it as soon as possible. He explained that delivery from ABAR was about a year to a year-and-a-half out. I had it in my head that I needed this furnace in about six months, but I didn't even know if this was realistic or not. I really liked Bill. From my experiences with him, I found him very receptive and helpful. So, it took me about two or three days till I could get up the guts to ask him which one of his competitors I should buy my furnace from. I told him, off the bat, that I wanted to deal with him, but couldn't wait that long. I respected his expertise and asked him where I should go. There was a big pause. Then he said, "would you be interested in a Jones furnace?" Immediately, I jumped at the chance. To this day, I don't regret that decision. So, as easy as that, we discussed the next steps. He would come to me in a couple of days and we'd work out what I needed, map out the furnace.

I had absolutely no misgivings about ordering that furnace from Bill, despite the fact that he had no company to produce it. I had complete faith in him. As soon as he asked if I wanted a Jones furnace, I said yes. A little bit later, I thought, well, I had jumped into that pretty quickly. But no regret about it at all.

I think Bill had been thinking about starting his own company for a time, though he never said anything. He knew where to go, and he resigned from a very good job. That idea of a "Jones" furnace didn't come out of thin air. At that point, we both had a lot to lose, but it was good timing for both of us. It was the right moment; I called him on the perfect day. Later on, I wondered how it had all happened, because it happened so quickly, but so naturally. I ended up buying three furnaces from Bill, and I was ready to buy another one when I ultimately sold my business.

I knew I could build that furnace, and Jim knew I could do it. I had an order if I wanted it, but no company or place for production. It was an interesting predicament. But I knew at that moment that it was time to go out on my own and break ties with ABAR. I went home and talked it over with Myrt. With her blessing, I then talked a bit more to Jim about this particular furnace, which I estimated would cost roughly around $250,000, about the same price as an ABAR furnace. I told him if he was really interested, I would prepare a formal quote. He told me to go ahead, and added, "Bill, if it's what you say it is, I'll give you the order for it."

I'd had a secretary at ABAR, Edith Laventka, who'd retired about a year before. I called her up and told her I was thinking of leaving ABAR and starting my own furnace company, and I needed to prepare a quote for a new furnace, which I had sketched out but needed typed up. I asked her if she would be willing to help me. She came to our house and sat at our dining room table with a typewriter I picked up from somewhere, and prepared the proposal for me. Of course, I paid her, and this was the beginning of forming our own company, Vacuum Furnace Systems, or VFS.

With this order all but finalized, Myrt and I arranged to meet with Charlie Hoeflich, the banker who took on ABAR's business after being unceremoniously dumped by PNB. We told him our plans. He asked us how much money we personally could put into this new business. It was a sobering thought, but we figured we could put up $40,000 of personal savings and mortgage our home in Chalfont for up to $40,000, so we had about $80,000 in cash. Combined with the order promised, we figured we would need about $250,000 more. Charlie examined our figures and suggested we might qualify for a guaranteed loan through SBA. But, he cautioned, there would be a great risk for all of us: If we defaulted on the loan, we would have only our bed. Everything else would be forfeited. Everything. He looked Myrt in the eyes and asked her what she wanted to do. With barely a moment's pause, she said she backed me one hundred percent. Charlie then asked me. I took a deep breath and said we were in.

Immediately, almost as if a buzzer went off to start a game, Charlie got to work securing the first steps of our future. He introduced us to Bill Aichele, who would become our loan officer (and, incidentally, would later become CEO of the bank). He set in motion the paperwork for a $250,000 SBA loan. As that process was being worked out, Charlie talked about our need for space. "You need a plant!" he said. "The Clemmer building on 309 is vacant and would be perfect for you." Within the hour, we met with the real estate agent and saw the building. As quickly as the meeting was arranged, the wheels were in motion again, this time to lease the facility. In one day, we put together nearly everything we needed to start VFS. Charlie again worked his magic when he suggested two accounting firms in our area. Although they were both highly respectable firms, Charlie, knowing my faith background, recommended we partner with Al Pritchard, at the accounting firm Niessen, Dunlap, and Pritchard. Charlie knew our values were in line with Pritchard's and that Al and I were like-minded individuals. As with almost every connection we made, that relationship would turn out to be profitable and long-standing. We were forging relationships with people and organizations that would stand for twenty, thirty years. To this day, the Pritchard firm handles our business. Al recalls the early days of our association:

An entrepreneur has to like what he's doing and put his all into it. Bill was smart. He used his professionals—the people recommended to him who knew the necessary steps to success. That's a mistake many entrepreneurs make, though. They don't look to the professionals to guide them. Bill did that, and still does, and he takes the opinions offered to him seriously. His association with Charlie Hoeflich was an integral step. If Bill and Myrt hadn't listened to Charlie's advice and followed through with his suggestions, it might have been very different. If Bill thought something was right, he would follow through and make it happen.

As we continued taking steps towards our independence, I reached out to my friend and ABAR colleague, Ron Zorn, and invited him, along with his wife, Charlene, to Sunday dinner at our house. Ron was the advertising agent at ABAR, and when he learned of my plans to start a new business and leave the company, he decided he would, too. Not surprisingly, he also did not get along too well with Don Frompkin and felt that soon he, too, would be replaced. He said, "Bill, if you're leaving ABAR, so am I. You just got yourself an Advertising Agent." Ron took a leap of faith and decided to join me and Myrt and our fledgling venture. But we still needed a name.

As we discussed the next steps, I told Ron I planned to incorporate the new company on Monday, the next day. I wanted his help in naming the new business. Well, this threw Ron for a loop. He was quite the deliberating fellow, and wanted to take some time to really think about the name. Under normal circumstances, he did not do things quickly, and though his decision to join me certainly seemed capricious, he wasn't usually a man to make snap decisions. Ron remembers:

I received a call from Bill one day, inviting my wife and me to his house for dinner. But, he said, it's not free. He was always very direct. He said, "I want you to think of a name for my new company." I don't know the exact reasons why Bill left ABAR other than that there was something that went against his conscience. It surprised me that he was leaving to form his own company. I thought he was firmly entrenched at ABAR; he had been the president of the company. And I did not know he was having problems there. I wasn't surprised by his entrepreneurial spirit, only that he was leaving a good position. But he did, so I started thinking of a name for his company.

To me, it was obvious. It had to be short and sweet, to the point. Something that would present a good logo. When I presented the name, Bill immediately liked it. He put everything he had into this endeavor. ABAR was infuriated when we settled on the name for the company. It explicitly stated our business, and it capitalized on the market. Because, what does ABAR mean or stand for? Nothing; it tells you nothing about the business. The name is the foundation of the company; you don't take that lightly.

Since I didn't want the company to be all about me, I did not want to give it my name. I wanted a name that accurately reflected our business and, of course, something that would set us apart from the competition. As I knew he would, Ron hit it out of the park. Monday morning, I called Ron to see what he'd come up with, and he confidently told me the new name: Vacuum Furnace Systems Corp. He explained, "The name says exactly what the company is doing. The furnace is a whole bunch of things bolted together. In today's world, there's a trend in calling companies like yours a system." I agreed, went to see Al Pritchard, and in late October 1978, we incorporated and officially began.

Ron immediately set to work developing advertising for us. In January of 1979, we hired our first handful of employees. Our first employee was Vicki Long, and she was my secretary. She was a friend of ours and a member of our church. Myrt had been talking with her one day about our new company and asked if she happened to know anyone looking for a secretarial position who might want to join our start up. Vicki replied, "Yes—me!" She left her position as a legal secretary to come work for us, and we were delighted.

Our second employee was Al Hagdorn, formerly the Vice President of Manufacturing at ABAR. Because of the immense backlog of work created by Don Frompkin's overselling, King Fifth Wheel began cracking down on production, and Al became a target. Not surprisingly, he was fired. He immediately called me. "Bill, I'm out," he said, and I hired him as our Plant Manager.

Our third employee was Jack Fair, the former Quality Control Manager for ABAR. He didn't like the new regime and was unhappy with the way things were progressing, and so he called me, looking for an opening with VFS. Jack also had good sales experience, and we hired him in a general technical capacity.

ABAR had a board of directors. Bob Gunow, Sr. was then the owner of Vac-Hyd, a Detroit-based aerospace company, which consisted of about five heat treating plants all specializing in vacuum. I got to know Bob over the years, and I brought him onto the board. He was part of the inner circle during the time I was struggling with KFW as ABAR's president. When I resigned from ABAR, he also resigned from the board. He then sold Vac-Hyd, and I invited him to join VFS as a manufacturer's representative. He became our best sales agent at the time and excelled in every respect, never to be replaced. He was the best manufacturer's representative we've ever had—before or since. He turned out to be the most successful representative in the history of our companies.

Ron Zorn, of course, continued to work with us, and then there was Myrt and I. I cut my ABAR salary in half, and that became my new salary. Still using our personal finances, we paid our employees and ourselves. The money from the SBA loan, although approved, would take several months to arrive, so Myrt and I continued to fund everything associated with VFS with our personal savings, including payroll. We also tithed to our church on that money—a tenth of our salary. Despite the dwindling funds, it was the right thing for us to do. After all, the church had continuing expenses, no matter our personal financial situation.

While we couldn't be as competitive as established organizations, we did offer the excitement of a start-up and ground-floor growth opportunities. For people passionate about technology and innovation, such a prospect is an exciting idea. If an employee performs well, the company does well, and the money will follow. Also, these people knew me, and they wanted to work for me.

Ron remembers the early days in a big, empty warehouse. "Bill was leasing the property for VFS—a huge building—and the first time I walked in, I saw that VFS occupied one little corner while the rest had been curtained off with big plastic sheets hanging from the ceiling. I said, 'Bill, what in the world are you going to do with this place?' He said, 'I'm going to fill it.' He had vision. So, we began."

In January of 1979, Fred Ripley was working as the plant engineer at J.W. Rex, a commercial heat treating company in Lansdale, PA, when he came across our small ad in the local paper. "It wasn't much of an ad," Fred recalls, "but it piqued my interest."

I offered Fred the position of Chief Engineer, though he was understandably a bit nervous. VFS was a start-up with only a handful of employees, just five or six. Having been employed by a solid, established company for about eight years, making a move to VFS was a risky venture for Fred, a married father of three small children. He discussed it with his wife, Judy, and they agreed he should accept the offer.

"It was a leap of faith," Fred asserts, "but those early days were the best. It was exciting to me and to everyone involved. It was fun." Fred had to sell his car to raise the $5,000 investment money needed to buy into the company. It really was a big leap of faith. But, as Fred said about it later, "There's no place to go but up when you're in on the ground floor." In fact, Fred's $5,000 investment netted him close to $1 million when we later sold VFS.

Then, there was Alice Shining. Alice was our first draftsman, who became a design draftsman. In the engineering department, an entry-level person is just a draftsman who will do detailed drafting work. As a draftsman gains more and more experience, he or she becomes a design draftsman. When Alice came to us, she was just a draftsman. She had been working part time for what was the predecessor of Boeing Vertol, but what was, at that time, a very small entity right at the Philadelphia airport; they were building helicopters. So, she was involved in the building of these helicopters. She wanted a full-time job, so she came to interview with us. Fred and I hired her together. When we interviewed her, the only thing we really had was the office part up and running. There was nothing in the plant. Literally nothing. But she didn't know that. When she left Boeing and came to work for us, she found out there was nothing in the plant and that the company thus far was only the office. She was absolutely exasperated. She said, "What have I gotten into?" We hadn't intentionally hidden anything; there simply wasn't anything to show. She didn't ask, and we didn't offer it. Alice quickly got over it and stayed on.

Alice became an integral member of our team, solving complex problems in a manner that was unique to her. I had received an order to do a hot zone rebuild for Metallurgical

Processing in New Britain, Connecticut. It was an ABAR hot zone, and I sold them our new, insulated hot zone design: The core of the hot zone is mounted on three separate metal rings. These rings were in fact the main structure of the hot zone—something like large-diameter cylinders. The heating element supports were all mounted off these rings.

Since the customer had had to rebuild that hot zone before, they had a spare set of metal rings. So, they shipped us these metal rings to serve as guides for our design. Now, we had to lay out heating elements in these metal rings. When you have something that's in the form of a circle, you first make them flat and then you roll them up into a circle. There were also other holes for heat-shield mounting and gas-cooling nozzles. We did not have the entire hot zone, heat shields, heating elements, gas nozzles, or drawings. So, it was a puzzle to figure out which holes mounted which components—it was not immediately obvious as to where these hole patterns were going to be, particularly the heating element, which was the question. To solve this puzzle, Alice literally took string and found the center point of the hot zone; then, she took pieces of string from each heating element support to the center, and she literally strung the elements up in line with the hot zone ring so we could rebuild the zone. Very clever.

We probably could have figured it out a different way with just a little bit of trigonometry but that's not what we did. After she strung this whole thing up, she came into my office and she said, "Bill, you know what? Those element supports are all at 30 degree angles." Well, of course, you don't make angles odd when you could make them even, so when she said that, the whole geometry all of a sudden appeared: There it was—a puzzle she unraveled.

Alice was truly a unique individual. She had a ramshackle sort of house that she rebuilt part of herself. She built a stone fireplace, with cement, by herself. She was Fred's right hand man, so to speak. She stayed with us until she retired. She was highly productive in everything that she did.

These were our first employees and the start of our exciting new lives. It was the middle of January, and we were eagerly anticipating the coming year of new challenges and opportunities. We were knee-deep in production for the furnace for Jim Williams, and working on acquiring new orders. It was shaping up to be a very busy and productive year.

And then, it nearly all stopped.

THE KING FIFTH WHEEL V. VFS LAWSUIT

The federal court lawsuit brought about by King Fifth Wheel accused me of using an ABAR patented technology in my new VFS furnace design. It was a total surprise and completely false, of course. I had always prided myself on my honesty and integrity, and I was angered that my values should be questioned. Be that as it may, the powerhouse that was King Fifth Wheel and their lawyers nearly shut us down as we tried to defend ourselves. It was David and Goliath, and Goliath had an army of lawyers at his disposal, keeping us busy with endless paperwork meant to grind our production to a halt. Though it only lasted a few weeks from start to finish—and though I knew we were in the right—the chapter was terrifying.

Almost at once, I called King Fifth Wheel's head attorney, Henry Scarborough, whom I knew very well. I told him I'd received the subpoena, and I couldn't believe it—that it was filled with untruths and was just plain crazy: I hadn't stolen any patents.

He simply said he couldn't discuss it with me and that was the end of the conversation. I felt like a door had been slammed in my face.

Myrt and I were, of course, concerned but knew we had right on our side. However, proving one's innocence in federal court is costly and not a little bit scary. We needed a good attorney.

There was a woman on the board of King Fifth Wheel, a cantankerous lady and a thorn in the Martin family's side. She'd inherited her stock ownership in the company from her husband. When she heard of the suit, she contacted me and said she wanted to join my company. Additionally, she offered the services of her son, whom she claimed was an excellent attorney. She would have him take our case, if that's what we wanted. I did not accept that offer. I felt it was too close to the Martin family, and would bring additional headaches we didn't need.

I knew the patent in question; I had worked on it myself, but it wasn't in my name. I also knew the design contained decidedly specific flaws that I set out to correct when I worked on the design for Jim Williams' furnace. I had been successful, so with my new and improved design ready to go, I had called Bill Cleaver—the patent attorney who came highly recommended by Zach Wobensmith, ABAR's patent attorney, while we were both at ABAR. Zach had described Bill Cleaver as a highly competent attorney—someone Zach had had to defend himself against and found a worthy opponent.

Looking back, I'm thankful I was determined to do everything by the book when we started VFS. When I had successfully corrected the flaws with ABAR's design, I called Bill Cleaver in early January 1979, prior to being served with the lawsuit. I asked Bill to review my new design. He agreed that it needed to be patented, and as quickly as possible, as he felt it was potentially risky. So, within about two weeks, we had the drawings completed and the application filed. That application would prove to be critical to our defense, and it reinforced my mandate that we dot our I's and cross our T's in order to maintain the highest integrity. But before we could defend ourselves, we needed to find an attorney to take our case.

When we were served, I went to see our attorney, Don Semisch, believing it would be a simple matter of time and paperwork to clear our name and make the lawsuit go away. Once Don reviewed the subpoena and saw it was filed in federal court, he said he couldn't possibly handle the case for us. It was too big for him. I was unprepared for his response, and it knocked me back a bit. Now we were without counsel and defense, up against a mighty team of lawyers who were backed by money. We were being ground to a halt and money was already in short supply. King Fifth Wheel knew about our startup finances, and they wanted to take advantage of our situation.

Don Semisch suggested we try a firm in Philadelphia and set up a meeting for me. There, I met with a junior attorney who reviewed the case. But if I was upset by Don's reaction to the case, I was devastated by this attorney's response. He said to me, "This thing is terrible. We're not going to take this case, because they have the cards stacked against you. I can't see how we could take the case." I persisted. Surely there was something they could do. After some discussion, he said he wanted to take it to one of the partners and review the case with him. It wasn't exactly the reassurance and pep talk I was hoping for, to say the least. We had naively assumed we could easily defend ourselves, and the reality that we could not was overwhelming. Even worse was the sinking realization that we could—and it looked like we would—lose everything and quickly.

I went home and told Myrt about the meeting. I told her I thought the whole thing was over. It was not a good conversation. Not knowing what could be done to save our company, our investment, all our hopes, we stood in the kitchen, holding each other, and cried. It was awful. We thought we were done.

The deposition was coming upon us, and the paperwork was never ending. Finally, we heard from the senior partner of the big Philadelphia law firm I'd visited. He said he wanted to meet with Myrt and me, so we headed back to their offices to talk this out. Miraculously, they had agreed to take on our case. They felt David might be able to take on this Goliath, after all. And the key to putting it all to bed was that application for a patent Bill Cleaver had filed on our behalf.

Since the patent was filed before the suit was brought against us, and because it clearly demonstrated significant changes from the ABAR patent in question, we were exonerated. With our attorney, we met one last time to settle the suit. No one from ABAR or King Fifth Wheel turned up for the final settlement. No representation from management, only their attorney. They knew they were beat. Even though we were small in comparison to the money and might of King Fifth Wheel, we won, because we had dotted our I's and crossed our T's.

Still, it was traumatic for all involved. Myrt and I had the most to lose, naturally, but others were involved and felt the stress of the situation. Ron Zorn remembers it as vividly as I do:

ABAR took VFS to federal court. Al Hagdorn, Jack Fair, Bill, and I were sued. It was a hugely expensive undertaking, but of course, we won the suit. Bill knew how to design the furnaces, Al knew how to build them, and I knew how to promote them. We presented a serious threat to ABAR. I can remember sitting in the office of a high-powered attorney in Center City, and the three of us discussing the situation, preparing for this lawsuit. It was quite a daunting experience. ABAR had money and powerful attorneys on their side. We only had each other and the Lord.

For Fred Ripley, it was a particularly difficult time. He had joined VFS only six weeks earlier, only to learn the company was being sued by a sizable and substantial organization, for patent infringement. The lawsuit held up the loan secured earlier for our start-up expenses, and, fearing for the stability of his family, Fred told me he needed to return to his former position. I completely understood, and between the two of us, we worked out an agreement that allowed Fred to work part-time at VFS, while the lawsuit continued. As soon as the suit was dropped, Fred returned to VFS full time and permanently. He was glad to be back, but it was a rocky start for all of us.

While there is inherent risk in any startup, the fact that I was accused of stealing cut me to the quick. I had worked hard at ABAR, building the company as I built my reputation in the industry. To have the executives at King Fifth Wheel turn on me in such a way was more than disheartening. It was disloyal. Even though their choice was "strictly business" and I understood why they brought the suit against me, the situation still gnawed at me.

I had always been an honest person who was raised by honest and trustworthy parents, and I followed their examples. From an early age, I recognized that people trusted me, with their radios, their lawns, their expensive television sets. As I grew older and developed a name for myself, others knew I spoke and acted with integrity. I learned early on that my word held weight; it mattered. In business, there are many opportunities to cut corners or exaggerate to make a point or a profit. I never felt the need to stray from the truth. Has my desire for honesty at all times caused headaches? Of course. There were many times a white lie or slightly inflated or deflated numbers would have eased some stress. But that has never been the way I operated. Especially as we expanded into the heat treating business—which has a reputation for being a dishonest one—my company's and my own personal reputation for honesty put us above the competition. It holds us to a higher standard, because I hold myself to a higher standard. In our case, honesty gives us a competitive edge, which is a bonus, but that's not why I believe it is the only policy in business.

Even before I found my faith, these values were of utmost importance to me. Later, when I became a Christian, they held even greater meaning for me. I knew I had to lead by example, to show a watching world how a Christian behaves, even when no one is watching. Whatever your beliefs, it won't do to have your business—which is an extension of yourself—going against your core values as a person. That's just a recipe for stress and heartache. Whatever an entrepreneur's goal may be, his or her business ethics must align with his or her personal beliefs.

It's also important for entrepreneurs, managers, bosses, etc. to keep their values always at the front of their minds, especially as business grows. It is very easy to lose sight of what is important when the dollars start rolling in. Though we were hardly rolling in money when KFW decided to sue us in federal court, the fact that I always stayed true to my character won out in the end.

GAINING MOMENTUM

In the start of VFS, I redesigned the furnace. This process was tremendously exciting to me, because it was *my* furnace. I was doing things exactly as I wanted, without interference from a parent company. Dr. George Bentley called it perfectly so many years ago: I would not be truly happy unless I ran my own business.

The first furnace that we built for Jim Williams, while similar to an ABAR furnace, did incorporate some different designs, particularly in the hot zone. We still used the molybdenum heating elements, and we used the molybdenum hearth rails, which we kept because of cost. However, we made several departures from what I was doing at ABAR. Of course, we continued with the round hot zone, but instead of building the furnace with metal heat shields, we built the furnace with a composite hot zone that combined Kaowool® insulation, graphite felt, and a graphite foil hot face. This composite was a contrast to the all-metal ABAR hot zone, which is a very expensive hot zone to build. The insulated hot zone is less expensive to build, but it also operates with half the electric power, so it is also an energy conserving design. Comparatively, Ipsen had an all-insulated hot zone, but their hot zone was all Kaowool®, which did not have the high vacuum capabilities. In the hot zone I designed for Jim Williams and VFS, the space combined a minimal amount of insulation with a graphite hot face to offset the temperature-limited Kaowool®—by adding this graphite felt onto the front and then the graphite foil hot face, we gained a couple of extra hundred degrees in temperature out of it and a gettering graphite environment. That was an important innovation: it was another leg up on our competition, who could not achieve the same results in their vacuum furnaces.

In addition to a changed hot zone, we also redesigned the gas cooling system. In the early VFS furnaces, we used what we called a recirculating gas cooling system, which utilized an external blower and gas-to-water heat exchanger. I removed the high vacuum isolation valves, for cost but primarily for reliability—the VFS gas recirculation valves were not 100% reliable. It sounds simple, but by removing those fairly big valves, we rendered that external gas system completely vacuum tight, like the rest of the furnace, which was important. No one else had built such a tight vacuum yet, and though the change wasn't exactly a dramatic moment, it was sort of like the arrival of the tubeless tire. The change made good sense, and we were the first to do it.

We incorporated those changes into the new VFS furnaces right from the beginning, and we were well on our way to establishing our presence in the market. We could have rested on our accomplishments right there and enjoyed the increased market share. But we didn't. Bolstered by our successes and the excitement of developing something new, we continued to think outside the box. We introduced a third VFS design, with the ceramic protection tube Type S thermocouple, a protection tube thermocouple. It wasn't actually my design. It came from General Electric in Detroit. All I did was cap the end of it. Another simple adjustment that changed the game. In capping the tube, VFS eliminated the risk of flooding the hot zone with air if the tube ever broke. This simple protection tube extended the life of the platinum thermocouple considerably, and that thermocouple design has become a standard in the industry. Our entire industry has copied that.

Innovating, solving problems, exercising my brain, and being a lover of all things technical, I was thoroughly in my element at VFS, and we were flourishing. Still, from the hard lessons learned from the King Fifth Wheel case, I made sure I kept all my details in order. It was important to me that we held ourselves to strict standards, so there could be no question of integrity. With this concept firmly in my head and with business taking off, there was an excitement that I hadn't felt since my early days at ABAR, where we felt we were taking on the world. Of course, I remember the VFS days one way, my employees, another. I wanted to accurately recount those days, so I reached out to a few former employees for their recollections. Ron Zorn, my advertising manager, was happy to recount some of his favorite memories:

The first ad we did, we took out a full page. I called it the "grey ghost;" it was a two-color ad in the industry's premier magazine. Bill didn't have a drawing, he didn't have a product, all he had was an idea and whatever was in his head, the designs and so forth. And faith in himself and in the Lord. He put everything on the line, and I began to do his advertising and publicity. Bill caught on very quickly.

Bill is big on press releases, and we did a lot of press releases. When he received an order, we issued a press release. When it shipped, we did another press release. One customer called him one day, and Bill asked how he heard about VFS. And the man responded, "Hear about you? Every time I open a trade journal I see your name!" That was the object—exposure in advertising is the name of the game. But it has to be good, it can't just be fluff. It has to have some substance to it.

Another way VFS gained exposure was through the color of the furnaces. Now, ABAR, in accordance with the indus-

try standard of the day, painted their furnaces dark blue. I told Bill he needed to use a color that would stand out. When you put a new furnace in a heat treating plant—such as a Pratt & Whitney plant with a dozen or so furnaces—people have to know which furnace is yours. It has to stand out. No one should have to walk over to the furnace to check the logo. So Bill told me to pick a color.

I went through the color charts—and color is extremely important in conveying your message—and I came in with this color chip: MAB Autumn Orange. Al Hagdorn looked at it and said, "Ron! You're not serious, are you?" I said I most certainly was. The color was so different from anything that had been done before, and that's what we needed. We needed something to catch attention and what catches attention more than orange? That's why hunters wear orange on their backs. So I convinced them. Al was reluctant, but Bill was quietly contemplating it. I suggested that Al buy a couple of gallons of the paint and just paint one of the furnaces, and if he didn't like it, he could paint the furnace again. He agreed. They were impressed, and we went ahead and shipped the bright orange furnace to the customer. About a week after the furnace shipped, Al received a call from the customer. Al said he was worried and thought, "uh oh, here it comes." The customer asked for the name of the color, and Al gave it to him. The customer said they liked it so much, they were going to paint the rest of their furnaces the same color. From then on, the VFS furnaces were Autumn Orange.

During the startup of VFS, my brother, Dick, played an integral part in many ways. Dick had been in the Navy, and afterwards, he learned to be an automobile body repairman. But he also learned to paint, and he was pretty good at it.

So, when we first started VFS, we didn't have anyone who could paint. We didn't have a paint booth; we didn't have anything. Myrt and I painted that first furnace we shipped to Jim

The beginning year of VFS.

Williams with a roller and a paint brush on a very humid summer day. To my chagrin, we did it on a Sunday afternoon after church. We went home from church, changed our clothes, came in and started painting. We were going to ship the furnace within the next day or two, so we had no choice. And, since we didn't have the manpower to do it, we did it ourselves. But then, of course, other orders came in and we had other things that had to be painted.

I asked my brother Dick if he would work for us as a spray painter at night after work. I paid him so much per hour, which we set aside so that he could buy stock in the company. Dick became one of the six stockholders of VFS, and he did so by painting. It took him about two or three years, working to buy the stock.

The time was the early 80's. Dick was working to purchase his stock, but his full-time job was with Roadway, as a truck driver. As Roadway is organized by the Teamsters, Dick was a union Teamster. At that time, Jimmy Hoffa was president of the Teamsters, and he was indicted by the federal government and put in jail. Amazingly, while in prison, Hoffa was still president of the union. Not only that, he came up for re-election during his sentence, ran for the office, and won. He ran his campaign from prison (this story has a familiar ring to some).

I talked to my brother about it. I said, "Dick, you know Hoffa's coming up for election. Who are you going to vote for?" Without missing a beat, he said, "Of course I'm going to vote for Hoffa. You don't realize, Bill, how much he's done for us." And he went on and on about how great Jimmy Hoffa was. So, sure enough he and all of his union brothers voted for Jimmy Hoffa when Hoffa was in jail.

Dick worked for several years and then he retired from Roadway. And when he came to work for us full time, he became one of the biggest anti-union people that you could believe. Why? Because he saw how a company could run without a lot of tension between the management and the workers. There had been a lot of tension between the management and the employees at Roadway. After working at VFS full-time, Dick had a complete change of heart about the value of the union.

In the beginning, when everyone worked to make the company a success, there was a palpable air of teamwork and unity. VFS spawned some wonderful relationships, born out of a mutual desire to innovate and succeed. The team we assembled took great pride in their work, and we all shared the same work ethic and drive.

One of the biggest factors of our success was our employees. Drawing on my experiences at MEECO and IDL, learning the difference between a manager who interacts with his employees and shares information and someone who doesn't, I developed a management style that provided all employees with the opportunity to learn what the company was about and to speak up about the work. Since my early days, I've always said I hire people who are smarter than I am. You need that; you need employees to feel empowered and know their manager believes in them. Especially after the Don Frompkin debacle, I wanted to be sure our team worked well together and that employees took initiative. I looked to be sure that each person was the subject matter expert in their area. I did not want a repeat of Don Frompkin versus Bill Hoke, or Sales versus Engineering. At VFS, I enjoyed driving the bus, but I learned to let each staff member take responsibility for his or her own area. I was still very much in charge, but I let each person do the job they were hired to do, a management style I've continued to this day, and it has served me well.

Fred Ripley, one of the first people to join VFS, shared some of his memories of those days with me, and he talked a bit about my management style. While at ABAR, I had practiced a linear style of management—there was a straight line going from me, as President, to all of my employees. I changed that at VFS, but I was still The Boss, and, as it was my company and my money on the line, I did not shy away from risk. Fred recounts:

We were discussing a building expansion of VFS, and meetings were held to determine the feasibility of such an expense. None of the managers were particularly inclined to bite off so much financial responsibility in one go and were

inching towards an agreement for only a partial expansion. Bill listened to all of the input and, after everyone had had their say, simply declared, "Alright, now I'll tell you what we're going to do." With that, we went ahead as originally planned for the full addition. End of the meeting. Despite opposition and some anxiety from the team, Bill had a lot of faith, a lot of courage in his convictions, and he decided to bite the bullet and go for this whole big thing. And it turns out, he was right. But it's a scary thing to do. We didn't have the money, we had to borrow it. But that's how you do it.

Why was I so confident that it was the right decision? Experience and my gut. I knew risk is a big part of any success in business, and what would it serve us to only build part of what we would eventually need? We'd only have to expand again later. If the idea had been completely without merit, with no real data to back it up, I might have waited, but it wasn't. I listened to everyone's input, and then, as was the case in so many other business decisions, I trusted my insight and my gut.

While VFS grew and continued to increase our market share, Abe Willan and Pratt & Whitney, who had been so influential and critical to my success at ABAR, remained interested in my work. Willan appreciated my hard work and my ability to find a solution for a problem, and he was a big help in getting us up and running. It was a huge support to our fledgling business, and I was always very appreciative of his loyalty to me. This continued until Willan retired, in the mid-1980's.

Shortly after Willan fully retired in 1990, however, I received a call from the Vice President of Purchasing at Pratt & Whitney, inviting me to meet with him. I went to his office; he sat me down, closed the door and, without much preamble, asked me just what I had on Abe Willan. Exactly how did I get so much business from Pratt & Whitney? He was downright nasty to me. I replied truthfully that I had nothing on Abe. There were no kick-backs, there was no collusion. He didn't believe me. He insisted there had to be something, because we'd received millions of dollars' worth of orders from Abe. He was determined there was something afoot, and he was going to get to the bottom of it. Well, there was nothing for me to say, and the conversation only lasted about fifteen minutes. I left, and since that day, I personally have never been invited back to the East Hartford plant. Though he held an investigation, there was nothing to uncover. We continued to receive orders, but I never stepped foot in those offices again. That discussion was offensive to me, and to Abe's memory. He was a truthful, straight shooting, hard-working man. All Abe had done was show faith in me and my abilities, and in return, I provided him with whatever Pratt & Whitney required or asked. With his support and encouragement, I thrived, both at ABAR and VFS.

Solar Atmospheres

When a project is in trouble, do not try to wiggle out at the lowest possible cost. Now is the time to spend the money and solve the issues. —Dr. Martin, King Fifth Wheel

As time went on and VFS flourished, I was becoming more and more interested in heat treating. Remembering my visits to Bennett Heat Treating Company in New Jersey—where they seemed to be minting money—I was keen to get in on this market. I distinctly remembered the piles and piles of work just waiting to get into their shop and all the trucks coming and going with work. Even at ABAR, when my days grew more and more stressful, I had mulled over the idea of starting a heat treating company of my own.

As I mentioned previously, I'd sought the advice of some experts George Bodeen and Sam Whalen, along with their wives, who had strongly advised against starting a heat treating company. "You can't compete," George had said. Both men felt the Philadelphia market was already saturated. Though their valid opinions took root, and though Myrt and I decided to wait, the idea of a heat treating company was always in the back of my mind.

Now running our own company and again feeling the urge to get into heat treating, we felt the time had come to finally do it. It was 1983, and we had more experience, and we knew what heat treaters were looking for in their furnaces because we built them. My son, Roger, had joined VFS by this time, and we spoke at length about it. He was also itching to branch out. He had gained some valuable experience in this area while he worked at ABAR and was certain we could be successful. "Though VFS was originally a furnace-making operation," Roger recalls, "I was all over my dad to get into heat treating. He listened and agreed we would, in time. But before we could do that, he argued, we had to build the furnace-building business, establish our name and our reputation. I was 100% in agreement with that plan."

We also needed the money to transition to the world of heat treating. If I could have, I would have gone into the heat treating business first. But we didn't have the money to do it then, either. We couldn't afford the expensive furnaces, and George Bodeen had cautioned us so strongly against it. So we decided to build furnaces first and establish VFS. After we were in business about two years, we had an established base and a good reputation, and the time was right to branch out into the heat treating business. The profits from VFS would help fund our next venture.

With the decision to move forward, I wanted to come up with a name that was unique, just as Vacuum Furnace Systems was unique. Tony Quaglia of Bennett Heat Treating had mentioned to me in one of our meetings that "vacuum" is just another atmosphere. While metals operate differently in a vacuum as compared to other atmospheres, metallurgy is metallurgy—the basics are the same. Tony's point was that users have to learn about vacuum. There are benefits of this non-atmosphere, but there are also liabilities that come with it. Vacuum is another atmosphere to study, and if we took the time to understand the atmosphere, we could learn how best to use it.

I wanted to come up with a name that people in the technical world would understand and that would speak to what we were all about. I also wanted to harness this idea of a vacuum atmosphere. I tossed a lot of ideas around. In the process, I thought about space, with outer space being a vacuum. The moon thus became a recurring thought: our furnaces could be evacuated to approximately the vacuum on the surface of the moon, and among technical people, that idea was reasonably well-known. But my fear was that the average heat treater probably would not know the vacuum on the surface of the moon. So, though Lunar Atmospheres came to mind, I decided against it for many reasons, not the least was the potential for people to make up all kinds of nicknames for the company, "loony" and such.

But then there was the idea of solar—the sun is the source of 99% of our energy. It's the source of all of our heat.

Now, in the scientific world of heat transfer, there are three forms of heat transfer. There is convection: Something heats the air, the air heats something else. Then, there is conduction: If you put your hand on a hot copper pipe or a hot surface, the energy (heat) moves directly from that hot surface to your hand. That's energy transfer by conduction. The third form of energy transfer is radiant heat: If you have a hot surface, it's not necessarily heating the atmosphere, but that hot surface is radiating energy, and we can feel it. The sun's heat to us is radiant.

Inside of our vacuum furnaces, the electric heaters are radiant heaters. These radiant heaters are built inside of a vacuum chamber out of which we pump all the air to form a vacuum.

Combining those thoughts—the sun, a vacuum, heat—I landed upon a name: Solar Atmospheres. And that's how I decided on the name of our heat treating division.

Roger was just as excited as I was to get Solar Atmospheres up and running. He recalls the fledgling business, which we initially referred to as simply VFS Heat Treat Division:

Shortly after we started VFS, we went to a technical scrap yard in Trevose, PA, called Crockett Machine, and we bought an old Stokes vacuum furnace that was in pieces. We probably only paid scrap value for it. It sat up there for years in storage. We purchased another small furnace, an Edwards vacuum furnace, a little laboratory-sized furnace. So, we started with used furnaces.

I pestered my dad until we finally got those furnaces up and going—around '81–'82. Our small shop was called the VFS Heat Treat Division. The first furnace we used was a Leeds and Northrup steam "homo" furnace. Our first customer that we actually billed for heat treating was a company in Harleysville called PM Fasteners. The job was a truss bolt that had hydrogen embrittlement. We were stress relieving these bolts in this furnace. They sent us these bolts by the truckload. I was in heaven because I was running these bolts, and I was doing this work and thinking, "Hey, this is neat." Of course, at the time, it wasn't a lot of work, but it was something to start. And that was my first job heat treating parts at VFS.

After that job, the heat treating business was up and down. We were in the process of building the two rebuilt used furnaces. They had to go through engineering, then we had to build the things and change this and change that, so there were a lot of modifications. Looking back, and I'm sure my father would agree, it would have been better to build a brand new VFS vacuum furnace—which came much later. But we didn't, and so we started out with used equipment, and that's how we got going.

VFS became well established; it grew. As a matter of fact, we expanded with an addition on the first building, the 1983 building. Then, my parents bought a piece of ground in the back, and we added onto the building with a high bay for building more furnaces and more office space.

When we first started the heat treating business, VFS was the cash support and helped us become established. It remained that way for several years until 1983, when my dad said, "Roger, we're going to make this a separate business." I was on board, but wondered what we would call this separate business. Would we continue to be associated with the VFS name? Dad had come up with a new name: Solar Atmospheres. I wasn't immediately sold on it—it sounded like we would be selling solar panels. I felt the name might cause confusion. I'm sure this was one of these epiphanies that he came up with in the middle of the night when he woke up in bed and said "I'm going to call it this." He explained how he came up with the name: The sun is an energy source in outer space and there is no atmosphere between the sun and the earth, only a vacuum. The "atmosphere" is what we're processing, either in a vacuum or in our partial pressure atmospheres of nitrogen, argon, or hydrogen. That's how he came up with the name Solar Atmospheres. It was ingenious and that's what stuck.

As Roger described, we needed furnaces, so we bought two used furnaces. One was a small laboratory furnace built by an English company, Edwards High Vacuum. The company we bought it from purchased it for some purpose, but they never used it. It sat in storage for maybe 10 or 12 years. We were called about it when they were disposing of their excess inventory, and they offered to sell it to us. I bought it for next to nothing, about $2,500. They had probably paid in the neighborhood of $20,000 for it, but at that point, they just wanted to get rid of it. Well, we brought it in, and we changed it around considerably. That became our first laboratory furnace, the HT-3. Just as in my ABAR days, it was important to me to have a furnace that we could demonstrate.

Next was a vertical, bottom loader furnace that I knew about and that had been at the General Electric switch gear plant on Elmwood Avenue in Philadelphia. They had developed the vacuum interrupter, which was a glass vacuum bottle with two electrodes that slammed back and forth inside of it, acting like a circuit breaker but with no arc. They pumped all the air out of the bottle and then sealed it—brazed it actually. The furnace wasn't too big; the hot zone was only about 24" x 24." It had a small ball screw drive on it—built by the Stokes Company in Philadelphia—but it was not like the ball screw drives that we used. It was literally multi-bicycle chain driven.

G.E. decided they wanted to buy a bigger, better furnace, and this little furnace was scrapped. I think they tried to sell it and nobody wanted to buy it, so the furnace went to a scrap dealer over in Trevose. When I was at ABAR, I knew the furnace was available, and we actually thought about buying it for ABAR. One of our men also suggested we buy the furnace. I thought, I don't want any part of that thing. But when I started VFS, we went over and looked at it, and we thought we could rework it. Which is what we did.

We completely redesigned that furnace. We were working with a hot zone that was about 35 or 40 inches tall and maybe about 24 or 26 inches in diameter. We installed a recirculating gas cooling system, added nozzles and so forth. And it worked. So, now we had that lab furnace and a vertical production furnace.

At some point, I looked at an Ipsen furnace and thought, "You know, we're selling furnaces in competition with this, so if I buy one, we can set it up and make it work, and then we'll be able to demonstrate the differences between the furnaces." We did just that.

But when I took that thing apart, I very, very quickly real-

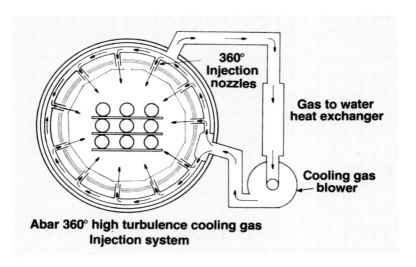

Abar 360° high turbulence cooling gas Injection system

Diagram of the Original ABAR Gas Cooling Design.

ized we wanted no part of that. We learned that Allison, the original owner, scrapped it because the chamber had developed water leaks. Once a furnace has water leaks in it, it's dead. The furnace is going to leak, and it will be too late to save your work—it will be ruined. Well, Allison scrapped the furnace, and I bought it from a used equipment dealer. Of course, they never tell you the history (at best, they are like used car salesmen, only worse).

After I bought it, I called the engineer, who was someone I already knew, to tell him I bought it. He said, "Well, Bill, I don't know whether you looked at the chamber, but we really worked on trying to solve the leaks in it." He continued, "We could never get the leaks out of it. Good luck." So the gauntlet was thrown.

I went to the gentleman who was making our vacuum chambers at VFS, Bob Caldwell, an excellent man. I told Bob, "I got this furnace, and it's got leaks all over the inner wall of the chamber." The front and back heads were okay but the inner wall was a disaster. I told him I wanted to change various things about it anyway, and to put some ports in. I said, "What can we do about this inner wall that's leaking like that?" He said, "Well, let's just reline it." In other words, we'll make a new steel rollup and lay it right over top of the existing one, then weld the lining all the way around. That's what he did. He ground out all these patches, and he put this new liner in the chamber, and it was absolutely tight. The rebuild was expensive, but it solved the problem. Allison could have spent the money for it, but they didn't have Bob Caldwell. That was the difference.

In the end, the rebuild was a bit of a jab at my competition—we couldn't use the Ipsen furnace as it was, so we reengineered it and made it a VFS furnace. I took out Ipsen's square box and replaced it with our round hot zone, with our jet-cooling nozzles and recirculating-gas blower, a heat exchanger, and a new VRT power supply. Then, we built a new control cabinet. We just reworked that furnace top to bottom. That became our first real solid production vacuum furnace, a converted Ipsen furnace.

Our rebuilt Ipsen furnace was the biggest and highest temperature furnace in the greater Philadelphia area. We re-engineered the hot zone to operate at over 2650°F. In fact, on several occasions, we took it close to 3000°F, which simply was not done in the commercial heat treating world at that time. That furnace was far superior after we reworked it. However, we learned something even more important: the bigger the furnace, the better. Thirty-six inch deep furnaces were in abundance at the time, but there weren't too many furnaces like the one we built, which was 36"w x 24"h x 48" deep. Because of the size, we could put more work in as well as bigger parts—you simply can't put a four-foot part into a three-foot furnace, so our investment in the larger furnace ultimately paid off.

Roger and I soon recognized that we needed an even larger furnace. We ordered a brand new VFS furnace that was 6-feet deep and had a work capacity of more than 7,500 pounds, which was another major advantage in commercial

Thermal Vacuum Stress Relieve in a Typical Round Hot Zone.

heat treating—both size and weight capacity. We needed bigger furnaces in order to run bigger parts that nobody else could accommodate, which gave us an edge. As a matter of fact, we got to the point where we had the biggest furnaces on the entire East Coast, so we were getting work from Florida, we were getting work from New England, we were getting work from the Midwest, all being shipped in to our plant because of our bigger furnaces.

Our other advantage was operating temperature. We made our furnaces run to quite high operating temperatures, which the Ipsen furnaces could never do—you couldn't really run the Ipsen furnace reliably over about 2200°F; we ran VFS furnaces to 2600°F. And we pushed them even further up—we've run some of them up to around 2800, 2900°F, which is quite hot. In fact, there aren't many jobs that you can do at that temperature.

Each of these moves focused on problem solving and diligence, something I'm passionate about. Many people just accept what currently exists, but I tend to push the boundaries. Part of such boundary pushing is about innovation; another part is about taking advantage of opportunities. Both served us well.

One of our other advantages related to quality. I've already written about the value I place in integrity. Integrity translates to quality, too. In heat treating, there are inconsistencies. Many shops aren't especially careful, and customers have often just had to accept that reality. But when we started Solar Atmospheres, we were determined to produce consistent good work—just as we had at ABAR, just as we were doing at VFS. There was no reason for me to produce sub-par work.

However, in the entire industry—going back to ABAR, Ipsen, anywhere else—there was no convenient way of measuring the part getting heat treated. The parts themselves were not monitored for temperature, only the hot zone via a control thermocouple. Once the furnace came up to temperature per the control thermocouple, using a rule of thumb universally accepted and used by the entire industry, the furnace operator would soak the load at temperature for one hour per inch of thickness of the part. So, a six-inch thick part would sit in the furnace for six hours.

That was a rule of thumb, and it was reasonably accurate, but it had many shortcomings. The heat transfer characteristics at low temperatures—around 1000°F, for instance—take much longer, particularly in vacuum, where there's very low heat transmission by radiation. On the other hand, if you're up at a high temperature like 2100, 2200°F, the process moves much faster. Time alone may not give you the whole picture.

Metallurgically, you can determine whether the part really came to temperature by measuring the physical characteristics of the treated part via a process known as metallography, wherein you slice the part and look at the structure under a microscope. There are other approaches for measuring the treatment, but each takes place afterwards, after the part has been removed from the furnace. Waiting until after treatment is like baking a cake, taking it out of the oven, and slicing it open to see if it's done—or, to your great dismay, that it's overdone. It's all after the fact.

In baking or cooking, a thermometer is placed directly into the cake or piece of meat being cooked. By this method, the cook can see it come up to temperature. In the heat-treating industry, we did not use this type of technology. However, the aerospace people did—they used thermocouples to confirm a part's temperature. However, it was quite difficult to get the wiring of the thermocouples in and out of the furnace since the wires had to go through special vacuum glands that were manufactured by a company called Conax. The Conax glands faced two problems: One, the glands were difficult to assemble; if the furnace operator didn't do it right, the gland could leak, which would ruin the vacuum in the furnace. Two, these thermocouples have a relatively short life; a furnace will only get so many runs out of a thermocouple before the thermocouple has to be changed. Replacement is all labor and a little bit risky—the technicians need to know what they're doing.

To overcome these problems and provide a better quality treatment, after VFS had been established, we built a jack panel into the bottom of the vacuum furnace (or in the cold wall side of the vacuum furnace). There, we had those thermocouple wires permanently wired through permanent glands so that technicians could simply plug into this jack and have multiple thermocouples attached to the part. The operator then would only have to put the thermocouples in the part, plug the wires in, close the door, then monitor the temperature. The surprising thing was, no one had thought of simplifying the process in that way before. We were the first. And again, the general commercial heat treating industry hadn't done anything like this at all, and VFS introduced the idea on an everyday-production basis. In the aerospace industry, there were some commercial heat treating people who were running aerospace work, and they had to put thermocouples in, but they only did it when they had to, and they did it a laborious way. We introduced this jack panel arrangement.

Furnace workload fixturing...
Molabar® fixtures provide low thermal mass, high temperature stability and significant production payload increases.

Full Fixtured Workload of Jet Engine Parts to be Vacuum Brazed in an Early ABAR Vacuum Furnace.

Once this method of measuring the heat and maintaining standards had been introduced at Solar, I told Roger, "Roger, we are going to use work thermocouples on all of our work. And we're going to track them, and we're going to put three thermocouples into every job and keep track of where the work is so that we know we've heat treated the job properly." As it would turn out, this was a new philosophy in the commercial heat treating industry. It seems a fairly simply idea, but no one had employed it before we implemented it. It would be a game changer.

We were in business for about a year or a year and a half when we received a box of small tooling from a company in Connecticut. The parts were all standard A2/D2, a certain type of alloy that everybody was heat treating at the time. The company told us what they wanted in the way of results: "process these, ship them back, and we'll pay you." We processed them. A week later, we got another box. Same thing. Another week later we got another box. Process them. Okay. After about a month of this, we get a phone call from their plant, letting us know that we had processed those three sets of parts exactly the same. We didn't know it, but they had conducted a round robin test of the industry. They had sent these parts out to at least three other commercial heat treating companies. We were the only company that duplicated the results each time. They wanted to come down and see how we did it.

They sent a group to visit us. We showed them our process, and they committed to sending us all of their work. We still have that customer to this day, incidentally—Helicoil.

With that experience, we began to publicize our achievement and the importance of measuring—and providing—the work temperature data. We could give our customers not just charts of the furnace but of the parts themselves. That was also a game changer.

When we first went into the heat treating business, not many commercial companies around us had vacuum furnaces.

A few did, but not many. With a vacuum furnace, if the product going into the furnace is clean, it will come out just as clean as when it went in. In other words, it's not oxidized. If a steel tool part goes into a furnace and gets heat treated in an air atmosphere at around 1800°F, it's going to come out all brown and black and blue—oxidized. Now, those parts need to be cleaned either by sandblasting or pickling in acid solutions to dissolve away the oxides. But put these same parts in a vacuum furnace, and they come out absolutely clean. Sometimes, a customer new to vacuum heat treating would come back to us and accuse us of not treating their parts, claiming we returned the parts in the same condition as the parts arrived to our plant. We would happily say, yes, we actually have treated them; that's the way they're supposed to look coming out of a vacuum. Some customers didn't believe us and demanded to see the hardness readings—they didn't think we knew what we were doing. But the beauty of the vacuum treating is the efficiency: those parts no longer need to be cleaned before shipping. Vacuum produces such nice, clean work that we can take parts right from the furnace, box them, and ship them. It's one of the main selling points of a vacuum furnace, and coupled with the work thermocouples, the result was repeatable. That helped put Solar Atmospheres in business. It was the first real rung on the ladder for us.

Meanwhile, my brother, Dick, was quietly gathering customers. He had worked in the plant when he first came to Solar, while he still worked for Roadway. After retiring, he came to work as a shipper receiver. We bought a new truck so that we could make pickup and deliveries and expand our ability to serve our customers. Dick started making these pickups and deliveries for us. As he was doing this, he did a fair number of "cold" calls. He would just go into the back of a machine shop and talk to the workers back there. My brother Dick could talk quite well, and he would ask them, "Well, what is it you're shipping out that's being heat treated? We can do it." Selling through the back door—he was pretty good at it. So we'd gain a customer here or there, just because Dick asked some questions and put our name out there. He'd just stop and chat them up. Next thing you know, we'd have an order. Out of all the other drivers we've had, none would do that but Dick. He was successful at it and, as a result, we forged new relationships and customers.

As we grew, Roger and I began spending most of our time with the business of Solar Atmospheres, leaving the day-to-day operations of VFS to the management staff. They were more than happy to have autonomy while Roger and I focused on growing the heat treating business. It was an exciting time, as Roger describes:

" *The company was growing, and we were moving forward. We hired a man by the name of John Kozelski, whose expertise was brazing, and he brought a lot of brazing jobs into the business. We started our first second shift in the mid-80s after we recognized that you need a quick turnaround in order to really see profit in this business. We also hired my uncle, who helped the trucking side of the business get off the ground. We were fortunate enough to gain customers in Philadelphia, but if you wanted the work, you needed to pick up and deliver. So we started a milk run with some of these customers, particularly in Lower Bucks County and in Montgomery County. We were running within a 50 mile radius of Souderton delivering parts.*

We wanted to get into the heat treating business because we knew that was where the money was. The furnace business was a good business to us, and still is. It is much more challenging, much more difficult. But it was what provided the funding for us to start Solar Atmospheres. We have a brass goose at home, which Myrt purchased somewhere as a symbol of what we were all about. We call it "the Golden Goose," after the Aesop's Fable. Now that Golden Goose represented VFS, not Solar. It represented VFS. We knew if we worked hard at it, VFS would provide the money needed to move on to our next venture. And it did.

Myrt and daughter, Holly Jones, at an early ASM Heat Treating Show.

THE SALE OF VFS

With VFS flourishing, and Solar Atmospheres taking off, Roger and I devoted more and more time, effort, and money to the heat treating part of the business. We had taken good care of the Golden Goose that was VFS and were rewarded with enough money to really let Solar Atmospheres take off. However, tensions began to build between VFS and Solar Atmospheres. There may have been those in VFS management who resented VFS profits being funneled to Solar. But when you have a startup business within an existing business, you use your existing business to start the new business.

When I decided to concentrate on Solar, I turned over the operations of VFS to the management team. As a manager, I've always had my hands in almost everything. The engineers would lay things out. I'd look at them. I would say "okay, go ahead," and they would be off and running. Even though I'd turned over day-to-day operations to the management team, I still had my fingers in almost everything. I knew the management team wanted to do their own thing without me second guessing them. I tended to do that, and understandably, they didn't particularly like it. That was the tension between us. They wanted the autonomy. Just like a teenager who comes of age who tires of Dad telling him what to do, the VFS management team wanted me off their backs. But it was still my company. Fred Ripley remembers those days vividly:

The typical conflicts between personalities and differing management styles aside, the VFS management did enjoy their autonomy. As Bill became more involved with Solar, the team was quite content to run VFS mostly as they saw fit. However, Bill still had the last word. Though he was working mostly with Solar, he was still the boss.

In early 1995, with this daily tension building between us, I thought, "Life is too short for this, I'll just sell it to them." After much discussion with Myrt and Roger, we decided to sell VFS to the management team so we could concentrate fully on heat treating and Solar Atmospheres.

Now, when Myrt and I originally set up VFS, it was just the two of us and our money, which we promptly ran out of when the KFW lawsuit was thrown at us. So, I had to raise funds. Dave Rinz, George Carter, Bob Crowell, Fred Ripley, and Bob Hoover were the original stockholders, and I sold them the stock in the company at a very reasonable price. In fact, I'm not even sure Dave Rinz purchased his stock; I may have given it to him.

As is the norm, I had my attorney draft a buy-sell agreement when the business began. All the stockholders, the original investors and those who would eventually make up the VFS management team, were written into this agreement, which stated that, if stockholders left the company, we had to pay the stock out, and that stock would not be replaced.

Friends like Bob Gunow and Glen Slotter invested in us. Some of our employees also invested. My son, Roger, and my son-in-law, Bruce Craven, also invested and became stockholders. My brother came into his stock secondarily. The outstanding stock was about 20% to those six or eight stockholders. Some employees came and went—in one case a man died, and so forth.

In addition to how the stock would be paid out, the buy-sell agreement stipulated that, if for any reason I were to sell the business, the stockholders—the management team—would be given the first right of refusal. This agreement was written to be fair to all parties—both to the principal owners (me and Myrt) and to the stockholders. However, I wrote the agreement in such a way as to be *more* favorable to the managers. I felt that was the right thing to do, though most anyone else would have looked out for himself first, managers second. That was not my way, of course.

When I finally decided I wanted to concentrate on Solar Atmospheres and sell VFS, a buyer materialized out of the blue, interested in buying VFS.

This buyer, along with a group of investors from New York, wanted to buy the company, and I considered their offer, since I was now firmly involved at Solar. The tensions between Solar and the VFS management team were high, and I seriously considered selling to this outside gentleman. But I had this agreement. I probably could have broken it, but that was not my way. So, when I finally made up my mind to sell VFS, I went first to the management team, in accordance with the terms of our agreement, to let them know there was an interested buyer and to remind them of their right of first refusal. I told them, "Look, there's an opportunity for you to buy the company if you want to." Not surprisingly, with terms almost too good to be true, they leapt at the chance to purchase my company.

We established a purchase price of a little more than $2 million for VFS. With a typical buy-sell agreement, the sale price of a company can be calculated one of two ways: The buyer can either purchase the assets of the company or purchase the company based on a ratio of earnings. As it turned out, the two were roughly a tradeoff. So, the price was established without negotiation. Again, it really wasn't terribly favorable to me, but I had insisted upon it at the time of startup. I felt it was the right thing to do, as these people were investing what little money they had in my idea. If I had sold VFS to somebody else, I know I could have negotiated a better price. I also know I could probably have bought out the VFS management team. But it was just time to move on.

With the completion of the sale, we told the new owners— our former employees—that, although they now had control of VFS, Solar Atmospheres would still be their customer. They were in our building; Myrt and I owned it. I was still going to have something to say about it. The equipment that Solar Atmospheres wanted to buy, we'd have VFS build to our specifications. Though I needed furnaces built, I wanted to be rid of the headache of the manufacturing business. The fact is, Solar Atmospheres was VFS' best customer. We were buying new furnaces every year (and continued to do so for many years into the future, when we eventually formed another company, Solar Manufacturing). We didn't want to build these furnaces or replacement hot zones ourselves. We didn't want to be furnace builders—we wanted to be operations people at Solar Atmospheres. And where else would we buy these furnaces? We'd have to go to our competitors, and I certainly didn't want to buy from them. The last thing in the world I wanted to do was buy a new Ipsen vacuum furnace.

Now, per the buy-sell Agreement I wrote at VFS's inception, I was required to give the new owners whatever help they needed—within reason—anytime that they wanted. Interestingly, the management team didn't want to consult with me. About anything. In fact, they just more or less ignored me.

Our accountant and long-time associate, Al Pritchard, reflects on the sale of VFS this way:

I was greatly involved when Bill decided to sell VFS to his management team. It was a very difficult time. I think some of his employees wanted to do their own thing. He gave them a great bargain. It was a very trying time. But I felt strongly that Bill had the advantage of being able to build his own furnaces, and, in some ways, it gave him a step up. I had no worries about his ability to build Solar into a successful company.

Incidentally, after the sale and the establishment of Solar Atmospheres as a separate business, there were a number of hourly VFS employees who wanted to jump ship and come work for Solar. They wanted to work for me and Roger. That felt especially nice, especially as after all the turmoil, instead of simply moving ahead, Myrt and I realized the process of selling to our management team ended up being terribly painful for us. Unbelievably, within just two years of settling the sale of VFS to the management team, they turned around and sold VFS to Ipsen. Of all the potential buyers, they sold to Ipsen, my nearly life-long competitor. We were stunned; it was not something we could even imagine happening. But we no longer had control over it.

Fred Ripley describes the troubling time:

When Bill and Myrt approached the management team with the offer to sell them VFS, I was unaware of any outside offers to buy VFS. Selling their company to their management team was simply a response to Bill and Myrt's desires to move on. All members of the management team, as far as I recall, were enthused with the prospect of buying the company.

The subsequent sale of VFS to Ipsen was a troubling time for both me and Bill. Ipsen's interest in the company preceded the actual sale by about two years, with Ipsen reaching out to George Carter a number of times. Each time, they were rebuffed. Finally, Ipsen suggested the team at VFS make them an offer. We came up with what we thought was a crazy number—$6.5 million—thinking that would end the conversation, and they would go away. But to everyone's surprise, Ipsen agreed to it.

VFS was in Bill's building. He wanted it back, and our lease was running out. We had been looking for other buildings or to build one of our own, but we were all at the age that none of us were too enthused about taking on a big debt to do that. That's why I think selling to Ipsen was pursued more than anything. And from my standpoint, the fun of running VFS had kind of run out. I was locking horns with some of the decisions that were being made, so I kind of went along with it. The buyer was there at the time, and that was the argument.

I wasn't aware that Ipsen had been courting the VFS management team with offers to buy. So even though Ipsen had been a factor for a couple of years, it was still a blow to me and Myrt.

All in all, selling VFS to Ipsen took about two years to settle. The management team sold VFS for three times what they bought it for. Fred wasn't happy about selling to Ipsen—"None of us were in love with doing that." He knew my history with this competitor. Fred also wasn't at all interested in selling to a German company. "I really didn't like the idea of selling a good U.S. company, which we'd all worked hard to build and where I'd spent 25 years, to go to a foreign company. That's what was being done at the time and so much of that was going on. I was just one of the partners, and that's the way it came down."

Fred resigned the day after the sale to Ipsen was finalized.

Though this was a sort of near tragedy to me and Myrt, I just accepted it. George Carter and Dave Rinz came to see me, just to give me a heads up. The deal was done and signed. When they told me, though, I wasn't angry. I didn't show any emotion. I simply said, "Well, this doesn't make me happy but what's done is done, so there's nothing that I can do. I guess we have to go on from here." That conversation with them didn't last ten minutes. The decision was over.

Fred also reflects on that conversation, though he had a different perspective on it. "Bill mentioned it was one of his saddest days when George Carter and Dave Rinz came over and told him what was going down," Fred recalled. "That was the first I was aware that George and Dave went to see Bill. To tell you the truth, it brought back my memories of one of the reasons why I left. They just went ahead and did that without saying anything to me or to our other partner, Bob Crowell. That was part of our problem, I believe."

In truth, the sale didn't distress me right away; it took awhile for it to sink in. Over a period of time, though, I did become upset.

They sold the company to—literally—an unrelenting competitor. Ipsen was a major competitor whom I had fought against for 40 years. It was as if Ford Motor sold to General Motors. After you go through such competitive fighting over orders—and really that's what it was: every order was a knock 'em down, drag 'em out fight—watching VFS become part of Ipsen was nearly too much to take. Ipsen was, and is, an immensely difficult competitor. Since my days at ABAR, I'd had years and years and years of fighting for every bit of market share we had against Ipsen. On a visceral level, I thought, "I can't believe you did that to me." Whether they understood it or not, their choice was a slap in the face. Myrt and I had no idea there had been negotiations and bids from Ipsen, so VFS's sale was unbelievably disrespectful and hurtful. Myrt felt betrayed. I came to understand the management team's position—they wanted out, and Ipsen offered a lucrative deal. But it didn't ease the pain much.

Roger felt the sting, too:

Though they weren't technically called a management team, there was a group of individuals who were running VFS alongside my father: George Carter, Fred Ripley, Bob Crowell, Dave Rinz, and Bob Hoover. When my dad decided to sell VFS to these gentlemen, there had been a bit of tension between VFS and Solar because Solar was growing. In hindsight—especially when the team turned around and sold VFS to Ipsen for more money—I believe my father would have never sold VFS. He regretted that.

Finding out from George Carter that VFS had sold to Ipsen definitely had an impact. It hurt me, but not as much as it hurt my parents, because my parents put their blood, sweat, and tears into starting from virtually nothing to build that business to what it was. And obviously, if my dad had known those individuals would sell it in that manner, I know he would have kept VFS. But today the heat treating businesses are more profitable than the furnace businesses. Ten times more profitable. So, we're better off for it, actually.

And Roger is right, of course. We are better off for it. However, running a family business presents some unique difficulties, especially when something like this occurs. When the sale of VFS to its management team was completed, both my son-in-law Bruce and my son Roger would have each received about $50,000. I went to both of them, and I said, "Well, we're going to write you a check; they've given us the money and your stock is paid out, so you're each going to get this money." I offered them an option: they could either take the money and keep it, or they could reinvest it in Solar Atmospheres stock. Bruce took a few days to think it over and finally said he wanted the cash. I cautioned him that I felt this was unwise, but he was resolute. Well, that put me in a hard spot with Roger. I told Roger I didn't feel comfortable with him being a stockholder while Bruce, his brother-in-law, was not. Because Bruce took the cash, I advised Roger to do the same. So that's what we did. That's one of those sticky situations you sometimes encounter in a family business.

Family dynamics and feelings of betrayal aside, the sale of VFS was a turning point for us. I came away from it with the advantage of knowing how to build furnaces and how to heat treat. I had more than enough experience on both sides of the industry, and all I needed now was the opportunity to use everything I'd learned.

ADVANCED TUBULAR PRODUCTS (ATP) V. SOLAR ATMOSPHERES

In the years after we'd sold VFS to concentrate fully on Solar Atmospheres, we'd successfully built a solid reputation as a premium heat treater and industry leader. We had been in the heat treating business since 1984, and the names Solar Atmospheres and Bill Jones were synonymous with honesty and integrity, which is unfortunately a distinction in the heat treating industry. We were still dotting our I's and crossing our T's in everything we did and doing our best to identify potential problems before they arose.

So when we were sued by a customer on the grounds of fraud and breach of contract, we were completely surprised by their claims. We knew we'd done absolutely right by this customer, but it made us stop and think: Could we have missed something?

In 2003, we were approached by Advanced Tubular Products (ATP), out of Kentucky, to heat treat some duplex stainless steel tubing. They'd heard of us, reviewed our website, and decided to come see our operation. We met with them and listened as they described their needs. It seemed a fairly straightforward project. Accordingly, Solar wrote up a quote describing the services we would provide, the price, etc. This quote, as with every quote we produce, quite clearly and explicitly spelled out our Terms of Sale and notice of limited liability. The quote was emailed and a hard copy was faxed to ATP, in accordance with our policy. ATP agreed to all terms, sent us some tubing to test, and we were in business. Our quote, in the absence of any purchase order or other documentation from ATP, served as the contract between parties. This would end up saving our company.

After work began on this order, we noticed we were not getting paid for our services. We were being strung out 60, 90, and 120 days. We received a call from the purchasing agent we were working with at ATP, who told us Federal agents had come into their offices in Lexington, Kentucky, shutting them down. He didn't know what was going on, and, unfortunately, neither did we.

Shortly thereafter, ATP contacted us again, but this time to say that the materials we treated were breaking down and not up to standard. As a result, Dyna-Coil, the company who'd received the tubing from ATP, would no longer work with them, and refused to pay them for their services. ATP estimated this cost them somewhere in the neighborhood of $10 million dollars in damages. They determined Solar was at fault for breach of contract and fraud, claiming we did not do what we said we would. They decided to sue us in federal court for at least $10 million, potentially more.

As we began to uncover the details surrounding ATP and this particular job, it became obvious to me that this wasn't simply about a claim of poor heat treating. I learned the owners of ATP were investors, attorneys who had purchased ATP with no experience in the industry. Additionally, the tubing we were heat treating for them was being sold to companies for use in oil and gas wells, another area in which ATP was completely inexperienced. As a matter of fact, it turned out the investors were having difficulty making ATP a profitable company. In short, ATP was broke, which is why Federal agents stepped in—with Dyna-Coil withholding payment for the supposedly faulty tubing, ATP went out of business. So, it seemed to me these genius investors decided that a suit against us would not only set them right but would allow them to take over Solar Atmospheres, a thriving and very profitable business. Quite a tidy way to get themselves out of trouble, if it worked.

As we are located in Pennsylvania and the work was being done in Pennsylvania per our terms of sale, they sued us in federal court, on our home turf. We hired the attorneys of White and Williams, and specifically, Jerrold Anders, to represent us. Although we were certainly on much firmer footing this time— as opposed to the King Fifth Wheel's suit against VFS—it was still an extremely scary experience. If we lost the case, we'd lose the company. This time, though, we had more experience and money. I felt sure we'd win the suit, but there was still a lot of prayer involved.

I suspected ATP of using other heat treaters for their tubing, and we couldn't be certain the faulty components had been processed by Solar at all. Still, lacking concrete evidence of this fact, I was concerned that we'd incorrectly treated the tubing. To be sure, I hired an independent PhD metallurgist to test the material. There was a company out in Detroit that had a pile of the tubing left over that hadn't been heat treated. I bought that material from them, and we reran it exactly as we had for ATP. Then, we had the treated tubing independently tested metallurgically, and it was fine. There was nothing wrong with it.

When I gave the case to Jerry to defend us, Jerry looked it over and he said, quite simply, our sales terms said that we were not responsible for any of this work; it didn't make a difference whether it failed or succeeded, and ATP, aware of our terms, had accepted them.

Jerry said, "I don't want to get into the technical nonsense, Bill. If this ever goes before a jury, and you try to defend this thing metallurgically, it's going to be a real rat's nest. So I don't want to do that." He said, "I want to bifurcate (separate) it, and I want to take this case and judge it on the merit of your sales terms—which are solid—and on the point that you have records showing that they knew what you were doing and so forth." ATP had accepted our terms, and that was it, as far as Jerry was concerned. So that was what he did. The first phase of the case concerned the contractual relationship between Solar and ATP, and the supposedly fraudulent statements made by Solar to ATP. The second part involved the issue of whether Solar properly heat treated the parts and any damages incurred by ATP.

Time dragged on, and depositions began. I attended every meeting, every deposition, to be sure I understood the full picture and knew exactly who was saying what. I was doggedly determined to be a part of each phase of the inquisition. At one point, I travelled to Detroit to attend a deposition. Jerry's father had just passed away, and the funeral was held on the day of the deposition. Jerry tried to reschedule the deposition, but the ATP attorneys refused to budge. They were so intent on making this as painful as possible.

Jerry handed the deposition over to another attorney on the case, Mike Onufrak. Onufrak was a decidedly confrontational attorney; he was a former prosecuting attorney in one of the counties in the state of Ohio. He was a tough egg, but effective.

When we were just about ready to enter the room for the

deposition, Onufrak quite suddenly turned to me and gave me some very clear advice. "Don't say a word. Don't move. Don't show any emotion or give any information to the opposing counsel. I want you to sit in that room like a stone. You are just an observer. Do you understand me?"

Did I understand? It was like a commanding voice from heaven coming at me, and I did exactly as I was instructed. I was completely still and emotionless as I listened. About half-way through the deposition, as the ATP folks were providing details, Mike turned to me and said to the other attorney, "I want to have a private consultation with my client." We left the room and he said, "You know, Bill, they both just shot themselves in the foot. That guy is a liar, and we got him." Just like that, we went back in the room. That's all he wanted to tell me.

As the depositions continued, Jerry was concerned there were questions of factual evidence, and because of this, he felt certain the case would go to a jury trial. The crux of the matter, though, as Jerry saw it, was ATP's claim of breach of contract *and* fraud. They could not sue for both.

First, the issue of breach of contract. When ATP approached us to do this job, we issued a quote, containing the terms of the sale. This quote was accepted by ATP when they sent us the tubing to test. There were no other contractual discussions after that quote was sent. In effect, they accepted our conditions by sending us the material to test and continuing with the job. Therefore, the terms of the sale were the terms of the contract between Solar and ATP. ATP was bound by that contract as well as the limits of liability contained therein.

We had made a slight misstep, though: ATP had never sent us a formal purchase order and therefore, they had no purchasing terms. Actually, this is a debatable business concept, since with no formal purchase order from the customer, the contract becomes questionable in terms of its validity. Lesson learned: Don't take an order without a formal purchase order from the customer and a signed acknowledgement or agreement. With all the business experience we'd accumulated to this point, we were still learning!

ATP alleged that Solar breached the contract because we said we could heat treat the tubing as required, but did not do so. Unfortunately for ATP, their allegations of fraud were based on the same claim. Jerry revealed the brilliance behind his strategy in his documentation of the case:

Just as in the contract claims, the central issue in the fraud case [was] what was negotiated for and accepted. The language of fraud is a mere expedient by which ATP…asserted an alternative, or backup, theory. The 'gist of the action' here is contract, and summary judgment must be granted in Solar's favor as to ATP's tort claim.

In other words, ATP accepted our quote as well as our terms and our limited liability. Therefore, the quote became our contract. Consequently, we were under no obligation to pay them any damages, other than the amount outlined in our limited liability clause—which limits Solar's potential liability to twice the amount of Solar charges. In this case, we charged ATP $13,530 to heat treat their tubing. Per our agreement, they were owed no more than $27,050. A far cry from $10 million or more.

As for the second part, Jerry's Motion for Summary Judgment sums it up best:

ATP's claim of fraud [was] based on the same factual allegations as its contract claim. ATP even goes so far as to incorporate the same factual averments in the First Amended Complaint. Accordingly, if ATP's contract claim is barred by the terms of the contract, then it follows that ATP's identical claim of fraud is barred by the "Gist of the Action" doctrine because ATP's "fraud" claim is nothing more than its contract claim under a different legal heading. In the

case at bar, the economic loss doctrine precludes recovery on ATP's fraud claim because it seeks to recover purely economic losses for allegedly failed commercial expectations.

Brilliant!

As this case wore on, the judge decided he wanted to meet with each party in the suit. He set the date, and Myrt and I had to fly up from Florida, where we had been vacationing. The plaintiffs flew in from Detroit. It was a big deal, this particular meeting with this judge in downtown Philadelphia. Before we went to the meeting, I'd said to Myrt, "We're going to have to think about how we present ourselves. We don't want to come off as country bumpkins, but on the other hand, we don't want to come off as rich bitches, either." So I bought a brand new suit, not ultra-conservative but middle of the road sort of thing, and she bought a conservative dress especially for this meeting.

The appointed day came, and we met with the judge. It went fairly well, but at the end of the meeting he said, "You know, I can't tell you how this is going to go. I haven't rendered a decision. But if this goes against you, you know it's going to be a phone book number." In other words, millions of dollars.

Then, it was time for him to meet with the plaintiffs. The two attorneys from Detroit go in, and they were both dressed in their dark blue suits. One had a handkerchief in his pocket. They were slick and sharp. In they went, and we left.

It was right around lunch time, and we went to lunch with our attorneys, Jerry Anders and Mike Onufrak. I said to Jerry and Mike, "Well, what do you think?"

Mike spoke up first. He said, "I don't think it looks good." He said, "I think this thing could go against you, and I think we ought to seek a settlement." In other words, negotiate directly with them for some kind of a payout.

But Jerry said, "No. I don't think so at all. I think we still have a very good chance. I do not think we should do that."

So, I took a napkin (this is me, this is how I am). I said,

"Jerry, I want you to offer them $500,000 to settle." I wrote the number down, signed it, and I gave it to Myrt, and she signed it. Then, I handed this napkin to Jerry. I told him that's what I wanted him to do.

He said, "I don't recommend this. If he calls me for a discussion, I'll consider it, but I'm not going to do anything until he calls me." Jerry was not going to make the first move.

So, we sat on it. And when the judge ruled, about three months later, it was in our favor. But that was not the end. They appealed it, as Jerry knew they would. The case went up to a three judge panel. This panel never talked to us, they just reviewed all the depositions, the particulars of the case, and so on. That took another couple of months. In the end, this case dragged on for almost two years.

Later the next year, Myrt and I were down in Florida again, and we received a phone call from Jerry. He said, "Well, Bill, you can go get a bottle of Champagne, we got the ruling back from the judge panel and they ruled in our favor." I was a little worried the ATP attorneys would appeal again, but Jerry said they were pretty much dead. "Look, they've now had two rulings against them. They've spent a lot of money. You've spent money, but I don't think it's going to go any further."

Sure enough, within a week the attorney for ATP called Jerry. He knew the ruling was against him, so he said, "Alright, now we're willing to settle." Jerry said, "What do you mean you're willing to settle? There's nothing to settle." Jerry called me and, with a laugh, he said so-and-so called me, and he said, "You know, Bill, he's dialing for dollars."

Basically, these gentlemen invested money in a company, kind of like venture capitalists, and it didn't pan out. They were looking to get their money out one way or the other. Unfortunately for them, they didn't read the fine print and their plan backfired. The fine print saved us, and the suit against Solar was dismissed. However, we did learn some valuable lessons from it all. My son, Roger, reflects on the case:

When the ATP lawsuit happened, Jerry Anders opened our eyes to some of the business practices that allowed some things to fall through the cracks—such as not securing a signed purchase order—and showed us where we needed to tighten things up. We were singled out by ATP because we claimed on our website that we were the best, we were the metallurgical experts. Their whole claim was fraught with fraud and lies, and ATP was already bankrupt. That whole period of almost two years, enduring all that, and all the things we had to do—it cost us about a quarter million or more dollars to defend ourselves. But we got out of it, and the case was settled out of court, thank goodness.

As an aside, Myrt later learned (and how she came by this information, I'll never know) that the lead investor in ATP was an attorney with a second wife who was a true "trophy wife." Since his company was bankrupt, the only substantial monies left were dependent upon the outcome of this lawsuit. She told him in no uncertain terms that if he lost the case, he would lose her! That probably didn't end well for them.

This case was many years after the King Fifth Wheel suit, and our circumstances were quite different. We were larger, more experienced, and had more money to spend on attorneys and a defense. But the two lawsuits underscore my constant—and consistent—belief in honesty at all times. Had we actually committed the fraud claimed by ATP, we would have admitted to that and paid out any monies due to them. But we hadn't, because we run our businesses honestly and don't cut corners to keep costs low or accept any other questionable methods as "business as usual." Of course, mistakes can be made, but I knew that wasn't the case here.

The accusations made by KFW and ATP—those of theft and fraud, respectively—both felt like a punch in the gut to

in favor of purchasing their own furnaces and doing it themselves, well, why shouldn't they buy their furnaces from us? I knew the business inside and out and already had an excellent reputation. Also, as heat treaters now manufacturing furnaces, we knew exactly what our customers would need, because we were also the customer. We understood the market like no one else—a niche within a niche! It seemed like a logical progression in my career.

But we also wanted to build our own furnaces as well as our replacement hot zones. We didn't want to buy them from Ipsen or VFS. The hot zones were expensive, and we felt we could build them cheaper ourselves instead of buying them from someone else. Not surprisingly, we also felt we could build a better vacuum furnace. There were certain engineering innovations that we wanted to put into the hot zones, which had continually evolved since we left VFS. We wanted those innovations to be in our new furnaces. Again, this is an instance where I looked at the market and saw an opportunity. Yes, there were already furnace manufacturers aplenty, but I wanted to design hot zones *my* way, for *my* company. I knew, if we started manufacturing vacuum furnaces, we'd be able to command a fairly large piece of that pie. With this decided, we founded Solar Manufacturing.

At first, we sort of felt like we were going backwards, once again getting into the headache of manufacturing. But on the other hand, there was a need. So, we reentered the furnace-making business and needed to hire people. Interestingly enough, we were able to hire some of the VFS people, who had gone to Ipsen with the sale of VFS. I didn't much care that they'd been working for my competitor. As far as I was concerned, our chickens were coming home to roost. A number of the people at Solar Manufacturing came from VFS, and they were ex-Ipsen people at this point. Eventually, the exodus forced Ipsen to make some changes. They developed an employment agreement stating every employee who signed an employment agreement would receive something like $2,500. Essentially, a non-compete with signing bonus. Many former VFS employees signed it, and a number of them have since greatly regretted that.

When I left ABAR and started VFS, the market conditions—particularly for vacuum furnaces—were more or less wide open. There was a hole that could be filled. But when we started Solar Atmospheres as a heat treating business, that was not the case. We were in competition with already well-established heat treating people, and it was an uphill fight. But we managed because we did things that other people didn't want to do, and we had a better furnace; one of our early VFS furnaces would operate at a much higher temperature than our competitors could. Our heat treating competitors didn't know vacuum as well as we did. That was a benefit of coming from the vacuum furnace manufacturing background; I knew my product well.

Well, with Solar Manufacturing, seeing our heat-treating customers looking for their own furnaces, I knew I could fill their need. So, I returned to manufacturing.

But we'd learned so much since we'd left VFS behind.

As the years passed and technology evolved, so, too, did the way our customers were using vacuum furnaces. I saw a growing need for larger and larger furnaces. The larger the furnace, the more productive the furnace. A job that might require four or five separate loads in a smaller furnace could now be processed in one go, saving considerable production time and money. Additionally, larger and larger parts that required heat treating were being manufactured; breaking those larger parts into smaller parts to fit in a furnace and then reassembling them post-treat was not an ideal solution. It was obvious to me that larger furnaces would become very valuable—both to Solar Atmospheres and to companies doing their own heat treating. So, we worked on establishing our reputation with the big furnaces and the ability to handle heavy weight. There is tremendous benefit to having larger and larger and *larger* furnaces, but our competitors couldn't see the market, or, if they did, *they didn't want to take the risk.*

This is a key point. Many people will see opportunities all around them, and they may even acknowledge the potential for success, but, being unable to take a risk, such people will let the opportunities slip by. Eventually, someone like me will simply look at the facts and say, "Well, no one else is doing it, and I know I can make it work," and snatch up that opportunity. Being well-versed in the market and a risk-taker, that's what I did when I saw the potential market for larger furnaces; making that decision was no problem for me. That's one of the things about being the owner of the company: you don't have to convince somebody else to trust your vision. If you're the owner of a business and you're going to invest in an idea and pay for it, you can sign on the bottom line and do it. When Myrt and I went into business at VFS, it was with the help of an SBA loan. We had to personally sign for that. Ever since, we've personally signed for every loan that we've taken out to do anything. This means that if the company goes bankrupt, it takes us with it. Basically, most accountants recommend against personal signatures. But, in all honesty, I don't see a problem with it. If you borrow the money, you have to, in fact, take full responsibility to pay it back.

In any event, Solar Manufacturing has succeeded since we founded it, but one of the problems we encounter is that, because we've been innovating and making these furnaces—particularly these hot zones—much better, they last longer. At ABAR, the hot zone might have lasted two and a half to three years, depending on how you used it. It was very expensive. Some of the VFS hot zones are 10 years old. The challenge is, since we've created better and better furnaces, our furnace customers are not buying replacement hot zones as frequently as they used to, so we're missing that sale. And just as I understand both sides of the heat-treating and furnace-manufacturing line, I understand both sides of the furnace-manufacturing and rebuilding-hot zones line: At Solar Atmospheres, we've learned to rebuild our own hot zones. We don't even buy from our sister company because they're more expensive. We can do it in-house, so we buy the materials and our maintenance men build our hot zones. These hot zones are tricky to make, and it takes a fair amount of ingenuity to do it, but we've trained our staff to do it because it's a considerable savings. But while it helps Solar Atmosphere's bottom line, it also adversely affects Solar Manufacturing's bottom line.

Solar Atmospheres was a customer to VFS, and then later, to Solar Manufacturing. And customers want things done a certain way. Now, when you have an outside customer, you can't argue with them. You can to a certain extent, but at the end of the day, that outside customer totally controls what he wants. Similarly, Solar Atmospheres is an independent company and Solar Manufacturing is an independent company. They each have their own presidents. They each are operating their own businesses, and they're trying to make money. We buy and sell from each other, so there's always a tension, and competition.

Frankly, if it wasn't for me sitting on top of it, there'd be much more turmoil. I have the final say, and I'll say, "No, we're not going to make that," or "We're going to give it to them to do now. Be quiet and pay for it." I settle these squabbles like a parent with children.

Now, what will happen when I retire? That's the $24 million question.

Expansion: Success & Failure

He called us for a meeting down in Naples, when they still had their home there. That's when we were setting up shop in California, and he was signing the paperwork. He said to me and Roger, "This is the last one." Now we have California set up, and we're working on South Carolina. He'll never stop. He'll never stop. —Bob Hill

O f course, as Solar Manufacturing took off, opportunities presented themselves, and I responded by expanding. But, sometimes things look better on paper than they do in reality. Most of our risks pay off, but some do not.

NEW ENGLAND

Around 1995, I bought a bankrupted heat treating company based in New England. We renamed it Solar Atmospheres New England, or SANE for short. The purchase was anything but. It turned out to be a painfully bad decision because of market conditions, because of labor conditions, and because we didn't have the right people. We did a lot of traveling back and forth to visit the new plant to help them get started. But the people there—they didn't have the expertise and knowledge we had. We used to get calls from them where they asked really elementary questions about materials. Those calls—and what they signaled—were troubling.

At first, the purchase had seemed like a good deal and a good opportunity, otherwise we wouldn't have done it. Though the original company had gone bankrupt, Solar had customers in that area, so we thought we could make a go of it. We completely turned the company around, and we made SANE into a sister of what we were doing in Pennsylvania. But we had hard competition up in New England at the same time as the metallurgical business in New England was really going down. There were unexpected electrical power costs, labor costs, and I rehired the original owner of the company—which was not a good move. The salespeople did their selling on the golf course—things like that—so we were constantly drained of cash because the sales people kept losing money. The low cash flow prevented us from doing anything else.

We owned SANE for about two years before getting out, and the experience turned out to be a failure.

For this plant, we built and installed two VFS vacuum furnaces, and they ran well. Our major customer was a company called Ametek, over in Middletown, Connecticut. They had a special project for which we had done some development work. Around the time we decided we'd had enough of the market up in New England and told our contacts at Ametek we were going to shut down our plant, they pleaded with us to reconsider. They said, "Look, we can't do this. We want you to stay in operation for the next six months, and we'll pay you whatever it takes to keep you here." So, we said okay. But we stated firmly that at the end of that period we wanted to leave. Our lease would be up on the building, and we wanted to get out of there. We couldn't survive in the rest of the business market. So, we let everybody go except one person, and we ran the company with this single employee.

Ametek then said they wanted to buy the two furnaces we had installed at SANE. We agreed on a price, and they bought them. Those two furnaces were probably worth 1.5 million dollars, but we let them go for less. All in all, we probably lost a million dollars up there, which was significant, but not terrible. We could absorb it.

After all the mess of SANE was cleaned up, we had recouped our losses and were doing well. Now, I could have beaten myself up over the failed project, but what would I gain by that? We must look at our failures as learning experiences, especially as an entrepreneur. Imagine, quitting when the going gets rough. We never would have established VFS, if we'd had that attitude! If we'd given up as soon as we faced our first real threat—the lawsuit from King Fifth Wheel—where might we be? Most likely, not the owners of a thriving and expanding business. We learned many lessons from Solar Atmospheres of New England, and we kept moving forward.

By this time, I'd earned my reputation for being able to polish up the nuggets overlooked by others and turn them into gold. So, why was I not able to make SANE shine? Well, as an entrepreneur, one takes many small, seemingly insignificant, steps before he gets to the big leap. Each of those steps is an experience, and if one pays attention, those experiences add up to a solid understanding of running a business, the intricacies of your industry, and so on. However, even with my experience and knowledge, I've found that I sometimes give people more credit than they're due. That was the case with the original owner of this company we purchased. Though he'd been unable to keep the company going before we purchased it, I decided to keep him on, because I believed that with Solar's support, he could turn it around. I trusted that the salespeople we kept on would invest themselves in the Solar way of doing things—working honestly and with integrity. They didn't always do that, and the company suffered for it. These challenges made for more lessons learned that we applied as we moved forward. Even though the SANE nugget didn't turn to gold, the experiences we took away from it would be invaluable in the future. Which is another kind of golden nugget.

As we were growing, I'd hired a number of excellent people over the years, one of whom was Bob Hill, hired around the time we acquired SANE. Now, how we came to hire Bob is an interesting story.

Many times in my career, there have been circumstances in which I meet or hear of someone in such a way that the experience reveals the person's true character as well as his or her skills, and I feel in my gut that this person will be a good fit for Solar. Unlike the people at SANE—in whom I'd mistakenly put my faith—most people we hire not only meet but exceed my expectations. I don't look at a person as simply a cog in my wheel. I look for the qualities like honesty, trustworthiness, integrity, and loyalty. Bob, like other employees we've handpicked for Solar, had all of those characteristics in spades.

Roger and I met Bob through industry meetings and such. Bob's father-in-law, Charlie Schafer, owned and operated a heat treating shop nearby, so we also knew him through this company. Bob's in-laws were, unfortunately, not the best business people. Their shop, Precision Heat Treatment, was one of the old types of heat treating place—with oil quench furnaces, induction, flame hardening, and so on. They even had an old Ipsen 924 vacuum furnace in one corner. It was the typical dirty, smelly shop most people picture when they think of heat treating. The shop needed updating and newer technology, but Bob's in-laws weren't interested in investing any of their profits back into their company or in borrowing from the bank. Not surprisingly, the business went into a steady decline. Bob was conflicted: he wanted to stay and help his father-in-law with the business, but he knew where it was headed.

While we still had ownership of VFS, Bob had started

feeding us work from his shop. The old Ipsen furnace wasn't producing clean work, and he couldn't send it back to his customers in bad shape. So, he sent the parts to us to heat treat. He tried to convince Charlie to buy a new hot zone from us, and Roger and I went to see them at Precision to determine just what they needed. After taking a look at their furnace, we agreed he needed a whole new hot zone. Charlie asked for a quote, and we provided a fair one. It looked like Charlie would order the new hot zone, but the next day, it was a no go. Charlie's wife Elma stopped it, much to Bob's dismay. At first, we thought the job was given to someone else, but Bob said they just weren't going to do it at all. They were just going to try to repair the old one and keep it running. So, Bob started giving us more and more of their vacuum heat treat work to do.

While we were certainly able to do the work better than they could, we were still novices at heat treating, and made some mistakes. Bob likes to tell the story of how we messed up one of his jobs. Not because we botched it, but because of how we handled it:

One time, I gave Roger a high-speed tool steel job, and he fixtured the finished machined end on a mesh screen. The screen left marks on the critical dimension. And, actually, Bill and Roger came down. I'll never forget the smile on Bill's face. And Charlie, the German in him, was all upset. But Bill just said, "You know, we're sorry, but we learned a valuable lesson." He had a check right there and wrote the check. Charlie was speechless.

The situation was quickly defused, and Charlie didn't incur any losses because of our mistake. However, novices though we were, their shop still couldn't produce high quality work like we could. Eventually, Bob was funneling so much of their work to us, he decided to just hand over his customer list for vacuum heat treating. He was tired of being the middle man, and he knew their shop was never going to produce work like we could for these customers. That customer list helped, in part, to get Solar Atmospheres up and running at full speed. It must have been a hard decision for Bob, but he knew we would serve the customers better than they could.

Shortly thereafter, Roger ran into Bob at our local ASM meeting, and while they were catching up, Roger could tell Bob was unhappy. He spoke to me about it, and we decided it was time to talk to him about joining Solar. Roger called him and invited him to join us for dinner. He met us at Benitz Inn, and we talked, but he declined our offer. We invited him to dinner two more times over the course of a year, and each time he turned us down, to remain loyal to his wife's family and their sinking business. We respected him for that, of course. We knew he was stuck between a rock and a hard place.

Because Precision Heat Treating was in disrepair, there had been a safety violation which required fixing, but Charlie couldn't afford it. The result was a large fire, and Bob was injured. He suffered third degree burns to his hand. That was the final straw for him; he had a wife and young children and wasn't willing to suffer more injuries or worse for the failing business. Sadly but resolutely, he told his in-laws that he needed to leave the business. His wife, Chris, supported him completely. He was offered a share of the profits when he left, but he refused the money. He knew Charlie should funnel it back to the company. While he was recovering from his burns, he looked for work elsewhere. He didn't call us, because he felt he'd turned us down too many times. So, he engaged a headhunter to look for work.

He was offered a job in Peoria, Illinois, and he was prepared to move his family for the position. I heard about his upcoming relocation, and decided it wouldn't do. I called him up:

I was cutting my grass, and Bill Jones called me. He said, "Bob, what are you doing?" He said he'd heard I'd left Precision. I told him I had, and he wanted to know why I hadn't called him. I had turned him down so many times, I didn't feel right about it. He said, "I don't care about that. What are you doing now? Can you be up here in half an hour?" I said yes, and went to see him in my shorts, covered with grass. I met with Roger, Bruce Craven, and Bill. After telling them about Charlie's business, Bill knew I was a wreck. He again offered me a job, but he said, "I want you to take a month off. We're going to start paying you today. Do what you need to do, and we'll pay you." He told me to take some time off and then "you're going to come work here. You're not going to Peoria, Illinois." What a godsend. I felt like God was looking down right then.

After Bob recovered, he joined us in 1995, shortly after we acquired SANE. He set about helping Roger run the plant and was promoted as the company grew. He became an integral part of our success and eventual expansion of Solar.

In 2001, as Bob was moving his way up through the company, he helped us see the potential of expanding Solar Atmospheres to western Pennsylvania. Although SANE had rendered us a bit gun shy, Bob's idea made for a great next step for Solar Atmospheres.

HERMITAGE, PA (WESTERN PA)

Around 1997, we had a customer, Allegheny Ludlum, out near Pittsburgh. They needed us to heat treat C.P. titanium coils. Now, these coils are a tremendously expensive product, worth about half a million dollars per coil. They were huge and incredibly heavy, weighing 15,000 pounds each. At first, we were trying to do the job in the Souderton plant, two at a time, trucking the materials back and forth across the state. It was a difficult journey, to say the least, though the customer assumed trucking responsibilities. Even with the difficulties, we were their heat treaters because we eventually developed a very precise cycle to anneal their coils to the properties they desired.

Eventually, though, Allegheny Ludlum considered buying a furnace to do it themselves in western PA. At the time, our furnace in Souderton, though large, was not large enough. We could only get two coils in the furnace at a time, and it was quite risky—we actually broke multiple furnace load rails trying to get the coils in and out, and we were close to damaging the material a few times. When Allegheny Ludlum told us about their thoughts of buying their own furnace, we convinced them that they would encounter multiple problems doing it themselves without understanding vacuum technology. So, we offered a solution: We would build a larger and better vacuum furnace to accommodate the load size they needed, and we would open a plant in western PA. No more trucking the titanium coils from one end of Pennsylvania to the other. We also knew there were two other major titanium producers in the Northeast Ohio area, so we began our search for a new facility for Solar.

The three major producers of titanium in North America were all located in western PA and northeast Ohio. Allegheny Ludlum (now ATI), RMI (now Alcoa), and Timet, now owned by Berkshire Hathaway. We centrally located the plant in the epicenter of titanium production. We signed a long-term agreement with Allegheny Ludlum, which gave them first priority in the new furnace. But with this opportunity came some apprehension from Bob and his wife, Chris:

When this opportunity came up, we realized we could either make a one-time sale to A.L. of a vacuum furnace for the price of one year's worth of heat treating coils and

thereby lose their repeat heat treating business, or we could build an entirely new plant to accommodate their needs and continue to heat treat for them. Bill Jones understood very clearly that we would rather have this work for an extended period instead of a one shot deal. Bill, Roger, and I saw a huge opportunity to expand the business. Bill and Myrt asked Chris and I to come over to the house one night. We talked about the new venture, and Chris finally asked the most important question. She asked, "Well, Bill, if you were our age, and at our stage of life, what would you do?" We were all sitting around Bill and Myrt's dining room table. And he said, "You know, that's a very good question, Chris." He said, "I would do it. We're going to put some unique equipment out there. This facility is going to be unlike any other, and I know your husband will be successful. That was a really good feeling for both of us.

With that, Chris and Bob were sold on the idea. So, Bob led the search for a new facility. After inspecting over a hundred sites, we finally decided on an existing building on five acres in Hermitage, PA, five miles before the Ohio border. We needed to buy the facility quickly; we had no time to build a new building, because the construction of a new furnace would commence immediately. So, as Bob set about finding the building, we set about designing the largest high temperature, high vacuum, furnace in the world.

Since Solar Manufacturing was still in the distant future, I needed someone to build this furnace, so I turned to my former company, VFS (now owned by Ipsen), who was now a vendor to Solar Atmospheres. The engineering for this new, 24-foot furnace was undertaken by a consortium of engineers. I was at the head of it, of course, but I knew a team of experts would build a better furnace. So, I had three engineers from VFS as well as Bob Hill—who was going to be the user of this very unique, never-before-built equipment—and Bruce Craven, a mechanical and plant engineer for Solar. We also had two outside consultants who were on the engineering team; one was the fabricator of the large vessel, and the other designed the load car underneath the chamber. This team met in our upstairs conference room every week to design that furnace. We mapped out what we were going to do, and then each person went out and worked on it. Then, we'd meet again, and we kept massaging the designs until we got what we wanted. It was really an example of excellent cooperation, though there was a reason why it worked so well: There was a head of this committee, and it was me. I wanted that furnace a certain way, and though I listened to what everybody had to say, I had the final word. My experience and my technical abilities commanded respect, and everyone on the team appreciated that. Additionally, I was the customer, and because I knew vacuum furnaces so well, my authority wasn't questioned. We all cooperated and pulled it off.

So, as a team, we designed and built that 24-foot furnace, purchased from VFS. The design and build were completed, all in Souderton, and we felt we had a success on our hands. However, the powers that be at Ipsen felt differently. George Carter, who once worked for me but was now running VFS, paid me a visit. He said, "Bill, the Germans (Ipsen) don't want any responsibility for this furnace. They don't want to test it. They don't want to turn it on. We want to turn it over to you." In other words, they didn't want any part of this experiment. They were worried it might fail and didn't want to go down with it. Of course, I had faith in the design and the engineering. I knew this was a solid furnace that would change the industry. I was happy to accept full responsibility for it.

I said, "All right, George, I'll do that." But I told him, "I'm going to patent the furnace, and I'm going to write you a letter telling you that we are going to take full responsibility for this furnace. You and Ipsen will be out of it, but I have the patent rights." They agreed. They really didn't think it was going to work.

So, we fully built the furnace in Souderton. We pumped it down and partially tested it, but we didn't have the power to heat it at Souderton. We needed that furnace in Hermitage quickly to meet the customer's needs, and to show the world that the project would be a success.

The furnace was delivered to Hermitage, PA, in seven truck loads. After we assembled the furnace, it was pumped down, and all the gas lines were checked out to be leak-tight. We then heated it up to full temperature, and I knew the whole venture was all okay. Bob Hill fondly remembers the test:

We built this furnace and we were ready for a trial heat treat run. We had been working tirelessly all week. It was 11:00 at night and everything looked perfect, so Bill says, "Okay, Bob, let's get a load in there." And I say "Ok, Bill, I want to process this much cheaper carbon steel material over here, low value material." Bill said, "No. You have five of those titanium coils." I said, "Bill, that's $3 million worth of work!" He said, "Put it in there." My heart sank, but that was what the boss wanted. That was the test. I know I didn't sleep all night. But, of course, I quickly realized that was Bill's DNA—confident, courageous, yet very humble.

Let me just say, we knew temperature-wise everything was fine. The furnace passed the temperature uniformity survey with flying colors. Vacuum-wise, Bill looked over everything. He's a guru on that. Bill and I were confident it was leak tight. I had total confidence pyrometry-wise, vacuum-wise the parts would be good. The thing I was personally concerned about was the new patented design of the load cars. We were loading 50,000 pounds of very expensive material on a load car never tested! Would the insulation prevent heat from attacking some of the key elements of the new load car? Would we ever get those five coils out of the furnace once we ran them? I was worried. I said, "Bill, what if..." He cut me off and said, "Put it in." I'll never forget what he told me next, "That's why we engineer things; you must be confident in your design and know it's going to be right." Well, Bill was very prophetic.

The next morning, we all came back to the shop. The cycle ran flawlessly—the vacuum level was exceptional and the pyrometry was unsurpassed. Then the moment of truth: we opened the doors. The multimillion dollar titanium coils looked pristine! But there was a final test to be done. We hooked up the coupling of the transfer car to it to pull it out. The 50,000-pound load rolled out as smoothly as it had gone in. All of us were surprised, except Bill. He is so confident in his engineering capabilities—he knew it would work exactly as designed.

Because I had done so many other things before, I didn't feel stressed using million dollar materials for a test. The furnace was a good, solid design, as was the car bottom loader. Without that, we wouldn't have been able to safely load the oversized, heavy, and expensive material in and out of the furnace without problems. When our other titanium customers saw that furnace, they all wanted to use it. It wasn't long before Bob came to me with another suggestion:

The first furnace was locked up for Allegheny Ludlum, but these other titanium producers wanted to send us work as well, so I went to Bill to tell him we needed to put at least another 24-footer in. Without hesitation, Bill gave his approval to build another 24-foot car-bottom furnace! As we were building that, I could see right away that we should probably pour a foundation for a possible third 24' furnace. But I was hesitant to go to Mr. Jones once again,

because I knew we were spending a lot of money. Finally, I said, "Bill, I can foresee one furnace for Allegheny Ludlum, one for Timet, one for RMI." I remember writing my projections of our ROI on a napkin at Zoto's Diner. That was all Bill needed to see. He said, "Bob, let's do it." That was a considerable investment in a short amount of time, $10 million. He was thrilled that his new "mouse trap" was working perfectly and that the titanium world wanted it!

Bob talked to me for about thirty minutes, and I effectively signed off on it in that thirty minutes. I knew it was the right thing to do and the right time to do it. How did I know? Instinct honed over years of experience in the industry. There's a gut feeling that something is right—you consult data and listen to advice, but there's a definite instinct that stirs when you are on the cusp of a good idea. And when you combine that with expert engineering and design, you know you have a winner. Although we knew it was the right time and the right direction, looking back on that first furnace, and the first thoughts of starting a plant in Hermitage, I had no idea it would become as big as it is today. Neither did Bob. It's a 60,000 square foot complex now, but it started with one 20,000 square foot building.

As Bob recounts:

In the beginning, I was out on the road selling all day from sunup to sundown, and Kevin Bekelja and Bob Sandora were building the plant. They were accepting all the equipment and building the infrastructure with the local contractors. When potential customers went home for the evening, I would come back at night to answer voice mails and emails. I'd work until 10:00 p.m. and then just hit the road again, in another customer's lobby by 7:00 a.m. Bob and Kevin really deserve the credit of building our facility. I remember looking

at the plant floor late at night, from one end of the building to the other, thinking, how are we ever going to fill this place? And by the grace of God and a lot of hard work, we filled it nicely. Within a period of less than six months from opening the doors, we were in the black. We turned the corner and were profitable. Coming out of an unsuccessful Solar Atmospheres of New England, this was a huge accomplishment.

During these 16 years, we've had our ups and downs, just like any other business. But because we were so dependent upon titanium to keep the Hermitage plant busy and profitable, we had to adapt when the market fluctuated due to a demand shortage and economic recession no one saw coming, in 2008-2009. You can't have all your eggs in one basket; my days at ABAR taught me that. Initially, eighty percent of our sales were titanium. Commercial and military aerospace customers, like Airbus and Boeing, were hungry for titanium, and it's an area we excel in at Hermitage. In 2007, Bob came to me, describing a new Boeing contract that would infuse $5 million a year into the business. In order to take advantage of the opportunity, I would have to build a 36' furnace to thermally treat the titanium seat tracks for the Boeing 787 Dreamliner. I agreed immediately to another $10 million project.

About five years ago, around 2011, Idaho National Lab approached us, on behalf of the Department of Energy (DOE). They were looking for American-owned companies with no foreign interest at all. They were also looking for unique equipment to process some exotic, top secret materials. They had a project for Homeland Security, which is all I can say about it. Well, to become involved with this, several of our key operating personnel, including Myrt, were required to receive security clearances. We received our "Q" clearances and built a clean room for processing classified materials as well as medical materials, and so on. We did receive sales from it, but it also felt as though we owed it to our country, too.

Now in Hermitage, we did $19 million in 2015, and we're about $18 million so far in 2016, with $20 million projected for 2017. We have about 52 employees, and we're still building onto that complex because there is a need. In fact, I have recently approved another $10 million project to build a new 18,000 square foot addition to house a 48' vacuum furnace utilizing my now-famous car-bottom patent. In Hermitage, we now have a need to process 40' long Inconel tubing for our nuclear ships in the US Navy fleet. I have total confidence in the philosophy that if we build it, the work will come as long as we have a good nucleus of contracted work.

And with the success of the Souderton plant and then Hermitage, I decided it was time to look at expanding to California.

FONTANA, CA (SOUTHERN CA)

We had some customers out in California, and I thought it might be a good idea to look at the market in anticipation of expanding Solar Atmospheres. However, the largest concentration of heat treating companies in the United States is in the greater Los Angeles area. While that fact seems like a huge strike against expansion into that area, it's actually a huge advantage. Why? Because there's this pie, representing the market. Now, all we have to get is a sliver out of that pie, and once we get the sliver, we can start to crank it open. I knew the business was there, we just needed to tap into it. As with any venture, I turned to my friend and associate, Al Pritchard, for his experience and advice:

The California plant was a difficult market to break into. Stricter regulations made it a bit of an uphill climb. We looked at a number of small heat treating companies out there, but weren't interested. We went to a company in

*Portland who had a plant in California, but we didn't like
that operation. I think Bill and I spent maybe two weeks out
there, visiting plants and customers. Then, Bill made the
decision to go ahead and open a plant there. So, we needed
to find a good location and hire someone to run it. Bill had a
candidate in mind, Derek Dennis.*

Just as with Bob Hill, my experience vetting and hiring
Derek Dennis was an unusual one. In retrospect, it sounds
a little crazy, but when I met Derek, almost immediately he
struck me as someone who not only knew his business, but
would excel at the challenge of starting a plant and running
it. I also knew from talking with him that he was someone I
could trust. "The way Bill went about finding Derek and offering him the position was a little different," Al explains. "When
Bill feels someone is right for a job, he makes it happen. Entrepreneurs tend not to have big personnel departments, so many
decisions are based on the owner's research into a candidate
and gut feeling."

My research into Derek, however, consisted of a three-hour
period the first time I met him. It was pretty much all I needed
to know, though, of course, he'd still go through our full interview process. I will let Derek tell the story of how we met and
of the ensuing push to get him to join Solar. It really is kind of
funny, and he tells it well:

*Mike Drakeley, who is my current sales director, used
to be Vice President of Sales for the Souderton facility. He
called me one afternoon and said his boss was visiting customers in my area and wanted to stop in and visit me. I
agreed, only to find out he was coming the next day and
couldn't really specify a time. He was flying out of San Diego
back to Philly, and he had spent all day the Thursday before*

up in Los Angeles. Bill came to see me that next day, on Friday, probably around 9:30 or 10:00 in the morning. I wasn't really sure why he was there, but I took him to the conference room, and we sat and discussed what the company I worked for did—Valley was a custom tube manufacturer for the aerospace industry. Bill was very interested, especially in the process. I thought that was kind of odd; why would he be so interested?

He asked to see the shop, so we put on safety gear and went out to see it. We spent an hour and half out in the shop, and I took him from operation to operation, and he had questions about every operation. What about this? What about that? We had some interaction with some of the employees on the floor, and I could just tell he was really enjoying the experience. But at that time I was thinking, "I gotta get some stuff done." So, I tried to start pushing him back into the office, but we went back to the conference room and probably spent another hour and a half in the conference room just talking about this, that and the other thing—and my thoughts on this and my thoughts on that. I thought it a little strange that he would be out traveling by himself, not with the sales person I interacted with in Souderton. (Now that I know him, I understand completely.) We spent about an hour and a half in the conference room, and I tried to tighten things up a little bit, because, let's be honest, he was a vendor, he was not really a customer, so I was spending a lot of time with a vendor. We talked and, eventually, I told him I needed to get back to work and finish up before the weekend. In response, he asked me to walk with him out to his car. Never has a vendor asked me that; never in my entire life.

I have respect for those in authority, so I agreed. We walked out to the car, Bill turned to me and said, "Derek, I'm really interested in putting a facility in California." My immediate response was, "Good, because we need it out here, we really need it." I hadn't the slightest inclination what-

soever what he was hinting at. So, he clarified. He said, "I don't think you understand what I'm saying." I asked him to enlighten me, and he explained that he wanted to put a facility in California and wanted me to run it.

I thought he was crazy, he'd known me for three hours at that point. We'd had discussions all over the board—faith, how we deal with certain situations, hypothetical questions. Looking back on it now, the experience makes more sense: At first, he was very interested in the technology and the processing that we were doing. Upon reflection, I realized that the questions then turned more towards me, personally. Which was not a problem; I'm a very open, very personable person, but it just seemed kind of odd. I responded to his very bold statement with a sort of appeasing, "Sure, sure." Bill continued, saying he hated to do this, as I was a customer. He said he felt horrible, walking through my facility and wanting to offer me a job elsewhere, that's why he asked me to come out to the parking lot. He felt very guilty about offering me this position, but he was dead serious. So, I gave him my card and wrote my personal cell phone number and email on the back. I told him to contact me, and we'd talk further. I never thought I'd hear from him again. I called my wife, Rachel, and I said, "You're not going to believe this," and I told her the story. She couldn't believe it, either. I thought maybe he'd offered the job to two or three other people. We got a chuckle out of it, and then I went back to work.

That Saturday morning, I was at the park with my baby daughter, when Bill called and left a message with Rachel. I called him back, and he said, "Derek, I'm down in San Diego at the airport. I got here early. I have two extra hours, and I'd like you to come down, so we can start talking about Solar California." I told him I'd love to, but I was an hour and a half from the airport, and I wouldn't make it in time. My wife was looking at me quizzically, and I told her it was the gentleman I talked to the day before. We were both surprised to hear from him. He understood and said he'd call me next week. I began to think maybe he was actually a little serious, but still didn't think it was an honest opportunity.

But then, Sunday morning, after he'd returned home from church, I get a call. It was Bill—though I'm sure he didn't notice the three-hour difference in our time zones, because I was at church and unable to take his call. He left me a voicemail message that he wanted me to call him back, so we could start talking about Solar California, and he wanted me to draft up a proposal of how I would see this go, and what I would envision this to be. I was dumbfounded, thinking, I don't even know what he's really envisioning, so how can I tell him what I'd want? I called him back, and we chatted for probably about an hour and a half, and that's where it all began.

In that hour and a half conversation, things started to feel very real. I definitely thought he was very serious. We had multiple discussions for about six weeks, and then he wanted me to fly out to interview with the management team. My background is lean manufacturing, and, at that time, the company I was with had recently brought me on board to prepare the company for sale. We were going through a sale at the time Bill was discussing all of this with me. We had been on the market for about two years. I had made an attempt to buy the company, but was outbid and the company was purchased for cash. With all of this happening, I had to be very careful about interviewing. So, Bill said he would take care of it. He advised me to take off on a Friday, and he and his team would fill me in that day over the phone. Then, they'd bring me in on a Saturday when no one was at the facility. He would set up strategic interviews.

I called it the "Solar gauntlet," because it was four interviews with three-to-four people on a panel, starting out with the family and going through Quality and just interviewing. Most of those people are still here, by the way. Solar has good *employee retention; good people, good company. Best company I've ever worked for.*

I actually get emotional when I talk about it. Bill is, without a doubt, like a grandfather to me. I cannot say enough about the man. He's unbelievable. I've worked for some good people before, and he is by far, hands down, the best person I've ever worked for. Bill and Myrt and Roger, just salt of the Earth people. I cannot say enough.

Well, I went through the interview process. Unbeknownst to me, Bill had sent out an email to the management staff and asked for feedback. It was 2008, around March or April, and it was a down time. Things in our industry were tanking. Of all the industries, manufacturing was really bad. Because of this, most responded to Bill that, although they had positive things to say about me, it wasn't the right time. I have all those responses. He has forwarded me all of them since then.

Because of this, Bill decided not to move forward with California. He decided to delay it until things improved. He sent me an email stating this, stating that they had made a collective decision not to move forward. From when I first met with Bill at my facility, through the interview process, about six months had passed. It was a bit of a whirlwind.

I was very busy in California, keeping things going in transitioning companies. But the email from Bill, stating that he had decided to delay the build and my hire was sent to the wrong address. He was off by one letter on my email address, and I never received that email. I was left wondering what was happening for months, even though Bill and I were still having little conversations here and there. About two or three months later, I'm still talking to him like we're moving forward, because he'd never said the project was dead; he simply wanted to delay it. One day, we were talking, and he says, "You know what, Derek, I've decided we're going to move forward on this." Up until that moment,

I didn't know that a final decision had been made months earlier. I didn't find out about that email until years after.

After I'd been hired, he was going through his email inbox, and commented that he'd like me to see the responses from the management team, regarding my interview. He sent them all off to me, and within those email strings was the one about not moving forward on the California project. That's when I finally saw it, and I noticed my email address was incorrect. I had no clue for years that there had been a decision and that Bill had reversed it until I saw that email. Then, I felt a little guilty, thinking I'd pushed Bill to move ahead with California.

When I gave several months' advance notice to my employer, they offered me the president's position if I would stay. They were restructuring. My wife and I had pretty much decided to make the move to Solar, but we gave it more consideration and prayed about it, and ultimately decided to make the switch. Never in a million years did I ever think that I was going to be a "dirty heat treater." In my industry, that's what it was. Heat treating was the dirty business.

It was Bill, no doubt about it. Valley, my previous employer, was a family business, two brothers. Their children were not involved in this business. They're typical California, totally different mindset company from Solar. My company car at Valley was a 550 BMW. It was all about the bling and the flash and everything. Solar is a real, true family, and they believe in modesty and those kinds of values. I liked what Bill had to say. Bill was talking about a family business and longevity and working together until retirement. All of that resonated with me. Not just good morals, an old-school set of morals. Good business morals, doing the right thing for their customers.

One of his secrets to his success is that he truly values honesty and integrity and character. Those things are not just vision and value statements, that's really what he is all about. Which is one of the reasons why his interview process is a bit unique. He wants to know his candidates personally, not just in terms of what they can do for his business. It's such a change in a methodology of interviewing people. The questions that he asks now you can't ask people. You can't ask people about their age and how many children they have and what your religious beliefs are and stuff like that. But he indirectly manages it. But the reasons he asks those questions are to really truly understand who you are as a person rather than trying to use that information against you.

Funny stories aside, once we had Derek, we still had to get the California plant established and make it profitable. I was right about Derek, of course. He was, and is, the perfect man for that job. As soon as the ink was dry on his deal, he set about scouting locations for the new plant. We couldn't find a suitable building, and we struggled a bit. Derek eventually suggested we just buy some property and build a building to suit our needs. I agreed, and made the decision to locate outside of Los Angeles. We wanted our employees to have a quality of life that didn't involve the hassle of driving to and from work, fighting the terrible traffic and congestion just to get to work or back home to family. That meant we would need to provide trucking in and out of the city, but that was preferable to having our employees dealing with that stress daily. Eventually, we found a property in an area known as "the Inland Empire." It was two and a half acres in Fontana, California. We started the process of building, which is not easy in California due to very strict environmental and other regulations. But Derek was adept at meeting that challenge and persevered. I will say that, again, it was providential. At that time, the market was depressed and the building's owner was anxious to sell. All things seemed to fall into place for us.

When we decided on a location, I was not present at the settlement, and while the building was taking shape, I did not fly out to California to check on the progress. I trusted Derek, and I knew he had everything well in hand. I knew he'd get the job done. In fact, I didn't visit the plant until well after it had been built, right before we had our open house. It was the first time I'd seen it. Derek had the building complete and the equipment installed and running before I laid eyes on it. Seeing the plant all at once like this was quite a moving experience for me, as Derek recounts:

"

When Bill did come to visit the facility, I picked him up at the airport, and it makes me a little emotional thinking about it. We're driving through the neighborhood—it's not the best neighborhood in the world, kind of a rundown area, but it was what we could afford. We came around the corner, and we're going down the long driveway. We come up to the gate, Bill gets out of the car, and he just stands there. We're in the parking lot, and I look over, and his eyes are all welled up with tears. He just looked at me, and I can't remember exactly what he said, but something along the lines of, "this has always been my goal. People have always told me you don't want to go to California, you don't want to do this, and I've always wanted a facility in California. This has been one of my life-long goals." Then we just stood in silence for about a minute, and he looked at me, and he said thank you. I was blown out of the water. I'm so emotional about it, even now. It took me awhile to recover from that, just seeing that he was so happy in our accomplishment and his accomplishment of building this facility. That was the best reward he could have ever given me. That was it, in a nutshell.

Truly, it was a beautiful sight, and the emotional factor cannot be overlooked. When you've worked hard for your success and hand the responsibility for some of that success over to someone else, you have to trust that person implicitly. Sometimes it's hard to let go of the controls and trust others, especially in business, where it often seems it's everyone for himself. But I truly believe in the people we hire, and I've always operated this way. I trusted Derek, just as I trusted Roger and Bob and countless other employees, and they've never let me down. Looking at that property in California and seeing how Derek and his team had brought my vision to its fruition brought many emotions to the surface. I was delighted. But now we had to get to work and bring in some business.

Derek took back to California four people from Pennsylvania who had been with me for quite a while. Many people jumped at the chance to move to the West Coast. Mike Drakeley, who has been with us for 25 years, was one of them. He's the Director of Sales in California. Mike Moffit, the Director of Quality, has been with Solar for about 18 years. Dan Barszcz, worked in the quality department in Pennsylvania, but is now the Director of Operations out there. And they've brought the Solar culture with them to California, because it's a vastly different place than Souderton or Hermitage. That's important, because we are building the same environment in California, even though it's 3,000 miles away.

Business is good in California, though we are still a relatively new presence out there. Last year, in 2016, we've done about seven and a half million dollars, so we're working our way up, and our goal is a $20 million per year operation. That's where we'd like to be. We're quite profitable; the profit margins are high, which is not easy in California. It's a rough place to do business. Our electricity is triple the cost of the other facilities; one major challenge is the electrical power grid, which has been decimated by the Jane Fondas of the world. We are really limited, power-wise. Also, our labor costs are reasonably high. California is not business-friendly, especially to industrial businesses. But we're making it work, and the plant is doing well.

GREENVILLE, SC (THE SOUTHEAST)

When I was signing the papers for the California plant—that day in Naples, with Roger and Bob Hill—I said it was going to be my "last one." It wasn't. Around 2012-2013, we decided we needed a plant in the Southeast.

As with all of our other plants, expansion into the Southeast was customer-driven. The heat treating business is regional—companies do not like to send their product long distances, because of freight charges. So, a job will go to someone local, if at all possible. In Pittsburgh, for example, we had a customer who was shipping product to us in Souderton every week. They were not very economical about it, and because of this, they eventually decided to purchase their own furnace, to avoid sending the job out. Of course, we responded by examining that area and other businesses and saw a need for a facility in western Pennsylvania. It was completely market-driven. California presented the same opportunities, with one-third of all the business in the United States coming from that state. Commercially, we knew there were a large number of our competitors in the Los Angeles area. I learned a long time ago that you want to go where your customers are. Why? Because there's an established customer base. There's that "pie" of customers, and we could carve out our piece fairly easily, thanks in large part to our biggest competitor—Bodycote—providing poor turnaround and customer service. We had a customer out west who preferred to incur the cost of shipping materials all the way from California to our plant in Souderton rather than deal with a local company. Even with the trucking time and costs, it was cheaper and faster for him to do business in Souderton than with our competitor. He also discovered our quality, customer service, and so on. It was a no-brainer for him, and opened the doors for us.

After California was settled, we looked around the country for additional manufacturing markets. Réal Fradette, Solar Manufacturing's Senior Consultant, prepared a considerable amount of market studies, and we identified the greater Southeast—from northern Florida to the southern part of Virginia, then west to the Mississippi River—as a manufacturing base. Through the Department of Commerce, I conducted a search of commercial operations, while Réal contacted many Chambers of Commerce, and all our searches seemed to center on Greenville, South Carolina. Once we had identified the area we hoped to break into, we needed to hire someone to find the location for the plant and to develop Solar business in the Southeast.

We wanted this person to be autonomous and a complete self-starter. We found Steve Prout in 2013. My son, Roger, and Bob Hill both knew Steve, as he had a strong heat treating background. They both highly recommended him for the position. Now, I certainly liked Steve, and he interviewed well. He seemed a good fit for us, but I had just a few concerns about bringing him on board. He had worked for two of our direct competitors—Blue Water Thermal and Paulo Products—and had an employment contract with Paulo Products. We contacted Steve's boss at Paulo, the director of the company, to ask for a copy of the contract. No one ever responded. That took care of those concerns for me.

As with Bob Hill and Derek Dennis, my interview with Steve was a little different from the average executive interview. Steve recalls our discussions:

When I came to Souderton, it was the first time I actually sat around and talked to many members of the management team. Greenville had not been named, if you will; it was referred to as a new facility in the Southeast. The idea was that I would come on board and begin the process of evaluating where we wanted a facility, based on the business we had and the business we thought we could grow into—

they wanted me to determine where would be the best loca-
tion. Many of those discussions were in line with what you
might expect in an interview. Everybody was trying to deter-
mine my background, what have I accomplished, and so on.
With Bob Hill, we already knew each other, and we had more
relaxed discussions rather than a formal interview. He knew
I came from a background that was very similar to Solar. But
my interview with Bill was interesting. In today's day and
age, you get into this kind of a role, and you're trying to estab-
lish that, technically and business-wise, there's a capacity
and an ability to operate that business profitably. You're pre-
paring for a discussion with this executive, to demonstrate
you're a capable person, a good candidate for this opportu-
nity, should the conditions align with your needs.

Although I had some of those discussions with Bill, the
primary conversation was about me, personally, and all
the details around who I was—about my family. All those
intangible things that I was not prepared to discuss in an
interview. As I was flying home and reflecting on the inter-
view, that conversation with Bill was impressive to me. He
trusted his managers would not bring someone for an inter-
view that wasn't capable. He wanted to understand my expe-
rience, but he was more interested in me, as an individ-
ual. He wanted to be sure he was bringing someone into the
company who he, and the rest of Solar Nation, could trust.
Will this candidate take care of my people and the name I've
built? That was encouraging to me, and one of my major
takeaways with regards to Bill, specifically.

Many times, you see things in an interview that you
carry into the position with high hopes, and you see some
things that maybe you want to see, but they're not an accu-
rate reflection of the company. Some of those initial impres-
sions I had of Bill have been confirmed, and it's been refresh-
ing, because Bill never hammered me with situational
questions—What if this happened? How would you han-

dle this? He was really looking at those intangibles. That was important to me, because it spoke to the autonomy and empowerment Bill gives his employees and to the authority his employees have to make decisions. He also gives you the opportunity to fail and holds you accountable. In this kind of role, you want challenges, but you also want to be able to take the initiative and run with it.

What I took away from my first introduction to Bill was that, for the first time, I had spoken to a true entrepreneur on an in-depth level, someone who truly loved the process of starting and growing a business. In my previous positions, I was speaking with the third generation. I had an opportunity to speak to the first generation here, the man who built it.

With my operation in a startup mode, I'm able to see Bill's true love of the technical side of the furnaces; this is where his true love lies. We benefit from that, because whenever I've had startup issues—equipment not necessarily functioning, etc.—he gets really involved. He is sending emails, he's asking questions, tracking things down, and so on. That's great; I see that as a welcomed involvement because he brings value. He is extremely knowledgeable in those areas, and as a result, his involvement does help. He has the ability to just allow you to run the business, but he does hold you accountable. But, as I am in a remote site, he hasn't been as involved as he could be, simply because he is physically not here.

I'll never forget when I first joined Solar: I came to Souderton. I was talking to everybody and discussing the location of the Southeast facility. We met at a local restaurant for lunch one day, and Myrt was there. We were giving Myrt an update on possible locations. When I took the job, my daughters were seventeen and fifteen years old, a rising senior and a rising sophomore in high school. I was looking at the prospects of moving two girls at a time when everybody advises against it. I had resolved to myself that they understood; they knew that we, as a family, needed to do those things that would be best for the long term. I thought it was a good opportunity for their faith to build, for them to give their concerns to God and let Him handle it. I looked at it as a faith-building process for them. I had shared a bit of this with Bill and Myrt, and relayed that the girls were excited but a bit hesitant about moving from their home in Huntsville, Alabama. Myrt very kindly turned to Bill and asked him why we couldn't just build the facility in Huntsville, so the girls wouldn't have to move. She didn't want to lose sight of us in the midst of what we're trying to do as a company. Unfortunately, we know it wasn't the right spot for the business.

Sometimes when you move from one area to the next for business, you don't always make money when you sell your home, especially in the current home market. So, when we were looking at a home in South Carolina, it was refreshing and touching that Bill would ask how things were going and how we were coping. In many situations, your new employer doesn't care if you've found a suitable home quickly or if you're settling in ok. That was another good lesson learned. I truly feel like I have been brought in as a part of the business and that they appreciate my efforts to grow the business. Being a part of something like that is special. I think that feeling has been most clearly communicated by both Bill and Myrt. It's pretty clear that they have concern for those details.

So, we identified Greenville as our location, and hired Steve to help us locate a building and set up the plant. As with so many of our projects, this was to be providentially orchestrated. There was a building that had been vacant for ten years. It was larger than we needed, but it was available for an especially attractive price. There had been some vandalism, but it wasn't severe enough to scare us away. The building suited our needs perfectly, and with Roger and Bob Hill assisting, Steve set about making it happen.

The market is a bit different for us in Greenville, because we don't have that big of a customer base—the "pie"—like we do in Hermitage and California. Fortunately, we had a few existing customers in Souderton who were actually based in the Southeast, and we were able to hand them over to Steve, to encourage Greenville's growth while he worked on building their customer base. This choice proved very helpful, because we lost a customer we were counting on to get the ball rolling just as soon as we were set up—they found a way to get around the vacuum heat treating process and cut us out of the production line. The "big fish" fell off the hook, so to speak. Nothing is guaranteed and you can never count on all the customers you've identified as potential clients to actually do business with you. We weren't devastated by this, but it did have an impact and made Steve hustle a bit more. We knew we were going to have to work at building Greenville and establishing ourselves. We've been in production since June 2015, though we don't have all of our equipment in a production state yet. We're still in the process of getting up to full stride, and all estimates indicate we need about three years before we break even.

The State of the "Nation" & Future Trajectories

Speaking personally, this business is Dad's enjoyment, thoroughly. He doesn't hunt. He doesn't fish. They recently sold their place in Florida, which my mom bought years ago as a place for them to go and get away from it all. But, even down there, my dad would spend half a day, usually the mornings, on the phone talking to someone back here. He'd be standing in the Gulf of Mexico in January or February, and he'd say, "Hey, Roger, my feet are in the Gulf, the water's like 70 degrees. What's the weather like up there?" And I'd reply, "It's minus zero, Dad. It's minus ten."

The business is Dad's hobby. He doesn't have anything else. If he could put a vacuum furnace or something in his basement, he probably would. We've always kidded him about that. As long as my father's health is in good shape, as long as his mind is sharp, he's going to continue to come into work for who knows how much longer. That's just the way he is.

I can say I've noticed over the past two years, maybe three, my dad has started to slow down a little bit. By that I mean he doesn't come into work at 7:00 in the morning. He might come in around 9:00. He's still here till 5:00—sometimes 5:30—at night, though. With the furnace side of the business, he's engaged, and he's involved, but he's letting some of those people do their own things. So, I think he's starting to slowly take a step back. He's going to be 81 years old next month, and he has to slowly take a step back, and it is going to be a slow step because I know it's hard for him to do that.

— Roger Jones

The current State of the Solar Nation is healthy. Myrt and I, with Solar, are currently worth a fair amount, about $1 million for each year of my life. Corporate-wide vacuum heat treating sales for 2016 were $48 million, and we expect sales to approach $52 million in 2017. We have expanded and have done well with each new project or acquisition. We now have four vacuum heat treating plants running: Eastern PA (Souderton), Western PA (Hermitage), California (Fontana), and South Carolina (Greenville). In November of 2015, our Hermitage facility broke ground for an expansion project for a 22,000 square-foot building to house the largest commercially owned vacuum furnace, at 6.5' diameter by 48' long, with a workload capacity of 150,000 lbs. That project was completed earlier this year and is the third expansion within the 15 years this plant has been operational. When Myrt and I first started VFS and later, Solar, I couldn't begin to imagine our company making a furnace that large. But we needed it, and we could build it. So, we did.

The Fontana plant continues to grow, with the many aerospace programs like SpaceX, Falcon 9, and Dragon providing us with much work and opportunity. Military, government, and medical projects are also keeping us busy in California. Vacuum carburizing has increased dramatically across the Solar Nation, and we expect that trend to continue. Like our plant in Hermitage, facility expansion is underway in California, and we are adding vacuum processing, air furnace, and parts cleaning equipment in an effort to keep up with—and keep ahead of—growing markets.

2016 was the all-time highest sales year for the Souderton facilities, at just over $18.5 million. This achievement was due largely to growing sales from new customers as well as increases from existing customers. In Souderton, as in California, vacuum carburizing has claimed a top spot among high-earning projects. As Jamie Jones, Solar's Vice President of Operations (and my grandson) notes, "Our special processes are a very important part of our success. One of the greatest jumps in sales is from our vacuum carburizing process." Medical processing is also very strong and will continue to grow. In fact, our medical room is busier from one month to the next. Though it is the oldest plant and contains the oldest equipment, Souderton continues to be a top performing facility. The age of the furnaces and their continued dependability is a testament to how well they were built and to our ongoing maintenance program, with our maintenance team under the direction of Dan Landis. The VFS and newer Solar furnaces are, quite simply, the best around.

The Southeast plant in Greenville, South Carolina, started in 2015 with two staff members working on drawings and approvals, and ended the year with eleven full-time employees, four vacuum furnaces installed, and all of the necessary quality accreditations to present themselves to the Southeast market as production ready.

As is often the case with a new venture, though, some unforeseen challenges beyond their control presented themselves, and forced them to slightly adjust the plans. Having shifted gears and timing a bit, they are back on track, targeting the aerospace and defense market. They closed 2015 with over $327,000 in the books, despite the few startup obstacles they encountered, and our shipments for 2016 were $2 million.

Their current opportunity pipeline is estimated at $3.1 million annually. I estimate this will put the company near breakeven.

Just a few months ago, Myrt and I added another business to our portfolio—Vacuum Pump Services Corporation—a manufacturing and mechanical pump–service business based in Hatfield, PA, which is close to our Souderton facility. This business is just getting off the ground, but we know it is an area that will grow. We have so many vacuum furnaces in use, and the pumps eventually need servicing. Well, we don't want to send them out to someone else to rebuild, so we have a company now that can service them and keep them in top shape for us as well as provide this service to others—even competitors. Even as we enjoy the current successes and expansions, we are also looking forward. We are never complacent, because the industry is constantly evolving. If you don't change with it, you will be left behind.

Bear with me for a moment, and read over Solar Atmospheres' Mission Statement below (developed by our Solar management team), because it plays a critical part in understanding the current and future state of The Solar Nation:

The mission of Solar Atmospheres is to add significant value to our customer's operations by thermally treating parts, principally in a vacuum environment, with an unwavering commitment to honesty in all relationships.

Reads like a pretty good, but pretty standard mission statement, right? But allow me to continue, for below that statement, we add some qualifiers:

We strive to fulfill this mission by:

Performing our work with an emphasis on quality and responsiveness (this is a key word)

Operating with an awareness and appreciation of the

value of our customer's parts while in our care

Forever looking forward in the area of technical capabilities (again, key words)

Demonstrating a willingness to accept the challenge (never complacent)

Providing and maintaining a work environment that is safe, clean, and reflects our respect for human dignity

Maintaining a workplace that is environmentally friendly

And finally,

Sustaining long-term growth and profitability (the commitment to remaining viable)

Responsiveness, looking forward, accepting challenges, and keeping in mind long-term growth and profitability—all of these concepts are critical to our success and are therefore woven into the fabric of our everyday work philosophy at Solar. This is why our employees are so keen and equipped to look at new methods and processes instead of committing existing ones to memory and repetition and being satisfied with the status quo. The future of any industry or business is nearly impossible to predict with any degree of accuracy, and our industry is no different. So many factors come into play—political, economic, environmental, and more. Even though you may be able to forecast, based on sales projections, contracts, etc., it is hard to know exactly which way the wind will blow more than a few years down the line. In fact, Michael Moyer, Solar Atmospheres' Director of Sales in Souderton, summed this up beautifully, as he looked ahead into what 2017 could bring:

Looking forward to 2017, there are some scary signs on the horizon. First, there is the election year which can be

a distraction to business. The global markets are on edge. There are huge drops in commodity prices (like crude oil) with rock bottom prices for primary metals. This will undoubtedly lead to the closing of domestic steel and manufacturing mills. There is a prediction that oil prices will stay low, extending the halts in oil/gas exploration and drilling. Iranian oil entering the marketplace will ensure prices stay low. The dollar is gaining on foreign currencies, meaning American products are more expensive abroad.

All of this points towards an ever greater trade deficit with the rest of the world. We are fortunate to be so diversified in the markets we serve, and I hope this insulates us somewhat from some of the uncertainty in the marketplace in the coming years.

Diversification. That's a key to our continued success. As we learned from experience at our Western Pennsylvania plant—when a drop in the titanium supply nearly crippled our sales—it is not a good idea to put all your eggs into one basket. Applications, and the projects we're working on, lead us to new processes and potential trends in industry. When you pay attention to how the industry is changing and can adapt to these changes quickly, you increase your business' ability to keep current or ahead of the curve.

Typically, in heat treating, when we receive nearly-finished parts to process from various manufacturers, we process and send them back. We are toward the end of the pipeline. Those parts and the production steps are already defined. But in the rapidly growing area of raw product processing (for Solar), they are not completed parts yet, and we are at or near the beginning of the process. Where some of these materials are concerned, we are the only commercial heat treating company processing these materials, For example, hydriding metals like titanium, tantalum, niobium, and other refractory-like materials. That is one advantage. Right now, the metals market is depressed, at almost a 25-year low. But, even with this, our business continues. If we see commodities prices rise, we will see even more business.

Additive manufacturing—the use of 3D printers to make parts out of plastics or metals—is a new market with tremendous growth potential. As the popularity of this technology builds, the parts needed to build and use these printers will need to be stronger, more useable, and so on, and that requires heat treating processes such as sintering. Different alloys are being made to work in the 3D printers, and sometimes those need to be heat treated before they can be used.

Virginia Osterman, Ph.D., a member of our Research and Development team, talks about some of the new areas we're looking at, in relation to 3D printing, as mentioned above, or in the world of Nano-powders:

We're testing the sintering qualities of these powders, and advising those companies trying to break into this [3D printing] industry on the best processes to use for these materials—how to develop the process within the vacuum furnace, which vacuum furnaces to use, whether to use an all graphite or all metal hot zone, and so on. We're acting in a consultant capacity for them, after testing the materials and figuring out all the critical information along the way, to help them achieve their best product.

Again, staying current with trends and projecting how these trends will change is a key part of our Research and Development department. As Don Jordan, Solar Atmospheres' Vice President and Corporate Metallurgist puts it, we are really Application Engineers. "Many of the processes are developed over years in academia. We take those and try to develop them as practical processes."

Looking not only at the parts we treat, but how those parts will be used, what the end product will be, and so on, leads us to look at our processes in different ways. We begin to see new applications emerge for existing technology. Rather than always trying to re-invent the wheel, we look at new ways of using the existing wheel, perhaps tweaking it a bit here and there for new applications. In this way, we can keep from stagnating and letting our equipment become obsolete. Don puts it this way:

"

Carburizing is a good example: It is a process that's been around forever. But we've developed it as a repeatable process, in vacuum, for a niche market. We did not invent it, but we like to think we perfected it, because we understood it better than most. We focused on new alloys being developed and how to carburize those. We are now seen as the number one vacuum carburizing company for military rotorcraft gears. We do R&D work with vendors for helicopter manufacturers who've received grants from the US Army and Air Force, with our name included in their reports. It's a big circle, which works out well for Solar.

When thinking about growing our business 25, or even 10 years ago, significant technologies such as 3D printing and nano-powders weren't on the horizon. We couldn't have predicted our position in these markets or how important they would come to be. New technologies are emerging at a fast pace, and staying on top of these developments is key to survival.

Don Jordan and my grandson—Solar's Principal Engineer, Trevor Jones—part of our research and development team, look at cutting edge and emerging technologies, with an eye for Solar's part in them. They wrote for Solar Atmospheres' 2015 Annual Report:

Research in conjunction with a small company contin-ues, involving sintering specialty Nano-powders to make thermoelectric generators that convert waste heat into elec-tricity. Universally, 68% of energy is lost as waste heat, so success in this technology would revolutionize the semicon-ductor industry, among many others.

What an amazing thought! Such work is off in the future and still on the cutting-edge, but we're keeping an eye on it. Again, such a turn is not something I could have predicted. There are also applications on the horizon that are considered exotic applications, and we have to meet the need, when it arises, to heat treat these applications.

We have also learned that to maintain pace with develop-ing technology, we need to design new furnaces to accommo-date new processes. For Solar Manufacturing—now a com-pany with $20 million in annual sales—this expectation means developing new furnaces and new furnace technology. In some cases, current vacuum furnaces can't handle the newest pro-cesses, or are no longer applicable. So, just as we adjust the applications, we adjust the tools to fit new developments in technology. Many of the older processes are no longer environ-mentally friendly—as is the case in salt-bath heat treating—and it is our mission to be as green and safe as possible, which means we have another reason to adjust our methods and equipment. As my grandson Trevor says, "It's all about materi-als evolution, and as materials continue to evolve, we are here to evolve with them." Materials are advancing, and we need furnaces that will operate at higher temperatures to process these exotic applications. Also, as the processes are becoming more enhanced, the furnace controls need to be continually improved and automated. As Trevor states, "You can no longer rely on operators to manually intervene with flow rates, pressures, temperatures, ramp rates, etc. The control system has to be the smartest piece of equipment to control the process." This is to say, innovation comes back, also, to repeatability and control.

We also see the need for specialized furnace manufacturing—no "cookie cutter" furnaces to suit every job. Customers need furnaces built to specific requirements. Larger furnaces will also be in greater demand, and this is an area in which Solar Manufacturing excels.

Yet another business Myrt and I established, this one about 15 years ago, is Magnetic Specialties, Inc. or MSI (now a yearly $3.5 million company). This is a slowly developing business for specialized transformers and magnetic components. The power supplies in Solar furnaces are all built by MSI, and the industry trend is leaning towards that type of power supply. We expect MSI to continue to grow as the rest of the industry jumps on board. We have a highly competent electrical engineer running that business, Mike Afflerbach. He is not only a hard working engineer, but a man who understands business and financials, which is a boon for MSI.

The metallurgical world has been relatively slow to emerge, compared to other industries. It is a slow, cautious science, but it needs to be. A good deal of the work that comes out of vacuum heat treating goes into highly sensitive infrastructures and sometimes volatile environments—airplanes, bridges, automobiles, medical equipment, defense, outer space satellites and probes, etc. A failure in one small part could have catastrophic consequences, so this work equates to a science that literally cannot fail. It was a metallurgical error that caused the Titanic to sink, not just the iceberg. The British-built De Havilland Comet—a four-engine jet liner—crashed several times before the metallurgical error was found; as a result, De Havilland couldn't give those planes away. This is why we test and test and test until we achieve results as close to one hundred percent perfect each time as possible. And still we keep working to improve the furnaces and the processes.

With all new materials and processes comes more quality control and regulation. Our quality department has grown substantially to keep up with the demands of the defense industry, aerospace, military, medical needs, and so on. OSHA and the EPA have become more and more influential, which will continue into the future and will directly impact our industry. In our California plant, we are already severely energy-limited in the summer, and this challenge will only continue and certainly restrict our operations going forward. We must learn to apply techniques and find ways to accommodate and improve our furnace operating efficiencies.

Overhead to support all of this growth has certainly increased, as well. But, here again, this process sets us apart from the other heat treating companies. Departments like quality control, research and development, and marketing don't typically exist in most heat treating companies, and the cost to keep these departments staffed and running well is a necessary expense.

As our Solar Nation continues to evolve, Solar Manufacturing will soon outgrow our footprint here in Souderton, and will most likely relocate to a larger plant in the surrounding area. In fact, we expect we will eventually need to build a new heat treating plant, as well. We are currently in the process of doubling the facilities in Fontana, and we have substantially added to the Hermitage site. Greenville has room to expand, as well, and I expect it will, once it is successful. This constant need for expansion is just Solar taking its natural course. It's the natural growth of a successful business.

I've said before that the heat treating business is regional. To that end, we are exploring another division in the Southwest—the "Oil Patch." Another possibility is the Midwest, the greater Chicago area. All of these developments are dependent upon the markets, of course. The point is, we continue to look for opportunities, often overlooked or passed over by our competitors because they're deemed "too costly" or "too specialized." In fact, this "niche within a niche" works well for us and helps us to diversify.

As we've grown, we've taken on some of the brightest minds, hired wonderful interns and young people who think in ways we never envisioned. They are the ones who will carry this technology into the future, further than we could have ever imagined. Our whole world here is looking forward, more so than many realize, and it takes intelligence and technical creativity to bring our vision to fruition. We are working with people right now who will be on the cutting edge of new technology and processes. The entire experience is enlightening.

THE SOLAR NATION, AFTER THE JONES FAMILY

Now, it's hard sometimes to imagine how Solar will continue after Myrt and I are gone. In fact, who will carry on with our work after the Jones family is no longer in charge? My son, Roger, is near retirement age, and we have grandsons Jamie and Trevor poised to take over when the time comes. But after that, who knows? It is said that a family business usually only lasts through one generation. We're into our third generation with Trevor and Jamie. We've had family meetings regarding the future of Solar, and Myrt and I have stated plainly and often that we don't want it sold. Roger, Trevor, and Jamie know this and will honor our wishes. We have also communicated this fact often to our management teams.

To prepare for a day when the Jones family is no longer an integral part of The Solar Nation, we have made sure throughout the years to hire individuals who are not only qualified, but who possess character and integrity, who hold similar values and work ethic similar to my own. No, we don't only hire Christians or only friends of church families or so on. But we do seek out honest, hard-working, ethical candidates who share our vision for an honest, hard-working, ethical organization. That sounds redundant, but an organization is made of its employees, and if executive leaders, managers, and employees don't share a common vision and all work towards it, the company stays as strong as its employee base.

We have worked hard to create that culture at Solar. Our employees completely stand by and uphold our mission statement, and this extends to each one of our plants, though they are spread all over the country. We populate new facilities with a few experienced people from other locations, who carry the Solar philosophy, work ethic and integrity to the new plant. They lead by example, and soon new hires learn the Solar way and enrich our organization's culture. In this way, our organization grows stronger, and the culture I've worked so hard to promote carries into the next generation, and so on.

What the future holds for Solar, I don't know. But I do know I'll feel good about stepping aside when the time comes. Our employees are remarkable people who can do remarkable things. I see no reason why their success won't continue long into the future.

BOOK
3
INNOVATIONS

Innovations

We spend money on R&D and have an R&D department. We are the only company in our industry to do this. We are also the only company in our industry with a marketing manager and marketing department. —WRJ

ABAR, 1964–1978

Over the years, I've been privileged to be either the first to design something new or to head a team paving new territory in our industry. It's quite reassuring, knowing you're contributing to history, and I'm pleased to say most of the innovations I was involved with are still in active use. Here are just a few.

The development of the Ring Hot Zone. This was such a game-changer, I gave it its own chapter in this book. For the full story of this innovation, see page 71.

Moly Nuts and Bolts. Though a seemingly minor change, this innovation was really quite a revelation in its day for our industry. We designed threaded moly rods and tapped moly squares to make moly screws and nuts, which allowed us to avoid riveting moly heating elements and other hot zone components. Moly is a very hard metal, like tungsten, and difficult to machine. The use of moly nuts and bolts was certainly new to me, and I reviewed this idea with my patent attorney at the time, suggesting that I wanted to try for a patent. Zach Wobensmith, our then patent attorney, was a really brusque sort of man. He looked at me, and said, "Bill, you're crazy. You can't patent the nut and bolt." That was the end of that.

Corning Glass Hydrogen Furnace. For Corning Glass, we designed a furnace for vacuum pump down, vacuum purge, and backfill with hydrogen gas to slightly positive pressure, and burn off hydrogen process gas. Hydrogen is highly explosive, so the thought of introducing hydrogen into the type of vacuum furnace that we built was an engineering challenge. And then there was the worry of whether the furnace might explode. Hydrogen is used all the time in furnaces that are not firmly sealed, so if anything goes wrong, they literally have blow-off panels that will relieve the pressure. But you can't do that in a vacuum furnace easily. Although the Corning Glass Hydrogen Furnace was not a really big furnace, we built it with every safety we could think of, and we never had an explosion. It worked just as designed.

Tungsten Mesh Heating Element Furnace. This first doesn't sound like much, but this furnace used a 12-inch diameter, 12-inch high tungsten mesh heating element. The furnace went to a very high temperature, 2800°C, measured with a disappearing filament L&N optical pyrometer. Now in these real high temperature furnaces, we tend to talk in degrees Celsius not degrees Fahrenheit. Roughly speaking, degrees Celsius is twice the temperature of Fahrenheit. So, we're talking about something here that's like 5,000°F or thereabouts. But the interesting thing about this furnace was that it was designed to run in vacuum or in one atmosphere of argon, nitrogen, or hydrogen—all three gases, as selected. It was a versatile furnace. The hydrogen was the most distinctive part of it, and at this very high temperature, running hydrogen was a real challenge at the time. This design was quite an accomplishment.

We actually had not tested the furnace at the plant before we shipped. It went down to Oakridge, Tennessee and was used in some way in their atomic energy program. Now, how they used this furnace, I have no idea. I tested it but I never put anything in it. It was tested using a sight port from the top of the furnace. This furnace used all-tungsten heat shields as well as a tungsten mesh heating element, a special element we bought from Sylvania in New England. This choice doesn't sound terribly important, but for that temperature, it was quite significant. We measured the temperature with an L&N pyrometer sitting up there on the top furnace head (lid). As an operator, you opened the sight port shutter and you sighted down into the furnace. And that's how you measured the temperature. It wasn't difficult with vacuum, nitrogen, and argon, but with hydrogen, you're literally on top of a bomb. If something went wrong, you went into orbit.

Oakridge put that furnace inside of a cement block enclosure, which, in order to accommodate the furnace and be safe, was a room about the size of an office. So, an operator or technician or engineer—whoever was working with the furnace—had to be inside this cement room and everybody else stayed outside. There was danger associated with it, but you went about operating the furnace in such a way that you didn't kill yourself. When testing, I didn't hold my breath or hesitate. I just did it. I had enough faith in what we were doing, and I knew that under these conditions, the furnace would not explode. We had engineered things correctly, and the furnace was built right. It was designed to do the job, and we did it.

Now, there are some other techniques to measure the temperature, but the most accurate way to know the temperature is to do just what I did. Which was quite scary. I suppose it was good that Myrt didn't really know how dangerous the build and test was. She really didn't know the depth of the danger, and

I never really fully explained it to her. I don't think she understands to this day.

Gas Nozzle Development. Equally important to heating these metals is how you cool them. And in the early days of ABAR—around 1968 or so—we had no real way of what we call cooling or quenching the heated parts. We had graphs to show how long it would take to cool metals in a vacuum, and it took about a day to get a product fully cool—about 12 to 14 hours to go from process temperature to ambient. In terms of productivity, that lag was a killer: Your furnace is just sitting all day while something is cooling off. There were various ways to speed up the process—keeping furnaces open with fans in front of them and so on, but never at high temperature.

Well, I happened to see a hydrogen atmosphere furnace that used a recirculating gas blower. It had a heat exchanger that brought the hot hydrogen up through this heat exchanger and down into a gas blower and back into the bottom of the furnace, circulating gas in order to cut that long cooling time. Then there was Charlie Hill, who had these gas cooling curves in vacuum with another set of curves cooling in what we called static atmosphere—just backfilling with gas cooling in something like nitrogen, with a small test load in one of our furnaces. Well, you could tell right away that backfilling with gas cut the time in half. But the gas was not circulating, and it was a very small test load. So, we knew that putting circulating gas into these furnaces would speed things up. The trick was, we would have to use an inert gas, something like argon or nitrogen or even helium.

In the early days of ABAR, I convinced my two partners at the time, Charlie Hill and Art Couillard, that we should have a demonstration furnace, so we built one of our Series 90 laboratory-size vacuum furnaces and had it set up and available as a demonstrator. That furnace was mine, and I ran it. We did all sorts of testing with that furnace and customer demonstrations. I ruined the hot zone a couple of times in various test runs—not good for our P&L statements.

Well, I knew this business about cooling, so I used this demonstration furnace to test some improvements. I put a single, 3/8" diameter stainless steel tube into the bottom of the furnace hot zone, and I connected that tube to a standard industrial nitrogen or argon gas cylinder, through a standard pressure regulator. Then, I clamped the furnace heads together so that I could exhaust the gas out of the top of the furnace through a chimney I built into it. I did that with one jet. Then I found if I could get more gas flow, the parts would cool faster. So, I built four jets, connected them together in parallel, and then took them out through the bottom and attached them to a couple of gas cylinders. While the tubes worked to move the gas, they were problematic because the system purged gas up through the hot zone, but threw it away. Once used, the gas was gone. And it was not cheap, even when a tank of argon was around $15 or so—with two tanks together, you're blowing away $30, every cycle. You didn't want to throw away $30 every run in a small lab furnace.

However, thanks to my modifications to the demonstration furnace, I showed that cooling parts with these turbulent gases was a good way to accelerate the part cooling process. When Ralph Swegman, the engineer from GE who bought that monstrous furnace, came into Philadelphia, I demonstrated my idea to him. And it was because of the demonstration that he bought that big furnace from us. He bought that furnace based on that one single demonstration.

Well, we had solved the cooling process, but we still had to develop a way to capture and recirculate the cooling gas. We tried a couple of designs where we had nozzles just across the bottom of some of these bigger furnaces with vacuum gas blowers, called Roots blowers. In those designs, I forced the gas up through the nozzles in the bottom, and it came out through the top, through an exit baffle in the hot zone, through a gas-to-water heat exchanger, and back into the gas blower again, so we were recirculating gas at reasonable velocities, at about 10 or 15 miles per hour. That's low by today's standards, but it was still respectable, and it gave us improved work cooling.

There were two things wrong with our early recirculating systems, though: First, our gas blower was not absolutely vacuum tight, so we needed to build a blower that was completely vacuum tight. With our early blowers, we took ordinary blowers like you could buy out of the Grainger catalog, and we put those inside of vacuum enclosures that we made vacuum tight. Then, we could force the gas through the furnace and back through a heat exchanger, which at that time was a shell-and-tube heat exchanger. Now we had something that was vacuum and gas tight. It could pump down into high vacuum, gas back-fill, and "gas fan" cool.

Our second problem was that having these nozzles in the bottom of the furnace gave us uneven cooling: All the cooling was in the bottom of the furnace, which resulted in distorted work in the furnace. I realized we needed to have something that was uniform in this ring hot zone. Fortunately, I remembered something I saw in a book, a quench ring, which was designed to use something like liquid nitrogen or CO_2 to gas quench induction-heated gears. It had holes all around, and they all squirted into the center. Using something like CO_2 or liquid nitrogen, the photographer had captured the gas streaming through all the holes. The cold gas formed condensation as it interacted with the air, so the photo showed a cloud of vapor streaming out of the quench ring. I saw that, and I said, "That's the way to do it. We have to have rings of these nozzles pointing into the hot zone in a circle in our round hot zone."

I built one of our bigger furnaces in a demonstration model with the nozzles for one of the ASM heat treating shows, and I connected it to a tank of liquid CO_2. I had a blower just blowing around in a circle, and then I injected CO_2 into the gas nozzles so that you could see the nozzles cooling the work load. Now, when I first built it, I used plastic lenses on the front and back so you could see right into the hot zone. I turned it on, and I couldn't see any condensation because there was no moisture in the air. I had to cut holes into the plastic to allow air to mingle with the atmosphere and then to generate the moisture of condensation. But I built a demonstrator to show those nozzles. It was the most popular demonstration at the show.

We didn't patent it, though, and it was quickly copied. There are ads everywhere, showing copies of the ring furnace with nozzles in the rings: one made in Canada, Poland, China, and another by our competitor, Ipsen, here in the USA. Even if I had patented it, eventually it would be copied. But we were the first to incorporate gas cooling nozzles in the vacuum furnace.

GE Evandale Furnace. For GE Evandale, in Cincinnati, we designed a big furnace for heat treating large jet engine case parts. The hot zone was about 8' diameter x 5' high. GE built the engines for a huge Air Force transport plane, the C5A—which is still in use today. At the time, those four engines were the most powerful engines built, so GE Evandale purchased this furnace to heat treat the outer casing of those engines. The furnace was a bottom loader, and it was the first big bottom loader that was ever built.

The build took place in the early days of ABAR, and we were in a tiny building. How General Electric had the faith in us to tackle such a large project is positively amazing. We had to build a building addition to construct the furnace. Now, the building wasn't huge, maybe 50' x 50' x 50', but I remember it cost $10,000 to build. When I sent the bid to GE, I included that $10,000 in the cost of the product. The building had to accommodate this furnace from top to bottom. We had a single rail crane that could pick the vessel up and put it onto the support framework and so forth. And it was about a ten-ton crane to pick the vessel up and set the vacuum chamber onto the support frame.

We built it a little differently than we do today. The furnace was designed basically by Charlie Hill and his designers, but the nozzle design was mine, which was very significant. This big, high temperature furnace (2400°F) is credited to both Charlie Hill and me, and to our Hunterdon V.R.T. Power Supply.

GE Lynn Furnace, with Charging Car. GE Lynn also makes jet engines, and this purchase was their first vacuum furnace. Charlie Hill designed the furnace—a vacuum brazing, horizontal furnace that was somewhat unique in that it had what I call a charging car. Originally, Charlie made the charging car horribly complex, but our chief engineer, Ben Kreider, later cleaned up the design to make it practical. In the end, the charging car (load truck) went in under the hearth rails and picked the work up and brought it out. Vacuum brazing was just coming into its own, and the jet engine people were just getting into the arena. GE was ahead here. Both GE and Pratt & Whitney were competing for various jet engine businesses, so when we put this vacuum brazing furnace in at GE Lynn, some of the plant mechanics came around and looked at it. I remember, I started it up, and a couple of the mechanics came over to me and said, "Bill, we would like to buy stock in your company."

I said, "Well, I'm sorry, you can't. It's a privately held company, there's no stock available." (By then, ABAR was owned by King Fifth Wheel.) And they were saddened because they recognized this furnace could do things that nothing else could. They were quite impressed with it. Interestingly, the higher ups in the company never said anything. Typical GE.

Ball Screw Drive. Charlie had built a classic, old-fashioned counterbalanced lift for our bottom-loading furnace; for the furnace we designed for GE Evandale, the bottom head came up and down, and it was on guides. But Charlie designed the system using big concrete block counterbalances, with four chains that came up and down over gearing, creating a counterbalanced bottom head. The setup was a heavy thing, and it was a little crude. It also wasn't especially smooth in the way it operated, so though the system worked and it did what it was supposed to do, we recognized that the design was not sophisticated or easy to use—almost like a barn door. Such low usability led to the development of the bottom head ball screw drive in use today.

Our solution had four big screws on either corner of the furnace—with special ball nuts on either end—and the drive of these were all interlocked mechanically with a motor and electric brake. This drive picked the head of the furnace up and put it in place and lowered it back down again. The drive also allowed for the bottom head to come out from under the furnace. In other words, you could bring the bottom head down, and the head would now rest on a cart. Then, you could pull the head out and load the furnace and then push the head back under again. That was quite an advancement, and we were the first to build it for a vacuum furnace.

Well, all these furnaces today use this ball screw drive, so our contribution was a real first for the industry, and it all came about thanks to our chief engineer, Ben Kreider, and design engineer, George Houser.

Rohr Furnace, Chula Vista, California. At the time, this furnace was the biggest furnace made by ABAR: it was 8-foot diameter, 8-foot high hot zone (Rohr named this the VAF 88, as in vacuum/atmosphere). Ben Kreider and I designed this furnace. At this time, our heating elements were normally all around the inside of the furnace—top, bottom, all around the side. Rohr was making the exhaust duct for the Pratt & Whitney engine to go into the then Boeing 707. That was what this furnace was designed to do: It was a double-wall cylinder brazement, and so here you had this circular-shape, about 6 foot in diameter and about 6 foot high. But Rohr wanted a heating element in the center, which they called a heating spike. This spike was designed to keep temperatures equal throughout, inside and out, because in a typical furnace design, you're heating from the outside. They brought the furnace up to temperature at the same time as we manually brought the spike up to temperature, watching the part temperature inside and out with work thermocouples. This furnace operated at normal temperatures up to 2250°F, with maximum temperatures to 2400°F.

So, we have all these outer heating elements and then we have this center heating element, the spike. It was unique, something that they wanted, so we did it. We brazed the first one on Christmas Eve, and that went directly from San Diego to East Hartford. Pratt & Whitney had an airstrip, so on Christmas Day, they air freighted that part. There was quite a bit of pressure to get the furnace built and working quickly, because Pratt & Whitney was very late getting those engines built. Boeing had planes just sitting on their runways in Seattle waiting for those engines.

Large Bottom Loading Vacuum Furnace for Rohr (VAF-88), Chula Vista, CA.

First Commercial Vacuum Furnace, ISCAR Blades, Israel. We sold the first commercial vacuum furnace in Israel to ISCAR Blades. It wasn't terribly big, but it was one of our horizontal models, with the ring hot zone and a work zone that was 24" x 24" x 36" deep. The furnace was the first one for Israel, and they were making forged jet-engine blades. They weren't making them only for use in Israel; they were making them and selling them back into the U.S.A. Myrt and I went over there, and I started up and taught ISCAR how to use the furnace. We were there for about six weeks.

Why did we stay so long? First of all, it was the first one in that country, and so there were a lot of things to check out—their gas facilities, etc. The furnace had been assembled but it had to be completely checked out, tested, and certified in the field. And it took me a couple weeks just to do that. And then I spent time with them teaching them how to use it. I had a couple of glitches that took me some time to work out, which were not design problems but were just a couple of instrument failures due to their 50 Hz power vs. U.S.A. standard 60 Hz. Nothing major and something that sometimes happens. The trip was also Myrt's and my first trip outside the U.S., and we were particularly pleased to go to Israel, the homeland of our faith, so we spent about two weeks of personal time there, also.

Pratt & Whitney Transition from Hydrogen to Vacuum Furnaces. In an earlier chapter, I told the story of finally getting my foot in the door at Pratt & Whitney and of eventually selling Abe Willan on the idea of vacuum furnaces over their much-trusted hydrogen roller hearth furnaces. They had four large roller hearth models. That first vacuum furnace I sold Abe became one of many. I'm not sure how many they bought, exactly, but it was more than a dozen. And by the way, these were half-million dollar furnaces. So, that was a huge advancement, for both ABAR and Pratt & Whitney. That in itself is interesting. But if you dig a little deeper into the back story, our role in this first becomes a fascinating part of America's history.

I read an article not too long ago that was written by one of the fathers of the titanium manufacturing process about the American U-2 spy plane. Much of this plane's history has been pretty much under wraps until just recently. This was a spy plane, developed by Lockheed Aircraft, which flew over Russia. Why was this article significant to me? Well, the U-2 was one of the early planes that used titanium metal, and unbeknownst to me, the Pratt & Whitney engine used titanium components.

This plane was flown in about 1955, when I had just finished college, and was a very advanced plane, with engines built by Pratt & Whitney. This plane was made to fly especially high and for long distances, soaring up to 80,000 feet. The only way anyone could see this plane was by radar.

This whole story is about the development of the most popular titanium alloy: Ti 6Al-4v, the development of which was somewhat shrouded in secrecy. Now, you cannot heat treat titanium in a hydrogen atmosphere, because titanium will absorb hydrogen and become brittle. All titanium comes out of the manufacturing process with a fair amount of hydrogen in it—several hundred parts per million—so manufacturers have to get it out right, otherwise the part will be brittle and will break. If someone tries to weld this material, it will bubble. So, the only way to get the hydrogen out is in a vacuum furnace. You put titanium into a vacuum furnace at relatively low temperature—around 1200, 1250°F—and you bake it in high vacuum. That way the hydrogen diffuses out of the metal matrix.

Now, if that hydrogen is present in titanium and needs to be released in a vacuum and if Pratt & Whitney only had hydrogen furnaces, they couldn't do it. How did they get it done? Were they sending it to someone else? I don't know, but I've thought about that a bit. You might get the worst of the impurity out in an argon furnace, but that will take longer and is tedious. Also, argon is potentially contaminating. Pratt & Whitney may have put the parts into a vacuum bell furnace—which was a furnace shaped something like a bell jar, with a hot zone that came over top of the metal alloy bell. At low temperature, you could pull a vacuum. However, bell jar furnaces weren't nearly as a good as a cold wall vacuum furnace, like our ABAR furnaces, and you could not get the hydrogen out as deeply as we could with high vacuum operation. With our furnaces, we vacated the hydrogen out to well below ten parts per million, with only a couple of parts per million of hydrogen left. But how did Pratt & Whitney achieve the necessary vacuum for a U-2? There were vacuum furnaces around, they were around in the 1930's, in the early days of electronics. But P&W didn't do it in a vacuum; I'm positive, because nothing was big enough.

I find all of this discussion of titanium parts in the U-2 engines interesting because even while I was trying to convince Pratt & Whitney about vacuum furnaces, they must have had these needs. Until I read that article about the U-2 plane, I did not know that titanium was in that U-2 engine. There are still things about that engine that are not known, and I'm not prepared to state my opinions about them here, because it's still classified information.

The Autoclave Vacuum Furnace Loading Door—In the early days of the vacuum furnace, furnace loading and unloading doors were either held in place with bolts like Allen capscrews or clamps of one sort or another, some pneumatically operated. Door bolts are inconvenient. The bolts can become cross-threaded and seize. Operators do not always tighten appropriately and door leaks can develop, particularly in gas quenching. Head clamps will not operate above a few pounds positive pressure. So the search was on to find a "pressure cooker" type of seal. We located such a design, which we called the "autoclave door." We bought the first ones from a company in Buffalo called WSF Industries who had a patent on the autoclave design. However the patent ran out and we were able to incorporate this design with improvements into the ABAR furnaces. The design is a stationary O ring in a groove machined into the flange of the front door (or bottom head of a vertical furnace), mating against another flange on the furnace chamber with an external flange ring that would rotate and seal the front door, similar to the seal of a pressure cooker that one would use at home. These autoclave door closures have operated to positive pressures in excess of twenty atmospheres (20 bar). They are relatively simple and trouble-free.

Example of VFS Autoclave Door.

Vacuum Aluminum Brazing—In about 1970 we were approached by Reynolds Aluminum, Richmond, VA, to do some experimental vacuum aluminum brazing in our Series 90 vacuum furnace. Two of their development engineers came to our plant and actually ran the ABAR Series 90 after I showed them how to do so. They spent about two weeks experimenting with different aluminum alloys and different gettering materials. We really had no idea of what this was all about.

However, it turns out that GE in Valley Forge, PA had a small vacuum furnace and one of three engineers had developed a process for vacuum brazing in this small furnace. This man wrote a GE patent for vacuum brazing of aluminum which was successful. This patent turned out to be a significant event.

A few months after the Reynolds visit we received a similar call from Alcoa's research department in Pittsburgh. They came down and we spent a few days with them doing some experimental brazing. It was learned rather quickly that it was necessary to use magnesium powder as a getter in the aluminum vacuum brazing process.

A few years later, both companies developed aluminum alloys containing a low percentage of magnesium, which acted inherently as a getter to promote the vacuum brazing process. For many years prior to this, there were aluminum alloys and brazing alloys that were the mainstays of aluminum brazing. Prior to this, aluminum brazing was done primarily in salt bath furnaces where the parts to be brazed were immersed in molten salt (special chemical salts, not table salt). It should be noted that the brazing of aluminum is done very close to the melting point of aluminum, so temperature control is essential. The salt bath furnace is inherently dirty because of salt dragout from the parts being brazed. The automobile industry had developed an A/C evaporator core which was quite dense and needed to be brazed. This was being done in salt bath furnaces, requiring a large investment in washing and cleaning the salt from the interior passages of these dense evaporator cores.

So there was a major interest in vacuum brazing to replace salt bath for environmental and economic reasons. Our next contact came from Philco-Ford and later from Harrison Radiator, a division of General Motors, to vacuum braze these aluminum heat exchangers. Specifically, we built a two-chamber lab-size vacuum brazing furnace for Philco-Ford where the vacuum furnace would be at the brazing temperature more or less continuously. The first chamber we would use as a vacuum lock for the work, pump it down, and then open a vacuum valve and shutter into the hot zone of the vacuum furnace, braze the aluminum core assembly, and then remove it from the hot zone back into the vacuum lock, open the vacuum chamber back to air, and remove the part so that we could sequentially braze parts quickly. This was a development furnace leading to large, semi-continuous vacuum brazing furnaces, first at Philco-Ford. The first production furnaces were not bought from ABAR but Ipsen, in spite of the fact that the development work was done by ABAR. Nevertheless, the first two Ipsen furnaces were only marginally successful in production, primarily because of the issue of magnesium contamination of the transport mechanism inside the furnace. Following this, Philco-Ford purchased two vacuum aluminum brazing furnaces from ABAR. These went into successful production in their Connersville, IN plant.

Later we were approached by GM-Harrison Radiator near Buffalo, NY, to supply a vacuum furnace large enough to braze two aluminum radiator cores for the automobile engine. We later supplied the same type of furnace for Reynolds Aluminum and Alcoa. These were batch-type aluminum brazing furnaces built by ABAR. Another order was for Hamilton Standard in CT. This rather large batch vacuum furnace was used to braze the air conditioner heat exchanger for the Boeing 747 airplane. We also built a similar furnace for a company in England for brazing large aluminum core heat exchangers. In following years, other production vacuum furnaces were built for Japan for automobile applications and for aircraft applications, by both ABAR and Ipsen.

In the middle of all this, GE had their patent and went after anybody doing production aluminum vacuum brazing with magnesium either in the alloy or separately, as this was the heart of their patent and the aluminum brazing process. GE decided the best way to corner Ford and GM was to license vacuum furnace manufacturers, which they did, one by one. This amounted to our not being able to sell a vacuum furnace to anyone not licensed by GE. In other words, the vacuum furnace manufacturers were made to be the policemen for the GE patent. GE made certain that if we did not follow their directive, they would come down on us like a ton of bricks. ABAR, as a Bill Jones decision, was the first to comply, and all of the other furnace manufacturers fell in line.

There is a lot more to the story of aluminum vacuum brazing, but my experience working with Philco-Ford in Connersville as well as GM at Harrison Radiator was not at all pleasant. The problems were with the production operators who made life really difficult for outside technicians and engineers working in their plants. I personally found this very onerous, and as a result vowed that on leaving ABAR I would never be involved with vacuum aluminum brazing or any other production process in an automobile manufacturing plant. I am not talking about suppliers, but in the area of the actual auto production plant.

The vacuum aluminum brazing furnace also had a fault. It would collect both magnesium and magnesium oxide on the cold wall of the chamber so that in a few months of operation it became necessary to remove the hot zone for a worker to go deep inside the furnace and scrape down the cold wall of the furnace. These furnaces were long, multi-chamber installations, something like thirty feet. Although the vacuum chamber was approximately six feet in diameter, going inside to the inner core was a fire hazard. A number of men were badly burned in this occupation, and to this day I do not believe vacuum brazing with magnesium is particularly attractive.

As for what we considered the ultimate application, the automobile radiator was of course the driving goal. However, the auto designers figured out ways to build the radiator with various forms of reinforced plastic end caps and the like, and/or epoxy sealing of the radiator tubes, thus avoiding the vacuum brazing operation. This has been a successful move for the auto manufacturers, as their primary goal with regard to this facet was to get away from a copper radiator, which was more expensive and with more difficult manufacturing techniques.

In any event, in moving on to my later experiences with VFS and Solar Manufacturing, we have avoided vacuum aluminum brazing applications.

First Commercial Ion Nitriding Vacuum Furnace Made in the USA—During my early days at ABAR, I came across an article in *Industrial Heating* magazine concerning the development of an electric vacuum process known as Ion Nitriding. The first United States industrial development of this process was by GE engineers for their steam powered electric generator gearing. I went up to GE to look at their development furnace. They had a simple power supply patent that they were willing to license for $50,000, but with no process knowledge or discussion.

I turned this down and we built a small laboratory size ion nitriding furnace around our Series 90 vacuum chamber. This worked under the direction of our then R&D Ph.D., Prem Jindal. So as a takeoff of this early work, we built a production model with a working hot zone of 24" x 24" x 36" deep. This was the first production size ion nitriding furnace built here in the United States, and we put the furnace into production in our new ABAR heat treating plant in Ivyland, PA.

Use of the Residual Gas Analyzer (R.G.A.)—In the latter part of my ABAR years, Bill Hoke, Ben Kreider, and I went to a company near Rochester, NY that was introducing a new, lower-cost R.G.A. After looking at a demonstration I bought one of their demonstration models and set it up on one of the early ABAR heat treating furnaces. It was a cumbersome instrument. I rigged a high speed pen recorder to it, similar to a "lie detector" recorder. At the time, Bill Hoke often remarked that I "was the only one who knew how to run and interpret the instrument," and he was right. Later in his career, Bill became a sales agent for a much improved, advanced instrument, making many sales. We later bought from Bill a new model for VFS.

The R.G.A. is a dedicated instrument for analyzing residual gas components in a vacuum atmosphere. It is useful for both R&D experimentation and quality control purposes. Today, our newer models are operated by Trevor Jones, who has the most experience and understanding within the Solar Nation.

VFS, 1979–2000

As noted in an earlier chapter, VFS started as a spinoff from ABAR. VFS sales started from zero and went to nearly $1M in its first year of operation and made a small profit: remarkable. The industry leaders in vacuum furnace production were

ABAR and Ipsen. Within five years VFS became a strong third in the marketplace, which was not necessarily a technological achievement, but certainly was a notable business accomplishment. It generated significant operating profits, allowing the purchase of our first rented building, tripling the building plant size, and establishing the First Solar Atmospheres heat treating plant next door to the original VFS site.

New Heating Element Insulator Assembly—This development was the keynote in the establishment of VFS, and is covered in a previous chapter as well as in the first VFS patent listed in the appendix.

New Composite Insulation Ring Hot Zone—This hot zone design was also discussed in a previous chapter. It was an important innovation because the furnace operated at lower power requirements and would operate at a higher temperature (2650°F) than the normal 2400°F ABAR or Ipsen design. This graphite foil hotface, graphite felt-Kaowool® design became the mainstay of the VFS furnace and has led to many more similar versions by both VFS and Solar Manufacturing.

Ceramic Tube-Insulated Platinum Thermocouple—This rather innocuous development, the platinum Type S or Type R thermocouple inside of a ceramic tube was a concept I copied from GE Carbaloy in Detroit, Michigan, to shield platinum from CO, CO_2, and H_2 contaminating gases in the hot zone that were shortening thermocouple life. GE did not have a patent on this design and the basic, simple idea of inserting the platinum thermocouple inside a ceramic tube through the high vacuum wall of the furnace was a concept not adopted by the greater heat treating community until VFS. We added some improvements to the original concept with plugs and jacks attached to the ceramic tube end on the air side, and additional improvements in the vacuum feedthrough glands. The ceramic tube we settled on was 99.9% high quality alumina. During fast heating and fast cooling, one had to be concerned about the ceramic tube cracking. However, this cracking due to heating and cooling did not occur. Where ceramic tubes have broken, it was due to mechanical abuse.

12' diameter x 10' high furnace for Vac-Hyd of Compton, California—At the time this car bottom furnace was built, it was the largest hot zone size, certainly in North America. Notable were the all-metal molybdenum (moly) heat shields, moly heating elements, and five-zone control, complete with top and bottom heating elements. The furnace operated up to 2800°F when new. It included three 35" Varian diffusion pumps and three Stokes / Roots blower roughing pumps. Also included was a 150 hp gas blower and heat exchanger for cooling the work through gas nozzles. The furnace also utilized a first generation Honeywell digital Programmable Logic Controller (PLC) with video screen that was easily programmable for furnace control. The instrumentation at the time was worked out by John Barron, VFS chief electrical engineer, and Nevagay Abel, electrical engineer.

Internal Vacuum Furnace Jack Panel Thermocouple Plug and Jack Innovation—Although this is a seemingly simple innovation, its major advantage was using a simplified thermocouple single vacuum feedthrough gland for permanent coupling of low temperature feedthrough wires to a jack panel plug inside the vacuum chamber on the cold wall side. This allowed operators to plug in work thermocouples easily and add thermocouples for temperature uniformity surveys. Every vacuum furnace manufacturer has now copied this design.

Closed Loop (non-aerated) Water Cooling Design with Rocore® Water-to-Air Heat Exchanger—A standard in the industry is a water cooling tower such as from Baltimore Aircoil to cool and recirculate the water from the vacuum furnace, and eject heat into the atmosphere. These cooling towers are also open to the air where the cooling water is thus aerated, providing more than enough oxygen over time to rust the vacuum chamber and any other iron alloy components in the vacuum furnace system. These cooling towers

Large vacuum furnace for VacHyd, Compton, Ca. Hot zone 12' dia x 8' high.

are subject to a ten percent water loss, blow down, against the flow in the furnace. So if you have 1,000 gpm, ten percent or 100 gpm is lost. This is expensive. Many municipal water authorities will complain about or charge for "throwing away" this much water. Further, the cooling water must be treated chemically to avoid corrosion and other problems in the system, but this requires weekly attention to monitor and adjust the chemistry. So we incorporated into our furnace designs a large water-to-air heat exchanger like an automobile radiator. Thus, the water is not exposed to atmosphere, avoiding oxidation and corrosion in the furnace. At all our Solar Atmospheres heat treating companies, we have utilized one large set of heat exchangers and multiple water pumps with variable speed drives to maintain a constant water pressure of 50 psig to the furnaces along with consideration for power loss with an emergency gas-driven electric generator.

Moly vs. Circular Graphite Heating Elements—In the ABAR furnaces, all of the heating elements were molybdenum. Our competitors used graphite, which has some arguable advantage when designed properly. So at VFS, Fred Ripley and his engineering team worked out a circular graphite heating element design using Poco graphite. This was a good design, and it eliminated the brittle nature of the moly heating element as well as the reaction of moly with both chrome and nickel vapor from the workload, gases which cannot be avoided in a high vacuum application. The early circular graphite heating elements did have interface connection problems. However, both VFS and Solar Manufacturing have incorporated continuous design improvements to solve these problems.

MSI Power Factor Corrected SCR Power Supply, MSI 2000—In about 1998, a company called Magnetic Specialties Inc., then in Trenton, NJ, called on me to build a solid state silicon controlled rectifier (SCR) power supply that has the major advantage of power factor correction and was not water-cooled (i.e., operated "dry"). The VRT saturable core reactor, which was a standard in the industry at that time, suffers to some extent from water cooling issues, and inherently in any saturable core reactor—VRT or otherwise—there is a substantial power factor correction. For example, suppose you are operating at a 50% control power. The resultant power factor will be 0.5, as opposed to at full 100% power the power factor will be 1.0. I was so impressed with the MSI power supply that I subsequently bought the company. However, the original MSI 2000 design was a specialized "home brew" solid state electronic control that suffered from reliability (down-time) issues. We were never able to completely solve the original MSI electronics and as a result, abandoned that technology. However, we do supply an MSI dry power transformer with a reliable Spang SCR drive which incorporates many of the features of the original MSI unit.

Pushing the Gas Quench Furnace to 300 hp Motors for High Velocity and Overpressure Gas Quenching to 10 Bar—There has been a continual desire by vacuum furnace users and heat treating companies for faster and faster gas quenching. The way to do this is with larger gas blowers, higher horsepower motors driving large fans up to 300 hp rating and higher, combined with higher gas pressures, as much as 10 bar or 10 atmospheres overpressure. VFS as well as its competitors was in the fray, and Solar Manufacturing continues to push this art along with variable speed drives (VFD) for the motor control.

Development of the 24' Car Bottom Furnace—The development of this furnace was accomplished by a team of engineers, and is fully discussed in prior chapter. Although at the time we could not visualize how this furnace would be utilized or accepted, it has turned out to be a unique design. Since the original VFS innovation, Solar Manufacturing has built perhaps ten additional furnaces of this type. The beginning of this advance, though, was in the later days of my VFS ownership.

Diffusion Pump Heating Element Improvement (ConserVac®)—Other than the power supply, the diffusion pump operating with a high vacuum furnace is the highest consumer of electric power. For example, a 16" Varian diffusion pump is rated for about 8 kW, equivalent to 80 one hundred watt standard electric light bulbs. One would never leave the plant with eighty light bulbs operating because it is so obviously a waste of energy. However, the diffusion pump is innocuous and can be overlooked. Conserving this energy loss for the diffusion pump is significant. Further, if one can set the power level lower when not in use, that is not pumping in high vacuum, heater life can be extended considerably. This insight led to the development of ConserVac®, which is a simple circuit that sets the diffusion pump power back about 50%. Normal diffusion pump heater life is approximately two years. With incorporation of ConserVac®, heater life can be extended to four to five years. Not only is this a savings in electric power, but the extended heater life is a reduction in operating costs and in maintenance. Replacing a diffusion pump heater can be miserable, because the worker is on his back, with insulation dusting into his face. The less often a diffusion pump heater needs replacing, the better in many ways.

Graphite Gas Quench Nozzle—In the original ABAR furnace, we used moly sheet metal-fabricated gas nozzles. These were difficult to install because the threaded connections would seize and because the nozzles ran cooler than the rest of the hot zone the moly would easily collect nickel and chrome vapor from the workload. The moly would then deteriorate, collapse, and nearly shut off the gas flow over time. So we experimented with other types of gas cooling nozzle materials such as ceramics, which all failed due to thermal shock. We investigated and standardized on machined graphite nozzles which threaded into a convenient metal or graphite connector. The graphite did not react with the nickel and chrome vapors. Thus the nozzles do not collapse and they are easily exchanged for service. A further innovation of the graphite nozzle was to taper the nozzle to enhance gas flow. The inlet of the nozzle was rounded to allow a smoother gas entry, and the taper allowed for increased velocity flowing through the nozzle itself.

Heating Element Ground Detector Circuit—Workloads coming in contact with the hot zone internal heating elements, or a heating element deflecting to come in contact with other hot zone components, or heating element insulator failures will cause heating element short circuits, and lead to melting and failure.

So I designed a simple six volt transformer and relay circuit to close on heating element contact to the hot zone ground. The relay would in turn light an alarm on the furnace control panel, thus warning the operator of a problem. This simple routine avoids a potentially expensive failure.

SOLAR ATMOSPHERES FIRSTS, 1983–2017

As previously stated, Solar Atmospheres was a spinoff company of Vacuum Furnace Systems, VFS. That story is covered in previous chapters. Solar Atmospheres initially purchased all their vacuum furnaces from VFS. After the sale of VFS to its management, and then the sale of VFS to Ipsen, a decision was made to start Solar Manufacturing in 2003. In this section, I will discuss the important Solar Atmospheres firsts. In a subsequent section, Solar Manufacturing firsts will be featured.

Single In-Plant Water Cooling System—with the establishment of Solar Atmospheres, rather than use multiple water cooling heat exchangers, water reservoir tanks and water recirculation pumps, I made the decision to design one large water-to-air heat exchanger, parallel water recirculation pumps, and a single water recirculation tank. The multiple water pumps are all controlled from variable frequency drive (VFD) controls in a feedback loop so that the inlet water pressure to the furnaces is controlled at 50 psig. This is a closed loop system, where the cooling water is not exposed to air, thus greatly reducing contamination to the vacuum chamber. The water chemistry is carefully checked and maintained for proper pH, turbidity, and electrical conductivity, thus eliminating major plugging and/or contamination of the furnaces.

Inert Gas Storage and Distribution—Many plants using vacuum furnaces have multiple gas reservoir tanks and in some cases even multiple sources of liquid nitrogen or argon. In our plants, we use one large storage reservoir for all inert gases, per plant. As part of our inert gas management, we monitor continuously and record for low dew point and low oxygen levels to approximately two to three ppm. We have also found that the monitoring of oxygen levels is more important than the monitoring of water vapor.

Large Vacuum Furnaces in the Commercial Heat Treating Industry—at Solar Atmospheres, we concentrated on design and development of large horizontal vacuum furnaces. The objective was to process larger components or parts that were coming onto the market, parts that others could not process. This led to the development of the 24' foot car bottom vacuum furnace in Hermitage, PA, as a startup Solar company. This furnace would accept very heavy workloads to in excess of 50,000 pounds, operate in high vacuum to below 10^{-5} Torr range, and included heating elements on the car so that heating completely encompassed the workload. It also had dual 300 hp gas blowers providing rapid part cooling. This furnace has operated to 2800°F and will in turn cool heavy workloads with nitrogen, argon, or helium gas. With the successful operation of this furnace, two additional 24' vacuum furnaces were built for the Hermitage plant and then followed with 36' deep vacuum furnace and to date a 48' deep vacuum furnace. Some of these furnaces will process workloads up to 150,000 pounds.

These furnaces have primarily processed multiple large titanium sheet coils, large titanium plate work, and titanium bars, all for hydrogen vacuum degassing and annealing. The most important titanium work processed has been the complicated titanium seat track for the Boeing 787 airplane. The seat track is a misleading term because in reality the entire bottom structure of the 787 is made up of these seat tracks. In other words, the seat tracks are a part of the core fuselage of the plane. These furnaces were also used in the development and final heat treatment of a Russian alloy, 5553, which is utilized in certain aspects of the 787 and other aircraft. In addition to the heat treatment of titanium coils, these furnaces have also been utilized for the high temperature annealing and solution heat treatment of grain-oriented steels in the form of multiple coils, and for use in high-efficiency transformers. These are just a few of the applications for the large car bottom vacuum furnaces. Subsequently we have added a 12' car bottom vacuum furnace to our Souderton, PA plant, another 24' for our Fontana, CA plant, and another 24' for our startup heat treating company in Greenville, SC.

Hydriding and Dehydriding of Refractory Metals like Tantalum, Tantalum Alloys and Niobium—the refractory metals are very expensive to produce. There is a significant requirement to recover scrap tantalum, hydride with hydrogen, then break up to chips and/or powder, and then put back into the refractory metal manufacturing process midstream, rather than starting with ore. This avoids a lot of chemical purification. Some of these hydrided refractory materials are further pulverized to powder and then placed back into the vacuum furnace and degassed to remove the hydrogen. The purpose of the hydrogen is that it functions as an embrittling agent so that the materials can be further processed.

Although not a refractory metal, titanium scrap is processed in the same way, and this is a significantly larger business for Solar than either tantalum or niobium. It is fair to say that Solar Atmospheres is the largest commercial heat treating company processing the refractory metals cited. Although this sounds like a simple operation, putting hydrogen into a vacuum furnace either at sub-atmospheric pressure or at slightly positive pressure requires consideration for safety measures to avoid a catastrophic explosion. Solar has addressed these safety issues as a first order priority.

Low Pressure Vacuum Carburizing—Low pressure vacuum carburizing was first introduced to the vacuum heat treat industry by C.I Hayes in the mid 1970's. Hayes used carburizing gases like propane and operated the furnace in the vacuum pressure range of approximately one-third atmospheric pressure. Unfortunately this led to soot deposition in the vacuum furnace itself, a deterrent to commercial operation. Subsequently the industry looked at other carburizing gases such as cyclohexane and acetylene. It quickly became obvious that acetylene was the gas of choice, and patents were issued to both a Japanese company and a Russian university professor for the use of that gas. However, the vacuum ranges were not well defined and it left room for others to seize the opportunity to utilize acetylene for operations, including Solar Atmospheres.

Solar developed a process from a concept, starting with

a retort and evaluating several hydrocarbon gases as candidate carburizing gases. The dissociation characteristics of the gases were analyzed using an R.G.A. along with combinations of carrier gases. Ultimately, the carburizing gas mixture was listed in US Patent 7,514035 B2 that we received for the carburizing furnace design. Solar Atmospheres now operates numerous low pressure carburizing (LPC) vacuum furnaces with sales in our top five of the heat treatment processes. Solar is now considered a leader in LPC technology for rotorcraft transmission gears.

Vacuum Purge Gas Nitriding—Carburizing is the most widely used process for alloy and or other steel components for surface hardening. Nitriding is another widely used process. Both of these have developed from standard atmosphere furnaces operating at atmospheric pressure: however, both have drawbacks in production and quality. The use of the vacuum furnace is faster, and allows for high quality processing not possible with standard atmospheric furnaces. Others have developed vacuum gas nitriding furnaces: however, Solar, using conventional vacuum furnace designs, developed a process to gas nitride using ammonia gas, and designed and built a vacuum-purge furnace with a novel lightweight graphite hot zone with gas cooling capability. We received US Patent No. 8,088,328 for the furnace design. The process reduces nitriding cycle times by half compared to conventional nitriding using an atmosphere retort furnace.

Surface preparation of the parts is critical with gas nitriding, and solar has developed an in-situ pre-oxidation step, proven to improve the nitriding results. The oxidation process was taken one step further by post-oxidizing the parts after nitriding for aesthetic and corrosion-resistance properties.

Other Processing with Vacuum Partial Pressures—
- Brazing at elevated pressures, to 10 to 50 Torr, to inhibit metal vaporization
- Annealing of magnetic alloys using hydrogen

- Annealing of brass at -5" Hg pressure to inhibit zinc evaporation
- Development of solution nitriding, or nitrogen surface hardening, of martensitic stainless steel and titanium alloys at elevated temperatures and varying pressures

Raw Material Processing—
- Nitriding of chromium and ferro-vanadium flake
- Reduction of powder metal oxides and minimization of carbide formation using a combination of partial pressure hydrogen, argon, and vacuum for high temperature sintering of transition element powder metal product
- High temperature chemical compound conversion of chromium and graphite to form chromium carbide
- Purification and annealing of rare earth and platinum group metal compacts
- Refinement of high oxygen tantalum metal to low oxygen tantalum metal using magnesium vapor
- Developed system controls to safely passivate highly reactive metal powders like tantalum and niobium with air in a vacuum furnace to prevent a pyrophoric reaction upon opening the furnace

Use of Variable Frequency Drive (VFD) for Motor Control—We have found controlling the gas quenching motors, some as high as 600 hp, with VFD controls, highly desirable. The primary reason is to operate the gas blower fan at maximum efficiency for gases with different densities, i.e. helium, nitrogen, and argon, which gives us the fastest performance with each of these gases and operation at high efficiency. Further, once past the critical cooling temperatures (e.g. below 800° F) and down to ambient temperature the motor speed can be reduced so as to reduce electric power consumption.

Another feature of the VFD is its usefulness as the power control on the vacuum booster pump. By incorporating the vacuum blower as a direct drive motor and then using the VFD as a speed control, we avoid the impact of an across-the-line motor starter to the gearing of the vacuum blower. This greatly increases vacuum blower life.

Conservation of Electric Power—This has always been a concern of our heat treat companies. Because of our higher efficiency hot zones, VFD motor controls, and monitoring of our electric power demand over the 15-minute utility measuring and billing, we have made significant cost savings. When looking at our energy cost of operations, according to the Metal Treating Institute (MTI) reports, Solar's utility costs are consistently lower than any of our competitor companies. This is quite an accomplishment, since our power source is electric and even comparing our utility cost as against companies using gas- fired furnaces, we are consistently lower in operating costs.

Our plant in Fontana, CA, is a particular problem. During the summer hours, between 11:00 a.m. and 4:00 p.m., we are highly restricted, monitored, and billed if we exceed certain electric power demand levels. Solar management, Derek Dennis, and Chuck Miller have devised electric power monitoring instrumentation that has multiple indicators throughout the plant so that operating personnel can maintain strict limits. This is the only way we can keep our electric power costs within reason and this is a careful balancing act with production, which means in summer hours we must operate off-daytime shift: either at night or on weekends.

SOLAR MANUFACTURING, 2003–2017

Solar Manufacturing was established as a spinoff company from Solar Atmospheres in 2003. So it does not have the longevity of service of ABAR, VFS, or Solar Atmospheres. The primary purpose of Solar Manufacturing was to design and build vacuum furnaces for the parent company, Solar Atmospheres. At the same time, we took on the design of new vacuum furnaces for customers other than Solar Atmospheres, and also rebuilding and repairing hot zones for other companies.

Hot Zone Developments—Over the course of these years, any number of new hot zone engineering developments were carried out. The most significant was in the area of reduction of energy losses and improvement of vacuum performance, but success came in increments. We developed graphite foil /CFC hot face and graphite hot zones similar to some of our competition. The design of a hot zone is a compromise based on desired reduction of energy losses versus vacuum performance. At Solar, we found that using graphite felt interlayered with graphite foil reduced energy losses considerably, and we licensed the design from a company in Phoenix, AZ (although it can be argued that they were not the first to use the technology). However, when our Principal Engineer, Trevor Jones, ran operating power loss testing on this design he found that at operating temperature, the power losses were as much as 25 percent lower than on our standard furnaces. However, the insulation design was almost twice as heavy as our standard felt arrangement. So that on heating the furnace, the power requirements were doubled, so that losses on the new design were twice that of the original felt for heating. We abandoned that design except for special order cycles, such as when long furnace cycles were the requirement, making the heating and cooling losses less important. In order to make these power measurements, we purchased an HP computer instrument that is very accurate.

Now, as noted, for a process that does not require high vacuum or a "noncontaminating" atmosphere on occasion we have used a hot zone with six inches of Kaowool® insulation, which is quite efficient and for certain kinds of magnetic annealing cycles, very suitable. So hot zone design can be suited to the furnace application.

Recently, over the last couple of years Réal Fradette and I have worked diligently on the development of a graphite board hot zone using graphite materials from Graphite Machining

Inc. This new board is very efficient and has less outgassing on pumpdown and heating. We believe it will be the insulating material of choice for the near future.

We have also learned, the hard way, that there are differences in graphite felt. The PAN felt has a high moisture affinity on opening the furnace for loading, and thus is a poor choice for batch vacuum furnaces where high vacuum conditions are a requirement. We have found through a series of tests that the rayon grade of graphite is superior and does not display high moisture retention characteristics. I must also say there are certain grades of solid graphite that are very susceptible to porosity and the retention of gases. For example, let us say we have a furnace filled with these porous graphite materials, like fasteners. On evacuation and heating, gas is driven out of these pores. Then on gas quenching, gas, very possibly under pressure, is readmitted to the pores and will not release until subsequent vacuum and heating cycles. This may not be a problem, except if you have stringent rate-of-rise vacuum standards which will require subsequent long-time, overnight vacuum pumping to meet the specification.

Improved Heating Element Retainer Support—This consisted of a moly all-thread rod that screwed in to the heating element ring assembly, and with suitable ceramic insulators, supported the heating element with electrical isolation. There were many of these supports in the furnace, not only for the heating elements but for the insulation as well. In order to retain the insulators and to position the heating elements, holes were drilled into the moly all-thread rod. This design was incorporated for many years. However, most recently these holes have been eliminated with the use of proper graphite spacers with a graphite nut and lock nut on the end of the support. Since there were hundreds of these support rods in a big furnace, the labor savings was considerable and the moly support was significantly strengthened with the elimination of holes drilled through the member. (US Patent No. 9,702,627)

Bottom Loading Furnace Ball Screw Lift—The original ball screw lift for the vacuum furnace was an ABAR design. However, Bob Wilson, V.P. of Engineering here at Solar Manufacturing, developed what I will call an inverted ball screw where the actual balls, the retainer balls, were stationary in the top of the chamber bottom flange and the ball screws rotated through the stationary ball retainers, thus lifting the bottom head into position and securing the bottom head to the vacuum chamber. This allowed for lifting heavier workloads, but more importantly kept the ball screw in better synchronization and much smoother operation.

Heavy Duty Work Loading Trucks—Solar Atmospheres installed a ten foot deep vacuum furnace and then a twelve foot deep vacuum furnace. It was our desire to load 10,000 pound and 20,000 pound workloads into these furnaces. The first work loading truck was designed by VFS, but could never achieve a 7,500 pound workload without deflection on the loading arms. It sounds simple to fix, but because of mechanical engineering issues, deflection in the back end of the work truck and other problems made this difficult. Between the early VFS and then Solar designs, we went through several iterations before finally arriving at a design that would not deflect. These work loading trucks were also motor-raised and lowered and we used electric motors to run the loading truck into and out of the furnace. Without these innovations it was just too difficult for heavy workloads to be loaded by manual labor.

Special Paints for the Cold Wall of the Vacuum Furnace—We (and our competition) prefer to paint the inner wall of the vacuum chamber to prevent rusting of the chamber from atmospheric moisture during loading and unload over time. For years, we have been on the lookout for coatings or paints that would give us rust protection and low vacuum outgassing, as well as stand up against the rigors of high temperature in the furnace. We have found such a coating in a stainless steel paint which we call SolarVacSeal™.

Hot Zone Temperature Uniformity and Gas Quenching—there have been numerous developments in the recirculating gas quenching design of the vacuum furnace. In the VFS furnace, a large insulating baffle was used in the rear of the furnace, so quench gas could circulate through the furnace hot zone, out through the baffle to the heat exchanger, back into the furnace, and then through the gas cooling nozzles into the hot zone. The engineering design is to have the maximum pressure drop across the gas nozzles to achieve high gas velocity. This baffle in the rear of the hot zone presents an engineering compromise. If one closes up the gap between the heat exchanger opening and the hot zone, you have a large gas pressure drop which is inefficient and reduces performance. If you open the baffle you have high temp losses, meaning poor temperature uniformity and the furnace will not meet temperature survey. So we desired to design a furnace with maximum gas velocity through the nozzles and at high pressure—up to ten bar. We knew the rear gas baffle would be a serious problem and would not hold up under the rigors of diverse temperature operation. Our Chief Engineer, Bob Wilson, and his engineers set out to design a retractable baffle (two sliding doors) so that when the insulated door baffles are closed, the furnace is thermally efficient, but during quenching these doors are open and present a low gas pressure drop. This was neither an easy design nor one simple to work the bugs out of. The insulated door panels are sliding frames, stainless steel, on hardened alloy steel rollers, and operated through vacuum sealing ports. After three redesigns, we now have several of these furnaces in the field operating very satisfactorily. The first furnace was delivered about three years ago to our Hermitage plant, which has been an excellent beta site. (U.S. Patent No. 9,187,799)

Internal Vacuum Furnace Gas-to-Water Heat Exchanger—The design of this fin and tube heat exchanger is critical for proper gas quenching of the high temperature gas exiting the hot zone. Here again there is an engineering compromise. The characteristic desired is to have the lowest temperature gas exiting the heat exchanger. If you make the heat exchanger so dense there will be a high gas pressure drop across it. The best compromise involves selection of the number of fins per inch and other heat exchanger design considerations. We have arrived at a design of eight fins per inch. The fins are made of heavier gauge copper with the first few rows of the heat exchanger made from 304 Stainless Steel. The reason for the 304 Stainless Steel on the hot face is to avoid hot gas impingement on the fins, annealing and bending the copper fins flat over time, which will block flow through the heat exchanger. There are other subtleties of design in the recirculating gas system, too numerous to outline.

Typical Solar Manufacturing vacuum furnace installation.

Three Zone Automatic Temperature Trim Control—
Our VFS hot zone power control used manual "Powerstats" per power zone, for manual presetting, for hot zone temperature uniformity across the furnace operating temperature band.

Although satisfactory for most users, an improvement for close temperature control is automatic multiple trim zones preprogrammed via the SolarVac® computer. This precise control programming has been worked out by our computer controls engineers, David Rossi and Bruce Slusser.

BOOK
4
A REFLECTIVE LENS

Myrt's Story

I told Bill when we were engaged that I didn't care where we lived or what type of house we had. We could live in a tent, and I'd be happy. Just as long as we're together. I meant it, and he knew that. —Myrt Jones

I had a less-than-stable beginning in life, which greatly influenced the paths I took as I matured. I was born on Friday the 13th of December, 1935, and thankfully, I'm not a bit superstitious. My parents divorced when I was two years old, and I spent some time in a foster home until my father could find a good place for me. Dad was a young, hard-working man of 22, and he contributed to my upbringing in whatever way he could. He was so faithful in visiting me. When I was three, my maternal grandparents graciously took on the responsibility of raising me, though my grandmother was not a well woman—suffering from hypertension during a time when there was little medical treatment available for it.

We moved from the Kensington area of Philadelphia to the

small suburb of Oakford, Pennsylvania. My grandfather, whom I called Pop Pop, was a plumber and a very hardworking man; my grandmother was a fabulous cook and a good homemaker. She never progressed past the sixth grade, but when the milkman came, she knew how to count her pennies and kept her accounts straight. She made pretty little dresses for me out of feed sacks. She taught me all about homemaking and how to keep a house clean. I remember once scrubbing the floor three times until she was satisfied with my work. She wasn't mean about it; she simply wanted me to do it until it was done right. We also had a chicken farm on our property. I took care of the baby chicks, and as they grew bigger, I gathered their eggs to weigh and separate for sale. Pop Pop also butchered the chickens to sell. As a young girl working beside my grandmother and learning how to run a household, I felt the nagging weight of childhood chores, but I did not realize how soon I would have to put all of these skills into practice. The chores would become my daily responsibilities.

Every summer, as a treat, my grandmother and grandfather would take me to an ice cream parlor down on Roosevelt Boulevard, called Cooke's on the Boulevard. It was special to me not just because of the treats, but because the name of the parlor was spelled just like my grandparents' name—Cooke. They served the most wonderful waffles and ice cream, with powdered sugar, and that was my little treat. We would also go for rides on the Wilson Line steamboat to Riverview Beach Park in New Jersey. We would go with our neighbors and friends for the day during the summer.

When I was twelve years old, my grandmother went to be with her Lord, and I was faced with running a household while attending school. Pop Pop, understanding that I was all he had, was very patient, and we both had to learn how to make a home together. As hard as it was, the experience wasn't as bleak as it sounds. Sadly though, our trips to Riverview Beach Park ended when my grandmother died.

While I generally enjoyed my childhood, I made a promise to myself that I would marry, have a family, and keep that family whole and intact. It was especially important to me that I be the mother that my own mother couldn't be for me. I didn't want my children to feel the fear of instability that weaved through my early years.

We attended a small Methodist church in our community, a church that was faithful to God's Word, and I sang in the junior choir. My love for singing continued, and I've been a member of many choirs since then. When I was thirteen, our Sunday School teacher took us to a youth rally, where I accepted Jesus into my heart. This experience gave me a solid foundation to build upon as I grew up. In fact, despite what the world would throw at me as the years went on, I remained steadfast. Eventually, Bill and I would become youth leaders and Sunday School teachers. My faith, plus the later security and strength of my marriage, would keep me from feeling panic when we hit troubled times. Though I was only thirteen when I accepted Christ, I never wavered in my faith.

Soon I was ready to begin high school. There was no high school in our area, so we were bussed into another community, to Lower Moreland High School, in Bethayres. In my new surroundings as a freshman, I was smitten with a blonde-haired, hazel-eyed Bill Jones, then a sophomore. I invited him to my sixteenth birthday party, and we've been together ever since. When I met Bill and grew to know him and his family—whether I realized it then or not—he represented what I had always wanted: stability and a traditional family, with a mother and father committed to each other and to their children. I knew with Bill, the promise I'd made to myself as a young girl would be fulfilled.

Bill and I became engaged in 1954 and were married after graduation, in May of that year. As a wedding gift, my father offered us a choice of a wedding or $500 towards Bill's college tuition. We chose the latter. That $500 may not seem like much, but in today's economy, it would be roughly $4,400, almost a year's salary for an entry-level position in those days.

Bill was my only true love, and he's always made me feel secure and safe, no matter what came along in our lives, including the bumpy and often uncertain road to and through entrepreneurship. Before we were married, I made a statement to Bill that I would be willing to live in a tent, as long as we could be together. That was more important to me than a big house, amenities, or money. It still is.

We were blessed with two children, Roger and Holly, and we were further blessed with grandchildren and great-grandchildren. Bill and I worked hard to not only provide for them, but to pass on the lessons of honest work and commitment that our parents and grandparents gave us.

I always had faith in Bill and his abilities. If he said he was going to do something, you knew he would do it. So, when he came home with the suggestion that he start his own business, I wasn't scared or overly anxious, just excited at the possibility of a new venture. Bill is a calculated risk taker. He knew that industry inside and out and, even though others cautioned us against it and outright told us not to go into business for ourselves, Bill's drive and passion convinced me that we could make it work. It didn't take much convincing, to be honest. His word was his reputation, and he lived it every day.

Even though Bill held stable positions over the years and earned good pay and bonuses, I understood his desire to do things his own way, and it was only after a long time in the industry, working for others, that he felt it was time. After working himself to the point of exhaustion, a health scare and trip to the emergency room with chest pains, I knew something needed to change. He was far too stressed working for King Fifth Wheel and ABAR. He needed a break, but not just that, he needed to do things his way. We decided that working for ourselves would be much better for us in the long run.

When Bill gave his notice, he turned in all his keys, credit cards and such, and left. Upon his return home from the plant that Monday morning, he received a phone call that all of our company insurance, along with our salary, was cancelled. No COBRA in those days! To add insult to injury, our son Roger, who worked for the heat treating division as a second shift furnace operator, was told to leave his job as soon as possible. Just like that, we were set adrift. With no insurance and no paycheck, we used our savings to get by. We learned how to tighten our belts. Though we'd never lived luxuriously, with monthly obligations, no paycheck, and our daughter Holly in college, we were really frugal.

Bill takes risks, but he's not naive. We knew we'd have to tough it out for a bit until we settled on a plan and secured funding. Although it seemed like a snap decision to promise to build a furnace without any means of doing so, it really wasn't. The idea only came to Bill after many, many years doing exactly what he said he would do for this customer, after years of working so hard for someone else. He knew he could deliver, it was just a question of how.

We were fortunate enough to have connections, and that really does help. We knew the president of the Union National Bank, Charlie Hoeflich, and sought his advice on funding for a small business. He advised us to apply for an SBA loan, but cautioned that, if we defaulted, we'd have to turn over everything we owned. Everything but our bed. If that doesn't make you stop and pause, nothing will. Charlie looked straight at me and asked if I still wanted to move ahead. He knew Bill's answer, but he wanted to be sure I understood what it all meant. I understood perfectly and replied that I was 100% certain of Bill and of this venture, and I backed Bill completely.

So, after much prayer, we started Vacuum Furnace Systems and took it one step at a time to answer the question of "how?" to deliver the furnace, as promised. The fact that we used every penny we had, our personal American Express card, and remortgaged our home to start VFS was nerve-wracking, but not scary. In practically a day, with Charlie's help, we had the loan paperwork completed, and we found a space that was perfect for our new venture. Though we were funding the expenses of this new venture with money from our savings as well as using that money to pay for our living expenses, we continued to tithe to our church. We could have stopped for a while, until the SBA loan kicked in and we had more wiggle room, but Bill and I believed strongly in continuing to give faithfully. The Lord would provide, and in the meantime, we would get by. It was all happening and, in truth, our heads were spinning slightly, but we knew if we thought this through carefully, followed our plan, and trusted in the Lord and each other, we could do it. And we did.

I didn't know anything about the working world or business, other than what it took to run a home. I'd never worked before, but I had managed our personal finances and made sure we were not only building our savings, but that we maintained excellent credit. Bill and I worked together to build our new business, and I did whatever I could, whatever needed to be done. He taught me, and our accountant taught me, and I learned as I went along. I was his Girl Friday, answering phones and paying bills, sometimes even cleaning the bathrooms and offices. We did it all, until we could afford to hire the right people. We even helped to paint our first vacuum furnace, the VF-II, on a hot, sticky day in July. One day, I was answering the phones and took a call from someone wanting to know about our furnaces. Well, we had a model in the factory, and I really didn't understand how those furnaces worked, but I told him we had this furnace that you just plugged in, and it would start right up! I went out to tell Bill about the call and he said, "Myrt! You can't tell people that!" So, I learned to hand off those calls to someone more knowledgeable. But that's how I learned to run the daily operations of a new business.

Both of our families taught us the value of hard work and doing a job correctly. My Pop Pop used to line cesspools with cinder blocks he had cut by hand. He was up and down a ladder all day long, doing incredibly hard work without complaint. It's what you did. Bill's family was the same, and the two of us put that work ethic to good use, working long hours every day. You did what needed to be done. Our employees, once we were able to hire some, saw how hard we worked and knew we were not only committed to the business, but to them, as well. They worked hard for us, because we worked hard for them. It was like a family, and all through it, the Lord guided us and put us in the right place or directed us to the right people.

But we weren't without our setbacks. We had a number of issues that threatened to close us down, starting with the King Fifth Wheel lawsuit. We were sued almost the moment we started our business. That was really awful, but we didn't give up, even when it looked like our plans were all over. I remember we came home from meeting with a lawyer who said he wouldn't take our case, and we stood in the kitchen and both just cried. We didn't know what to do or how we would continue. I remember reading the Psalms to Bill, to try and comfort him. Just a short while later, maybe a day or two, the lawyer called us and said he'd changed his mind. He wanted to sue the big corporation on behalf of the little guy. We were the little guy. We went to see him again to discuss the case, and he told us he'd take us on with a $25,000 deposit towards a retainer, to start. Well, we didn't have $25,000. In fact, I had all of $2,500 and that was for payroll. I took out my checkbook and showed him. I said, "This is it, this is all we have." He said, "I'll take that." And so I wrote him a check, not knowing how we would pay our employees.

Bill and I drove back to the plant in utter confusion. How would we explain this to our employees? We were going to gather them together immediately, but we didn't. I guess we wanted some time to think of what to say. But I went into the office and absentmindedly began opening the mail. And here, the Lord's hand reached out and shined a light on our darkness. I opened an envelope containing a payment from a habitually late customer, Metallurgical Processing Company. The owner, John Ritolli, sent an advance payment, something he never did before. Unbelievably, this early payment was in the amount of $2,500. And just like that, we had enough to cover our payroll. We knew that wasn't coincidence.

The lawsuit was settled without financial injury to us. After all the hardship they caused us in an attempt to shut us down, KFW never showed up in court.

Bill and I knew each of our employees and thought of ourselves as a big family. When it was someone's birthday, I baked cupcakes, and we celebrated with them. Each Halloween, I would dress up in a silly costume, and we'd all have a great time. Of course, as the company grew and expanded, we grew too large for me to personally celebrate each person's birthday or bake enough cupcakes! However, the feeling of family and respect for each of our employees continued.

But as close as we were to our VFS family, we still faced troubles like any other organization. Over a period of about five years, a trusted employee embezzled about $250,000 from us, using VFS to purchase equipment for his side business building and supplying parts for race cars. When we found out, we were devastated. We trusted him—how could he betray us? It hurt, and I was ready to have that man thrown in jail. But Bill wanted to spare the man's family the grief of having a husband and father in prison. As much as I'm a Christian and believe in forgiveness, that employee hurt us so badly, and *I wanted justice.* After all we had worked for and how hard everyone had worked for us, stealing from us like it was his right infuriated me. I couldn't stand it, but in the end, I deferred to Bill's judgment and mercy. We did not file a legal complaint against him, so he never went to prison. That opened our eyes, though. You have to protect yourself and your employees from those who would take advantage.

As we expanded and began to build a small empire, we still encountered setbacks. Though things mostly fell into place for us when we needed them to, life throws you some curve balls and you need to be able to bounce back quickly. In 1991, we received another curve ball.

At 4:15 a.m. on a bitter cold February morning, I received a phone call. Solar was on fire. At that time, we parked our trucks inside the plant, and one of them caught on fire. To make matters worse, the sprinkler system never went off. Unfortunately, Bill was out of town at the time. Hearing the sirens and knowing they were for our company made my heart sink. I was on my way quickly and caught up with the fire engines. The road was blocked and the fire police wouldn't let me through until I told them I was the owner of the building on fire. As I approached Clearview Road—where Solar was located—and saw our twin blue towers reflecting all of the flashing red lights, with firemen all over the place and billows of black smoke pouring out of the dock doors, my heart sank lower. I can't adequately describe the feelings I was experiencing. One of our employees, Sherri Cardillo, had arrived at the plant for work, and she and I watched helplessly, sharing the traumatic experience and trying to comfort each other.

Roger told us later that, after he came into the plant and cleared the smoke out, removed the trucks and could see everything clearly, he noticed we had three or four furnaces running automatically, and they were all still running. Like nothing happened. So, he let them complete their cycles and then shut them down. Even though the fire had burned about 100 gallons of diesel fuel—leaving a black, sooty mess in both the plant and the offices that had to be professionally cleaned—we were back in operation basically the next day.

Thankfully, no one was injured, and we rebounded. But what amazed me was how we all banded together—all the employees—to salvage our jobs and areas that needed attention to get our business functional again. Through it all, I thanked the Lord for His goodness and mercy. Of course, we no longer park trucks in the plant.

There are so many success stories and cautionary tales we could tell, just like any entrepreneur. But the real story is in the everyday work. For all the right people in the right place at the right time, if we didn't do the work, we wouldn't be where we are today. We're so grateful for every helping hand and each vote of confidence, but you have to do the hard work every day. And the only people who can truly appreciate and understand how Bill and I have developed our businesses—and everything we went through to get here—are the people who walked through the valley with us. We've taken many risks, but the Lord has seen us through many trials. He has truly cared and ministered to me in my life, and Bill and me in our life.

Because of this adventure Bill and I took together, I went from a happy wife and homemaker to a business partner. It was a big leap, but we did it together—always together. While my duties no longer require 40 hours a week, I'm still an integral part of the business. I am the co-owner and Corporate Treasurer of Solar Atmospheres. I share part of the major investment in the buildings and businesses. My name appears on all major loan documents requiring signatures for personal guarantee, such as our line of credit with the bank to keep the companies operational, a total of over millions of dollars. I am part of all decisions on added ventures for Solar. I sit in on all Board of Directors' meetings. I attended all of our ASM heat treating shows since the beginning of VFS, and attended most MTI meetings as well. I am known by most of the business people in the heat treating and furnace fields. Major ventures are always discussed with me, particularly if funds are in consideration. Bill and I are supportive of one another and are usually of one mind on most decisions. Bill has always treated me as an equal in our ventures, never as "the little woman" who was simply trying to help out. Because of this, we have a strong marriage and a strong business partnership. We respect each other.

I want to stress how we were lifted up time and time again by the kindness of others, some strangers and some friends.

With each step we took towards building our business, we knew we wouldn't have survived without all these people and their advice, services, counsel, prayers, business, and generous terms. Because it not only meant the world to us professionally but also personally, we became determined to provide the same support for others. We wanted to be generous and give freely to those in need, and not just monetarily. The kind word, the encouragement, the recommendation, the referral, the advice, it all goes a long way to helping someone find their way in business or in personal pursuits. We knew that to be successful in all things, we needed to set the example and live up to it every day. Hopefully, that will be the larger part of our legacy as entrepreneurs: not just our net worth, but our contribution to humanity.

My Brothers

"No man is an island." —John Donne, *Meditation XVII*

Much has been written about twins, and the special bond between them. Many have asked if my twin brother, Dick, shared my enthusiasm for all things electrical and technical. The truth is, he did not. Neither did my older brother, Elmer. However, my interests and pursuits never kept me apart from them. While we certainly took different paths in life, my brothers, in addition to my parents and the many people I've met throughout my career, helped mold me into the man I would become. Since many have been curious about my brothers, I thought I would include a little something about them both here, since they are integral to my story. Though they didn't join me in my pursuit of innovation or become entrepreneurs themselves, they are no less important to my life story.

ELMER JONES
Elmer is five years older than Dick and I, born in Abing-

ton, PA in 1930. Five years' difference in age between us meant quite a gap in our growing years, with substantial differences in interests and directions.

When he was 16, Elmer spent his summer on board a sea-going barge, the "Windford Sheridan," which was anchored in the upper New York City bay. His commitments were from June to September, during which time he never went ashore. The onboard conditions were a bit primitive: no electricity or bathing water, only a small tank of drinking water. His duty was primarily "chipping paint," a really dirty and nasty job. Difficult and uncomfortable as it was, the time served a great learning experience for him.

Elmer attended Lower Moreland High School in Hunting-ton Valley, and was in the Commercial Course, which was a later career advantage. During high school, he lettered in foot-ball, which was a big deal in those days. His position was as a Right Running Guard. He was a true athlete, something in which I never showed any real interest.

In 1947, at the age of seventeen, Elmer left high school at the end of his 11th grade year and joined the US Navy, attending Boot Camp in Great Lakes, Ill. At that time, Navy men were trained by the Marines, particularly on the rifle range. Interestingly enough, most Navy men have little time for the Marines, though they are technically a division of the Navy. While enlisted, he studied for and earned his high school GED and graduated with his high school class in 1948.

Elmer trained as a Fireman, Second Class, and was assigned below decks in the engine room of a cargo attack ship, the USS Oglethorpe. He saw service in the South Pacific. Shortly after this assignment, Elmer spied a notice posted by the ship's command for someone who could type. Elmer took the position. After working in the ship's office for a time, he earned the rank of Seaman First Class, where he worked directly under the Executive Officer and stayed with the ship for two-and-a-half years. During that time, he passed his tests for Yeoman Third Class.

He then transferred to Washington, D.C., and served in the Bureau of Naval Personnel, where he met his wife, Ida—after graduating from high school in her native rural Arkansas, Ida began work in civil service in Washington, D.C., and was assigned to an office in the same department as Elmer. In May of 1950, they married. Ida was a solid Christian woman and—a bit later in life—taught Sunday School and served as an unpaid Methodist Church treasurer for many years. She was a dedicated, faithful wife to Elmer and mother to their two girls.

Elmer then returned to sea duty and served another two years aboard the USS Blackbird, an experimental, sea-going mine sweeper that towed an experimental "electronic fish" looking for classified undersea objects. Coincidentally, my brother, Dick, also joined the Navy, and both of my brothers served together on the Blackbird for over two years. (at Dick's funeral service, Elmer quietly remarked to me, "Dick was a good ship's sailor," in other words, he followed orders and did his duty).

At this time, Ida and Elmer had moved near the base in Panama City, Florida, with their newborn children—being an enlisted-man's family was never easy, traveling from Navy base to base.

For enlisted personnel, the "navy way" meant several years shore duty and then back to sea. So, Elmer was assigned to a navy base in Argentia, Newfoundland, which was a navy intelligence base and then part of the American "Dew Line," with navy aircraft on search patrol for possible Russian intervention or spy planes across North America. Ida and the children followed to the base. While on assignment, Elmer worked considerable overtime to sort out and reassign critical intelligence files. For this effort, Elmer was awarded a "Special Commendation" by the base commander at a highly unusual "Captain's Mast." In navy lingo, a "Captain's Mast" was usually reserved for wayward personnel as some form of punishment. Not so for Elmer.

Elmer and Ida Jones at "Captain's Mast" Special Recommendation Award.

Along the way, Yeoman Jones was—through a series of studies and based on his work ethic—promoted to Chief Yeoman. It is well recognized among navy personnel that Chiefs are the backbone of the service and are considered the go-to men to run the ship and get things done.

After his promotion, Elmer returned to the Washington, D.C., area, assigned to the then-Joint Command, in Maryland, an underground joint military command center. Ida and the family returned to a home Elmer and Ida built on the outskirts of Manassas, VA, which was, at that time, just a small town about 40 miles south of Washington, D.C. Today Manassas is all part of the greater Washington sprawl, with major traffic issues.

Ultimately, Elmer served 20 years in the navy before taking retirement, but looked for a new assignment. With navy experience, he easily received an appointment with an electric utility, the Northern Virginia Co-Op. He served in many interesting capacities, working directly for top management, and was assigned to head two field offices—one in Leesburg, VA, and a second in MinnieVille, VA—running both concurrently until his retirement 26 years later.

Interestingly, my father, though never a military man, had a similar career with the Philadelphia Electric Company, starting first as an electric meter reader and progressing through the ranks to head the Suburban Electric Power Meter group in Jenkintown, PA, before retiring after 46 years of service. He knew a great deal about three-phase electric power and trigonometry, and he taught me the basics of power factor theory, vector math, and the problems of electric power demand control, all useful to me to this day. Both my father and Elmer were self-taught and take-charge men. Both taught me a great deal over the years.

RICHARD (DICK) JONES

Sadly, my twin brother, Dick, passed away during the writing of this book (mid-2016). What follows is the eulogy I wrote for his service.

As twins, my brother and I were of course born on the same day. My earliest memories of Dick were in our big bedroom in Bethayres, where my other brother Elmer also had his bed. We were typical boys of the era, doing all the things that boys do. One particular memory was of the three of us building model airplanes. These were stick-and-paper and painted models of real planes. A foot or so long, they were tedious and time-consuming to build. They were rubber band-powered, but actually flew.

I would have to say Dick was not an academic type. It could be said that he certainly enjoyed his young life to the fullest. At age 17, my father enlisted him in the Navy. And so, Dick went to boot camp at the Naval Training Center, Bainbridge in Maryland. There was a graduation day, and my parents and Myrt and I (before we were married) went down to Maryland and saw the graduation, which was complete with the sailors marching, a close-order drill, and the Navy band. It was a thoroughly inspiring day. Dick served on two ships, first with my brother Elmer, on the USS Blackbird—a very interesting small ship of an experimental nature; it was designed with a torpedo-like fish that they towed behind the boat looking for objects like submarines. Following the Blackbird, Dick served on the USS Samoset, an ocean-going tug. Most of his time was spent in and around the Gulf of Mexico and up and down the East Coast.

Dick had a red Harley Davidson motorcycle. During one winter, while in the navy, he decided to drive his motorcycle home from Florida. Of course, on the way north, the weather changed dramatically. He nearly was frozen to death, and he stopped at our Aunt Ray's house in Claymont, DE. Aunt Ray was one of these very loving types who would put her arms around anyone and do anything for them. Dick probably knocked on her door half frozen in the late afternoon. Aunt Ray took him in, sat him down, and fed him black coffee and a big steak made especially for him. He talked about that for the rest of his life.

After his four years in the navy, he went to auto-repair school on the GI bill for a year or so. Dick learned to do all sorts of mechanical work, including painting. He worked for an auto-repair shop for a year. Then, his major working career was with Roadway trucking in Line Lexington, Pennsylvania. Dick could talk for hours about Roadway. He spent 20 years there before he retired. Dick was a full-blown union Teamster. One of his bosses at the terminal was a man about five-feet-two-inches high. When this man wanted to talk to the drivers, he stood on top of a stool so he could talk directly to the men's face, a no-nonsense manager. Dick had issues but nonetheless respected him. The Teamsters had an election for president of the union while Dick was at Roadway. Jimmy Hoffa, was running for re-election from jail. Before the election, I asked Dick, "Are you going to vote for a jailbird?" Dick said "He's done so much good for us! Sure I am, and so are all the other brothers." Jimmy Hoffa was re-elected.

Dick worked for me during the Vacuum Furnace Systems (VFS) startup, where he painted all of our vacuum furnaces with the famous orange color. Vacuum chambers, control panels, everything—before we had a spray booth. He had to be very careful. I made a deal with Dick. I told him, "We are desperate for cash, and I can't pay you. Keep track of your hours at the pay rate we agreed on, and we will put that amount toward the purchase of company stock." This eventually amounted to five percent of the company. Dick completed that assignment and won the stock. Then, he came to work for Solar Atmospheres full-time when we required trucking routes. When we started Solar, he became our shipper-receiver and the first delivery pick-up service in the field.

Dick had a wonderful gift of talk. He would stop into plants we were not doing any business with and talk to the man at the back door, asking for heat treat business. Surprisingly, he brought in quite a bit of business. He was the only one who has done that before or since. That is the kind of can-do person he really was. So, Dick was not only in charge of shipping and receiving and trucking, but also a stockholder, and with this, his mindset changed with regards to unions vs. management and directing people.

Dick was a bit of a roustabout, and his daughter-in-law Sonia always referred to Dick as a "buckaroo." Not sure what she meant, but I think we all get the picture. In 1991, we had an evangelistic event in Bucks Mont known as Encounter '91. An evangelist, Steve Wingfield came to town, and the organizing group—Bucks Mont Coalition for Evangelism—had us erect a tent the size of a football field. I was on that committee, along with Ray Mininger and at least twenty-four others. I asked Dick to help with the tent, and he did. After the tent was up and the meetings started, I asked Dick to come to the meetings—because after all, he had helped put up the tent! Dick said, "I didn't agree to that part." But he came to the meeting on a Wednesday, and he was glued to the 100-voice choir, in which

Myrt was a part, and to the speaker. Following the speaker, there was an altar call, and Dick raised his hand. I was sitting next to him in the second row, and asked him what he was doing. Dick said, "I will come back tomorrow night with Pat, and we will both go forward together." That is how they both came to faith.

I thought it best they not follow me into the Lansdale Presbyterian Church, where I was an elder. I didn't want to overwhelm him, to which I am prone. I suggested Immanuel Leidy's Church, and they joined and attended faithfully. Dick was an usher and collected the offering, and he helped with the annual Strawberry Festival as he was able. He did this until his Parkinson's overtook him and he was too shaky to continue. Over the years, the pastors have been truly faithful to Dick and Pat whether they attended or not, and they called on Dick and Pat at least once a month for many years.

There is much more to be said about Dick's life. During his last days on earth, he tended to live in the past, which is common with older folks like us. Even in his last days, he referred to his work assignments at Solar or at Roadway. He was happiest talking about these things—sometimes even about things that aggravated him.

In the words of my older brother, Elmer, to me on the phone the other night, I would like to say to Dick, "Fair winds to you, and following seas," a classic navy expression, among men of the sea.

Faith & Providence

It is important to treat employees (and customers) with the old adage, "Do unto others as you would have others do unto you." We believe honesty in all matters is paramount for our business. —WRJ

The reader may very well wonder why I've included a chapter on faith in this book about entrepreneurialism. We've all heard the expression "Take a leap of faith." Well, there's something to that saying. As an entrepreneur and owner of several businesses, I have experienced times that call for faith over other business principles—faith in yourself, in your abilities, and in your experience, your wisdom, and—of course—your employees. However, for me, there has been a greater, deeper faith that sustains, no matter what happens in my professional or personal life, and that is my faith as a Christian. I would like to share with you my personal journey of faith.

Firstly, do I run a "Christian" organization? No, I do not, for several reasons.

In matters of faith, as a Christian in the workplace, there is not much one can do to set any kind of Christian testimony within a company except to lead one's own life before a watching world. However, as the head and owner of the company, I am in a much more powerful position. I can set policy, and make discipline decisions. I don't believe in pushing faith issues, so we are not a "Christian" company.

It bothers me to no end to go into a restaurant and find a little book where Christian companies can take out advertising, because that book's just branding. When you look through the book, you find all sorts of companies you know are not Christian at all. I think if you are running a small grocery store, a barber shop, a doctor's office, you can take the position that you are a "Christian" company. You may only hire Christian people, and you can run the company from a completely Christian viewpoint. However, I do not think it is possible for my companies to operate in that way. We have customers throughout our businesses and around the world with different values, and we cannot push our own values onto our customers. Nor can we hire only Christians. We hire people of all faiths and ethnicities—in other words, all who are qualified. If a person applying for a position is qualified and can do the job, s/he should have that position. But make no mistake, my faith has most definitely impacted and affected how I conduct business.

From the very origins of Vacuum Furnace Systems, I was pleased to be able to start fresh, with a clean piece of paper, and to set new policies in motion, based on previous experience. Additionally, I was able to set some things right from the start, with a Christian view. From the startup of VFS, many vendors and friends came to our aid in ways we could never imagine. Particularly noteworthy was the Stokes Company of Philadelphia, the Pierce All Pine Company of Oaks, Honeywell of Fort Washington, Tudor Technology of Horsham, Bearings and Drive of Souderton, Amax Molybdenum of Cleveland, Ohio, and the Hunterdon Transformer Company of Flemington, New Jersey. These companies—and many others—extended to us nearly unlimited credit and service, all assuming we were going to make it. Such generosity far exceeded our abilities at the time and was nothing short of heaven-sent. So many pieces of the startup puzzle seemed pre-ordained, and Myrt and I knew it was all *providential*. We couldn't have orchestrated it all better if we'd tried. Long before I had the notion of starting my own business, the wheels were set in motion for me. We gave thanks early and often for the blessings we were receiving and would continue to receive.

Working with other people of faith is a joy. When your values align with others', you know it will be a fruitful partnership, even in times of distress, which we discovered early on. Adjacent to VFS was the Norman Good Plumbing and Air Conditioning Company. About three years after VFS was established, we had a major electrical accident that temporarily blinded our lead electrical engineer and burned two of our workers. Following the accident, I shut down the plant for the rest of the day and called for a time of prayer, which we all did together. Shortly after, I went next door and, in near tears, told Norman Good what had happened. He put his arm around me, and told me that his facility was available in any way I wanted, to help pull us out of the mess. He also offered prayer for VFS, on the spot. We did pull out of the accident with few ill-effects, except for minor injuries and a slightly singed spirit. Again, other companies and our community showed their support and caring, beyond business relationships and profits. When we experienced episodes like this, we experienced the love of Christ in the form of selfless giving from others. More so than any public declaration of faith or scripture hanging on a wall, that willingness to help, offer prayer, extend one's own hand… that's being a Christian, and that's how we prefer to do business. Time and time again, we learned the mercies of God. We didn't take them for granted.

So why is this faith so important to me? Because I came to faith in Christ late in life, and I fully understand the impact and change my faith has had on my life and on my opportunity to influence others.

My father was an agnostic, and he held a non-Christian view. He was not a total nonbeliever, and he was not anti-faith; he was just neutral. However, he bought into the lie that it was best for his children to find their own faith and to make spiritual decisions for themselves. Thankfully, my mother had better vision and sent me and my brothers to the closest church to attend Sunday School and summer Bible School.

Mother was raised as an Episcopalian. Her father, my grandfather and namesake, William Lamb, was a believer, though he did not attend church. We used to visit him occasionally on Sunday afternoons, and particularly in the summertime, he liked to sit in a chair under a tree and read his Bible. I remember that very well.

Having been raised in the Episcopal Church, I believe my mother went through the church Catechism classes, and I believe that was how she came to faith. She was not an outspoken, born-again Christian, but her faith was obvious. Mother came with us to church in our early years, beginning with nursery school at about age four. The church was very nice inside, with a pipe organ; not immense, but nonetheless a nice church. There, we learned some early biblical teachings and simple Bible stories from the King James Bible. One of my fondest memories of this church was a big sandbox in the basement, about six feet long and three feet wide, filled with pure white sand, probably from the New Jersey beach. Aside from anything else that happened there, playing in that sandbox was really nice.

Unfortunately, around the age of fourteen, my brother Dick and I walked away from the church. A major reason why I drifted away from faith was my father. We often said on a Sunday morning, "We don't feel like going" for whatever reason.

And he said, "It's up to you; I'm not going to make that decision for you." That ambivalence is an absolutely wrong thing to do, because churchgoing is not a decision you leave up to your children. It is a decision you make for them, and in my opinion as long as they are living under your roof, if you go to church, they go to church. I feel very strongly about that.

Though my brothers and I left the church as teenagers, I knew all of the basic Bible stories, things like Noah and the Flood, the Creation, Adam and Eve, and David and Goliath. The gospels did not have any influence on me, except Jesus' miracles such as the feeding of the five thousand and the various miracles in the New Testament. They were all taught from one of the approved Scriptures, like King James.

However, in those times—that is, the 1940's and 1950's—there was considerable Christian influence in all walks of life, including public schools. Each student was given a Bible and a hymn book. We read the Scriptures in class and learned to sing the great hymns of faith. The meaning was never explained, but the reading and singing were dutifully carried out each day. Though my church upbringing was beginning to fade away as I entered junior high and high school, the Bible readings each morning in home room remained a constant—albeit unrecognized—influence. Each student was assigned a verse, a different one each day. There were thirty children in my home room, and because we went to the same school 7th grade through 12th grade, that was the way it was through all of my junior and senior high years. That daily exposure obviously leaves an impact. You may not think it at the time, but it does.

The principal of our public school at that time, Mr. Hoke, was an Episcopalian. He was really a godly man, but, like my mother, not overtly so. It was obvious in the way he conducted himself, but he didn't shout it to everyone. I can remember, though it only happened once or twice, a member of the Gideons would come and speak at our high school and distribute Bibles for all of us to keep. At the time, I would say none of this had an influence on me, but I would have been wrong. Some 20 years later, the stories and lessons of Sunday School and my exposure to the Scripture in school would rush back into my soul and result in a revelation in my life.

In my college years, there was none of that influence. Penn State was neutral. There was no Bible reading, there were no Christian assemblies. But there was one professor, Mr. Hanney, who was obviously a Christian, though not outspoken. In one of my math classes, he drew two trees on the blackboard and then drew a vine that spanned from one tree to another. He showed us that this vine could be described by a quadratic equation. He then said, "If you think man invented mathematics, you are wrong. This was from the beginning, and it is all of God." That is all he said; nothing more, nothing less. Mr. Hanney was a respected teacher, and obviously he had some Christian faith and values that he imparted.

Myrt, on the other hand, was a Christian when I met her in high school. She came to faith when she was thirteen years old while attending a small Methodist church that was rather fundamentalist—that is, believing in the literal translation of the Scriptures. Her grandmother used to take her to church, and Myrt continued to attend after her grandmother's passing. Very important in Myrt's life was her Aunt Myrtle. Aunt Myrtle used to call her young niece every Sunday to ask if she had been to church. And she kept at her, even after Myrt was an adult and we were married. Myrt and I thought she was just being a pain, but we later realized her Aunt was simply concerned for her. Worrying that Myrt—with only her grandfather to guide her—would stop going to church after her grandmother died, Aunt Myrtle was determined to continue the work Myrt's grandmother had started. Myrt's grandmother had been the real Christian influence in Myrt's life. Aunt Myrtle was just continuing that influence.

Thanks to her grandmother's and aunt's diligence, Myrt had been a devout Christian since she gave her life to Christ at thirteen. She had the spiritual base that I lacked, and she would be a major influence in my conversion.

Myrt and I were married by the time I finished Penn State and went to work. We were living in an apartment in Ambler, Pennsylvania and Myrt went to the local Methodist church faithfully. I did not. On Sunday mornings, I stayed home. By then, Myrt's attendance at church was of her own decision; Myrt's aunt no longer checked in each Sunday to make sure her niece attended church regularly. Roger, our first child, was baptized in that church, and Myrt and I stood together at the baptismal font during the ceremony.

We then bought a small house in New Britain, and Myrt began attending a Methodist church in Doylestown. We were just starting out and had very little money. A year or so after we began attending, the church wanted to build a new church building on the outskirts of town and began a campaign to raise funds. Two of the lay people came to visit us, and they wanted to talk to us about how much we were giving to the church; they wanted us to make a pledge. As a matter of fact, the pledge they wanted us to make was for two dollars a week. I didn't say yes or no, but I later said to Myrt that it was out-rageous, and it was something we were not going to do. I was totally against making a pledge, because I thought we should not be put upon like that, even for two dollars. Of course, we could have afforded it, but that was not the point.

However, in the course of this building program, the church had a fundraising night, and they invited the whole congregation. I went to this Sunday evening dinner and I was impressed—terribly impressed—with the way the ladies put that dinner together. It was really a good meal, and it was all home cooked, as we do in the church. It was really done right. After the meal, we heard a speaker, a contractor from New Jersey. He talked about tithing, and about contributing to causes like a building program. He talked about his own life, and what he had done. He wasn't being braggadocious about it. He was a young man, maybe ten years older than me at the time, about 35. The way he spoke about his contributing surprised me. It amazed me that he would contribute that kind of money, which was to us at that time an enormous amount. The way he spoke about his faith impressed me also. I didn't do anything about it, but it stayed in my mind.

While working at Instrument Development Laboratories, I was greatly impacted by a tragic plane crash, which took the life of a promising new employee, Dick Zeller. We had an open position for an Application Engineer, and a likely candidate, an affable young man named Dick Zeller, flew up to Boston for the interview, which I arranged. The interview went well, and we offered him the position. Dick was excited at the prospect, as he was newly married and his wife, Phyllis, had recently given birth to their first child just six months earlier. Don Hall, our Sales Manager, drove Dick back to the airport to catch his plane home. While unloading his bags, Don accidentally let the car roll forward a bit, to which Dick laughingly called out, "What are you trying to do, kill me?" With that, Dick Zeller rushed off to meet his plane.

As Don Hall was driving away, he watched Dick's plane take off. As the plane was ascending, the Eastern Airlines Electra ran into a flock of birds. It crashed, killing everyone on board.

Don was devastated. Dick, who just a short while before had been laughing and joking with a life of promise ahead of him, was suddenly dead. Don called me, and I was shocked to my core. Sadly, I had to make the call to Dick's wife and break the news to her, that she was now a widow. The grief in her voice was unbearable. Though I'd only met Dick Zeller a few times and didn't know him well, I felt her unbearable sadness. She was probably only 24 or 25 years old, with a six-month-old baby. Although money can't console a loss such as this, Dick had opted to purchase airline insurance, at my insistence, before taking his ill-fated trip. The day after the accident, a courier arrived and delivered the insurance benefit to Phyllis.

Of course, several of us from IDL attended Dick's funeral. While there, I met Phyllis' father, who was a medical doctor with a practice in Vineland, New Jersey. We talked about the tragedy and its lasting effects. He said something to me I will never forget. He said, "In this life, there is no progress made without the shedding of blood."

What I didn't realize at the time was his comment was based on Christ's blood, shed for us. It was particularly profound. I didn't understand that part of it, but I did know that the man was hurting deeply after the loss of his son-in-law, and I thought it a brave comment and a testimony to Dick's life.

I was not yet a Christian, though, and I dealt with the blow as a non-believer—I felt the pain of loss and sudden-death, but had no faith to sustain me and help me through it. Shortly after Dick's death, Don Hall recognized that I was out of sorts, and perhaps not quite over the accident. He contacted Dr. Bentley in Boston and asked him to speak with me. Dr. Bentley took a train from Boston to spend some time with me. This choice impressed me; he took days out of his very busy schedule to make sure I was handling the loss. Though I've always been able to deal with a great amount of stress and I've always had a positive outlook, it did take some time for me to move on from Dick's death. Ultimately, I think the tragedy may have added to my frustration with, and apathy towards, my career at IDL. It was like a house of cards, and Dick's death was the final blow. I moved on to my next step in my career, but I never forgot Dick's father-in-law's words to me: There is no progress made without the shedding of blood.

In the course of my job changes, around 1962-63, I went to work at ABAR. At ABAR, Charlie Hill and Art Couillard were both solid Christians. I'd had discussions with Charlie and Art about matters of faith, to which I always responded that it was personal, and I did not want to talk about it. I thought religion should never be discussed with either customers or employees. They were not pushy about it, but I knew where they stood, and they knew where I stood.

During this time at ABAR, before my conversion, I had met Bud Brock. Bud introduced me to his new technology, which we adopted—the VRT. It became an integral part of our furnace technology. As our relationship grew, Bud also influenced my opinion of Christmas or holiday office parties. Though I was not yet a Christian, Bud was. He never preached to me, but he modeled for me—whether I recognized it or not—how a Christian behaves and cares for others.

I have never been a big drinker, I do have a drink on occasion, but I've never been fond of "tying one on" or carousing with business cronies. However, I never made a statement against that sort of thing, until Bud Brock called me, asking me to ban our Christmas office parties. Now, Christmas parties were all the rage in the 1950's and 1960's. In those days, it wasn't unusual to pull up to a gas station on Christmas Eve, and have the station owner invite you into the shop for a drink. While you were on the road! Drinking and driving wasn't the scourge it is today, and drinking at a Christmas party then driving home was the norm. On Christmas Eve day, employees would come to their offices or factories with alcohol in their thermoses instead of coffee. By noon, no work was done. Parties were in full swing, and production of any sort wound down. Seeing this, I decided to close the plant on Christmas Eve day, as well as Christmas Day. I wanted our employees to spend the extra time with their families, rather than drinking at work and driving home. Even with the extra day off, Christmas parties were still part of the culture, and I didn't dissuade our employees from enjoying them, until Bud called me with a terrible story that changed my mind.

Bud Brock's company had, as usual, celebrated the coming Christmas holiday with a party, and a number of people drank to excess. One of his employees, a young man with a wife and two small children, drove drunkenly away from the office but never made it home. He crashed his car and was killed. Bud had to deliver the awful news on Christmas Eve to that man's wife. She lost her husband, the children lost their father. All because of a Christmas party and an attitude of "live and let live." Bud was crushed, and I could understand why he was so determined to spread the news about the event. He wanted desperately to prevent another tragedy.

I listened to him and agreed wholeheartedly. As an employer, I couldn't bear the idea of putting innocent families in danger, all because of a party. Better these people go home to their loved ones and enjoy their Christmases together than whooping it up at a company party and inviting tragedy. Bud's impassioned plea and the genuine heartbreak he felt touched me deeply and has stayed with me to this day.

Despite the shining examples of Bud Brock, Art Couillard, Charlie Hill, and my own dear Myrt, I remained steadfast in my belief that my life without faith was just fine. Though Art and Charlie knew I felt discussions of religion were inappropriate at work, they would still, every now and then, refer casually to their faith. Eventually, Charlie introduced me to a radio program called "The Twentieth Century Reformation Hour." It was produced by Dr. Carl McIntire, a graduate of Princeton Seminary, and it aired on our local radio station, WBUX. I found the program one day while driving to work, and, curious, started to listen to it. Carl McIntire was into conservative politics; as a matter of fact, he was more into conservative politics than he was into faith, it seemed, and many people held that against him. Nevertheless, he was a solid Christian man. Carl McIntire would come into the studio and just sit down and talk, unrehearsed. I don't think he had a script in front of him, maybe not even a note. The man had a very good mind; there was no question about that. There was another man who was always on the program, called "Amen Charlie." Very quietly, throughout the program, he would say, "Amen. That's right," or "Amen, Doctor." I was impressed with this, because, to me, it added a mark of authenticity to Carl McIntire and his program.

I had been listening to McIntire for a year or more, when I learned he would be speaking one Sunday evening at the Calvary Baptist Church in Lansdale. It was a terribly foggy night; you could not see one hand in front of the other. However, Myrt and I wanted to go. I wanted to go and meet Dr. Carl McIntire. And so, in the thickest fog I've ever seen, we managed to find our way to the church. All we could do was follow the white line on the road. We were literally God-directed that night. Dr. McIntire's presentation that night wasn't a whole lot different than his radio program. But on the way out of the church, I shook hands with the pastor, E. Robert Jordan, and I told him, "I'd like to know more about this church, and I want you to send me some literature" (as a good engineer, I collect data). Pastor Jordan asked for our telephone number and our address. We gave it to him, and within the week Pastor Jordan came up to see us.

I didn't know it at the time, but Pastor Jordan was a real shouting Baptist—an altar-call-at-the-end-of-every-service sort of minister, in the manner of Billy Graham—a pastor who said all were sinners and going to hell if they didn't repent, believe, and be baptized. All hellfire and brimstone. In person, in a one-on-one conversation, however, he was an entirely different individual. You could sit down and talk with him in a conversational way, without all the admonitions. He made some gospel presentation to me, but not much. We talked about church, and I said "Well, I don't know. I don't go to church. I have not gone to church, but I have come to the point where I realize that I learned an awful lot in Sunday School. So, I think it is important that my children go to Sunday School."

And he said to me, "Bill, we would, of course, like to have your children for Sunday School; however, I want you to think about something. If you take this path, your children are going to be just like you. At age fourteen, they are going to walk away from the church. It is absolutely important that you set the standard, that you take them to church, and that you come to church." And of course he added, "that you come to faith." He was right. The next Sunday, we went to church. We have never stopped. And that is where it started.

We did not join Calvary Baptist, but that is beside the point. I didn't like the pressure of the altar call. I felt that it was an emotional response, and I didn't want to do it. I didn't want to take that step. So, we started attending a local Presbyterian church. It was more like what I was used to growing up, and there was no hard pressure regarding coming to faith. From my younger experiences in church, I remembered the warning against taking communion if you are not a believer or if you are a young person and have not yet made a decision of faith. That warning was presented early and often in my life, and I knew that taking communion was a serious step, requiring serious contemplation and commitment. As an adult, I knew that I could not take communion if I wasn't a believer. Until we began attending this Presbyterian church, I didn't feel ready to take that step. However, as a result of a communion service, I finally did. And so, I made a profession of faith.

That service was obviously a pivotal moment in my life, but I was really changing all along. I then took communion, probably before I should have, but that didn't make any difference. I met with the Session—the governing body of the church—and Myrt and I both joined.

As soon as we joined the church in Lansdale, I rather quickly became convinced that we should tithe, which is freely giving one-tenth of one's income to the church. Gone was my anger over contributing. Because it was a biblical commandment, in both the Old and New Testaments, we began tithing. However, in tithing, I did not feel that it was right to tithe on your gross pay, but to tithe on your net pay. Why? Because Jesus told us to render to Caesar what we had to render, but he didn't say we had to tithe on it. Right or wrong.

Since the early years of giving, our contributions have been considerably above a tithe, but that's how we started. This was during the Goldwater era, and Myrt and I became involved in the Goldwater campaign and the politics that were part of it. I am convinced that conservative politics and Christianity walk pretty closely.

Because Lansdale Presbyterian Church was a small church, with about 50 members, almost immediately after we joined, we were taking a more active role. I later learned that the Sunday before we came to the church, a prominent couple had left the congregation. The following week, we joined. A good friend of mine later told me, it was as if God sent a replacement for that couple, and I think He did. All the way around, it worked out *providentially*. We became active in the church in a number of ways. Myrt sang in the choir (in fact, she has sung in the choir of every church she's attended since she was twelve years old). After six or eight months at Lansdale, the pastor asked us to teach Sunday School, so each of us had a Sunday School class. I ended up with a junior high class, teaching something we call Bible Doctrine—a three-year class, Catechism study based on the Westminster Shorter Catechism, a statement of faith that goes all the way back to the 1600's.

After we'd been at the church over a year, another pivotal moment presented itself: There was an election for trustee, and I was nominated by our Session. It was an open election, and another church member, a grandmother figure I'd known since my childhood, nominated someone else to run against me. The person she nominated had been at the church for a long time, so to put me, a relatively new member of the church up against this long-standing church member was not a good sign. This election mattered to me; I wanted to be a trustee. I don't know why, but I did. Not surprisingly, I was not elected.

However, within six months, there was an opening for a member of Session, which is the highest office, next to the pastor. I was nominated and elected as an elder in the church.

Before taking the ordination vows, which in the Presbyterian Church are the same as for the pastor, I sat down with our pastor, Pastor Clark, regularly for a period of about three months to study the Westminster Confession of Faith, which is the doctrinal position of the church. The pastor and I needed to know if I agreed with this doctrinal position. I studied the Confession fairly thoroughly with him and agreed to it. I found a couple of items a bit difficult to immediately accept—such as the since-revised statement about the Pope being the instrument of the devil. Though there were points I disagreed with, I wasn't prepared to challenge the Westminster Confession of Faith, either. I was about 34 years old when I was elected as an elder, and I have remained a ruling elder all the way up until a couple of years ago—in total, for about 45 years. I served consistently, year-after-year-after-year. In our church, we don't have elections every year. If you become an elder, you stay on until you retire or resign. So, I became a ruling elder in the church.

Those events started a whole new era in my life. Naturally, my Christian walk affected my business thinking, and the way I conducted business. For example, we had an important customer in Newark, New Jersey, named Bennett Heat Treating, and I had some interactions with the principals of that company. The co-president of the company was a man named Tony Quaglia. The other co-president was Dave Mazer, a good and devout man of Jewish faith. Tony Quaglia had a terrible vocabulary. It was profane, and when he spoke, every other word was a curse word. One day I was with Dave, who never uttered a foul word, and Tony. As Tony spoke and swore, I turned to face him, and said, "Tony, do you realize that the language you use is absolutely demeaning to you, to your business, and to God? I think you should think about that." At that time, Tony was close to 60 years old, and I was in my thirties. For someone of my age to say something to this older, quite successful businessman was an extraordinarily bold move. But I did it. Tony Quaglia never uttered a bad word in my presence again.

What it did in his personal life, I have no way of knowing. But he got the message loud and clear, and he knew I was a different kind of a person.

Shortly after my conversion, we had a distressing and unfortunate occurrence at ABAR which tested my management skills as well as my newly acquired moral imperative. Our parent company, King Fifth Wheel, had a Christmas party. They would work until noontime, and then have a party with drinking and other things going on. At this point I was a Christian, and I still had the memory of the tragic accident that killed Bud Brock's employee after too much Christmas drinking. So, I had strong reasons for disliking these parties. Unfortunately, we were in the same building as King Fifth Wheel, and their parties could not be ignored. We would shut down at noon, paying our hourly employees for the full day. In an attempt to play down the allure of the KFW Christmas party and to dissuade any of our people from sticking around to attend, I suggested our employees go home and enjoy time with their families. I told our people that I did not want them to attend this Christmas party, and as far as I knew at the time, no one did. Except one.

One of our field service men, a married man with several children, decided to go to the KFW party. There, he met a lady who was in the accounting office of King Fifth Wheel. They became, as people like to say today, an item. A few weeks later, this man came to me and told me of his plans to divorce his wife and marry the accountant. I told him he shouldn't do it. I implored him to think about what he was doing, what it would do to his family. I tried to point out the position he'd put the company in, to help him see sense. I reminded him that a field service man could not work at ABAR while having a relationship with one of our accountants with access to all of our financials, including payroll. He was steadfast and wondered just what I was going to do about his decision. I warned him quite clearly that I would not have it. He was resolute and insisted on his plans. I ended the conversation with a promise to consider the implications and get back to him.

I talked about it with my pastor and described the situation. I told him I was of a mind to terminate both of the parties because of their fraternization and because of what I considered to be an illicit relationship. Pastor Clark told me he agreed, because the relationship was both morally wrong and likely to set a bad precedent in the company. He supported me. At the same time, the head of the accounting department, a Catholic named Joe, went to his priest to ask for advice about the same issue. Joe and I met within a week, and Joe's priest had advised that it was wrong to take away a man's job over a personal decision. The priest thought the company had nothing to say regarding such decisions. Here I was, at cross points with the head accountant of our parent company. I made my mind up about it, and fired both of them. There was some turmoil about it, but I'd made my decision. How things ultimately worked out for that couple, I don't know. But for him to walk out on his wife and children—I just could not see that. I was so concerned about this man, his family, and the effect this relationship would have on other employees, I felt I had to take a strong stance against the apparent "whatever goes" attitude. We need a moral compass, and I was determined to be one for that young man. As I've grown in my faith and matured as a businessman, I understand this is not a popular approach to such a problem. But we lead by example, as Christians and as leaders in business.

The VFS employee who absconded with about a quarter of a million dollars' worth of materials was another crisis that brought my faith to bear on a work situation. Sometime before this experience, our accountants had discovered a flaw in our purchasing system and warned us that something could happen that could be a problem. I ignored the suggestion that we change things, which was a mistake on my part, as this employee eventually made use of this flaw by stealing from us.

Myrt and I were in Florida at the time it was discovered, and George Carter, our plant manager at the time, fired the culprit on the spot. I might have done things a little differently had I been there. Myrt and I met with our attorney at the time, Don Semisch. Myrt was in favor of prosecuting the man, and so we talked the situation over. Don was a Christian and an elder at Willow Grove Presbyterian Church. The question was, should we prosecute this man? I remember the words of Don Semisch at that time. He said two things to me: first, that he understood Myrt's position. She was the mother hen protecting her brood. Don's second point was that a quarter of a million dollars is a few VFS dividend payments (though not true at the time!). I took a deep breath, and decided not to prosecute. What does that have to do with matters of faith? Well, you can take someone when they are down and step on their neck, or you can forgive. I didn't think of forgiveness as much as I didn't want to be the one to cast a stone. I told Myrt, and she agreed, though she still thinks I was wrong. But she acquiesced.

ENCOUNTER '91 & HOPE '96

Myrt and I have been privileged to be a part of local evangelical programs, another important area of our walk. I became involved in Encounter '91 first, a Steve Wingfield evangelistic campaign that ran for a week. It was a Billy Graham-style event, patterned after Graham's evangelistic crusades. There was a big tent set upon the grounds of Christopher Dock Mennonite High School. I was asked by Ray Mininger, a local Christian builder, to serve on a facilities committee to help set up the tent and provide other services. I had good history with Ray, and I respected him. If Ray or his father, Harold, called and wanted something, you did it. When Ray called upon me for help, and asked me to serve on the facilities committee for Encounter '91, I agreed to do it.

While on that committee, I asked my twin brother Dick to help us perform a number of tasks. I was concerned about

Dick, as he professed no faith. But I knew if I involved him in the event and drew him into the projects of the committee, Dick would be exposed to faith in a way that might be more palatable to him. I was right. Dick helped us and was a true asset, but, more importantly, he was witnessing God's Word in action. When Encounter '91 got under way, I invited him to one of the services. At first, still resistant, he did not want to come. But he relented, and he and his wife Pat came to the event. As a result, they were converted. I was elated.

My brother had never been baptized, so when the time came for Dick to join the church, he had to be baptized. I asked the pastor of Leidy's Church, where Dick and Pat were becoming members, if I could be part of that service, and he agreed. I was part of the baptismal service for my twin brother, and I was quite pleased about that. Had it not been for Dick's involvement in Encounter '91, would he have come to the faith? I don't know, but I'm deeply grateful for the event.

Five years later, the local pastors wanted to have another event as part of the Bucks Mont Coalition for Evangelism (BMCE). The pastors met with Charlie Hoeflich, the CEO of the local bank and the chairman of Encounter '91. Charlie had immersed himself in Encounter '91, with all of his extensive community contacts, which were far more than I had. Pastor John Niederhaus called me on the phone one day and said the pastors had met and agreed to ask me to consider being the chairman of this new evangelistic effort, called Hope '96. The event was to feature evangelist and pastor Dr. John Guest, whom I did not know. I was dumbfounded. To try to step into Charlie Hoeflich's shoes was almost beyond comprehension to me. But I decided I would consider it.

I talked it over with our pastor, John Clark. Pastor Clark said, "Bill, if you feel led to do this, I think you ought to do it." Then I thought I should talk it over with Charlie Hoeflich. So, Myrt and I went to Charlie's house, and I wanted to know all that was involved. I didn't make an immediate decision, but as he was walking us to our car, Charlie said, "Well, Bill, I know the Lord has called you to do this, so I don't think you have any choice." Driving home, Myrt and I decided we would do it, and that began my involvement in Hope '96. I took a year's sabbatical from my job to do it, and asked my secretary at the time, Faye Loughridge, to join me. Solar Atmospheres Inc. paid our salaries.

After personally hiring Ray Mininger's company for the renovations, I took over an unused classroom at Biblical Seminary in Hatfield, PA, and turned it into an office for Hope '96 (it is now the President's office). Myrt and I decided taking a year off from work to do this was the way to go. After all, there would be a lot of planning in the months leading up to the event and many committees to form, including one for a two-hundred voice choir and a youth committee. Maxine Waldman, head of Zion Choral Society, was a dynamic person and the only one I wanted directing the choir. She would do it, but only if she had complete control of the music. I agreed, and she knew just what to choose.

The director of our youth committee, Eunice Landis, came to me and asked for $20,000 to bring in a contemporary Christian youth band called Third Day. I said, "You are out of your mind! We can't possibly come up with that kind of money." But she eventually persuaded me, and that's what we did. The first night of Hope '96 was Youth Night, and we had distributed lots of flyers out about it. Just before that first night, we suddenly started to get tremendous interest from near and far about the concert. We received calls from youth groups as far away as Atlantic City. As the numbers grew, it looked like we might have about 12,000 kids coming, with room for only about 7,500 in the tent. I was scared to death. What if things got out of control? We had plenty of security, though, and they assured me they would have things well in hand.

The night of the concert, I was contacted by a lady known as "Prayer Kathy," who had a considerable prayer following.

She called right out of the blue, and asked how I was doing. I told her I was scared out of my wits and worried we might have a riot. She said that she had thought so, and wanted to give me prayer support. She prayed, and the event went off beautifully. As a matter of fact, that night, a member of the security team had confided in me about his young daughter, whose life was troubled. This young lady made a commitment of faith at the event.

But hers is not the only story of conversion. While taking up residence in the Encounter office at Biblical Seminary, I was approached by a concerned student from the Seminary. He had attended the Encounter meetings and came in to see me. He told me that he and his wife had been having marital troubles and came to the meetings seeking answers. He told me that as a result of their attendance, and after a conversation with John Guest, they had made some decisions to put their life back on track. So many similar things happened during this event, and we touched around 500,000 people. It is amazing to think you've been a part of something that touches so many lives. The events were broadcast on the radio as well, and Philadelphia's Channel 6 interviewed John Guest on television. The average attendance at the event was 6,000–7,500 each night.

Encounter '91 and later Hope '96 were major events in my life. Never in my wildest dreams did I think I would be a leader in an event like Hope '96. It proved to me that I was more than capable of managing people and projects—and not those just related to my particular industry. That's important, because so many people feel they are qualified in one area particularly and feel their skills won't transfer to another. It's my belief that, if you pay attention and learn as you go, you can apply these lessons to any part of life. If you are an effective manager in retail, for example, you can apply those skills to another area, like becoming a Deacon or Elder of a church or can serve on a community board and help to manage the day-to-day needs of another organization or project.

Incidentally, during my year-long absence from my company, it thrived. In fact, it ran without a hitch, even without me, thanks to the solid management team in place. I would never have believed that possible when I worked at ABAR, where I believed the whole place would crumble without me. I had clearly changed my management style for the better since those linear, top-down days, and that change proved highly successful. Cultivating a company culture of honesty and integrity—as well as hiring competent managers and allowing them to run their departments—enabled me to temporarily place my business in others' hands without concern or incident. Not many people would be comfortable leaving their business for a year, but I was.

Sometimes evangelizing takes place one-on-one rather than in crowds of 7,000 gathered under a tent. In the middle of our VFS years, the Varian Company, which makes high-vacuum diffusion pumps and other high-vacuum equipment, sent their local salesman to see me, and he continued to call on us for a number of years. One day, he came into my office to see me on a routine sales call. He mentioned that he was trying to improve his vocabulary and broaden his language skills. He told me he was studying the dictionary. I replied that the dictionary was the wrong place to study, and told him that he should study Scripture instead. Many of our root words are found in the Bible. I suggested he make a study of Scripture. I bought him an NIV Bible and mailed it to him with a note suggesting that he start with the book of John. He came back a few months later and told me that this gift had revolutionized his life. He realized it was not the verbiage, but the meaning. He had actually come to faith because of his reading. He was single, and he said he had gone about setting his life in order and had found a local Presbyterian church to attend and was in the process of joining that church. About a year later he came back, and reported that he had found the love of his life at that church. She was a college professor at Princeton. How about that?

In this memoir, I have discussed many providential things that have happened in my life that are almost unexplainable—a turn of events, a perfectly-timed referral, an early payment from a habitually late customer. Without a doubt, the hand of God has been upon us.

Philanthropy

B efore coming to faith, contributing to worthy causes or local organizations had no priority for me, and I've discussed how I responded when the church we attended asked us for a weekly contribution to a building fund. But, to discuss philanthropy, I would like to start with a word about tithing. That is not normally thought of as philanthropic, but it is something I think each Christian should do. It is an extremely important part of a Christian's faith. I am strongly convinced a Christian cannot walk only by faith. A Christian must lead by example, and part of that includes giving. There may be reasons why a person can't tithe, and I am not going to look down on them for it. That is between them and the Lord. But I think it is an extremely important part of one's faith—offering tithes or service in kind. As a good friend of mine, theologian Dr. Karl Heller, says:

Tithing is based on a law of the Old Covenant (Testament), but clearly is only a recommendation in the New Testament, based on one's ability to give. For my own guideline about giving, I have used John Wesley's inspired and very simple formula for economics: 'Make all you can, save all you can, give all you can.' And that can sometimes mean even more than money.

There is an old saying in the business world that "You have to put your money where your mouth is." That is an extremely crude way of putting it, but on the other hand, I think Jesus and God—one and the same—have commanded it. Giving of your blessings, specifically, your income, is essential. That is philanthropic in itself.

As discussed above, I have been tithing since about age 32 or 33. We tithe on our net income, but our income today includes our investment money, so we don't just tithe on my salary but on everything else. We have a number of rental properties, and we tithe on that income as well. We do not tithe on corporate operating profits, because we put all of that money back into the company for reinvestment and corporate development. We don't keep that money; we never have. That is how we have been able to build our companies. We do take a salary, though, I am not the highest paid employee in our companies—maybe about fourth. Several of our presidents are paid more than I am, which is ok with me. At this point in our lives, Myrt and I don't need the income. We have income from our properties and other investments. And so, we tithe on that income, and I think that is important.

Over time, there have been events that have come up that needed funding, and we felt strongly that we should contribute. When our church embarked on a building project, we made a major contribution. We financed the project with ten year bonds, which we would not do today. At the end of the ten years, we simply turned the bonds back to the church, not asking to be paid back. I was also head of the finance committee during another one of our building campaigns, which meant I had to be one of the major contributors, and I was. We have had several building campaigns we contributed to, but the most significant one involved our mortgage at the church. Myrt and I decided that the mortgage was hurting the church. Our congregation had to make those monthly payments, and that was taking away money from other things the church could do. So, Myrt and I paid that mortgage off.

A little while later, at the church we attended in Naples, Florida, we encountered a similar situation. That church was struggling fiercely in its finances, and Myrt and I decided to pay off that mortgage, as well. It lifted that monthly burden off of them.

When I was on the board at Biblical Seminary, we had a fund-raising campaign for a major renovation project. I became the head of the finance committee, along with local businessman Lester Clemens, and we each contributed a million dollars to that building program, a considerable decision for Myrt and me.

I include these details, not to brag about them, but to highlight the importance of giving. If a person makes money, fine, he's entitled to it. He worked hard and earned it. But he must contribute to society and give back what he can. For Myrt and me, our church and similar Christian organizations take precedence, but we have given to many philanthropic causes in the last twenty years, to the tune of around $10 million. Again, this information is not here to impress anyone; I simply feel people need to know what they can do if they have the money, rather than spend on airplanes, boats, and trips around the world. And, if one is a Christian—as Myrt and I are—such giving is imperative.

Aside from that, we have also made contributions to worthy individuals outside of our contributions to our church. These are pre-tax gifts. Myrt and I have been abundantly blessed, and we feel it's important to bless others, if we can. Sometimes a friend is struggling with finances or in need of something we can help provide. We have bought houses and cars for individuals as well as paid tuition for others. Now, there are difficulties in giving money to needy individuals. I would like to give it through the church so contributions can be tax deductible. In our church, the deacons are leery of that; they are sometimes concerned about "washing" the money in a sense.

Myrt and I have also started a charitable foundation, a 501c, as a way of continuing our philosophy of giving to those in need and of preserving our legacy. The William and Myrtle Jones Foundation was formed in 2015 as a charitable organization focused on philanthropy, voluntarism, and grant making. It is controlled by our son, Roger Jones, our daughter, Holly Craven, and one of our attorneys, Rob Pritchard. Every year, 5% of the net corporate earnings will be contributed to the fund. As of 2016, we have already contributed $600,000 to the foundation from our personal funds. This money will be donated to worthy organizations in perpetuity.

We give whenever and wherever we see a need. For us, it's a personal choice, and we receive calls and emails regularly, asking for contributions. I won't say we have a particular system of deciding who gets what; it's a heartfelt decision. There are so many worthy causes, and we respond to requests for help after natural disasters or tragedies, like the September 11th terror attacks. The point is, we give. I think it is important that everyone supports our fellow man and passes along the blessings that each of us has received. Otherwise, what good is all the money each of us has earned and saved? And, as the old saying goes, you can't take it with you.

Here is a partial list of organizations we've supported. Perhaps this list will encourage you to do likewise.
- American Red Cross
- American Society of Materials (ASM), Cleveland, Ohio and

Liberty Bell Chapter, Philadelphia
- Biblical Theological Seminary, Hatfield, Pennsylvania
- Cypress Woods Presbyterian Church, Naples, Florida
- Flight 93 Memorial, Shanksville, Pennsylvania
- Friendship House, Immokalee, Florida
- The Gideons
- The Grand Old Gospel Fellowship, Lansdale, Pennsylvania
- Hopewell Hospice of America
- Immanuel Leidy's Church, Souderton, Pennsylvania
- Lansdale Presbyterian Church, Hatfield, Pennsylvania
- The March of Dimes
- Mennonite Relief Fund
- Mental Health Education Fund
- Muscular Dystrophy
- Paralyzed Veterans of America
- Penn Foundation, Sellersville, Pennsylvania
- Rockhill Mennonite Community, a continuing care retirement community, Sellersville, Pennsylvania
- The Salvation Army
- St. Jude Children's Research Hospital
- St. Philip Orthodox Church, Souderton, Pennsylvania
- Support for Missionaries outside of our denomination, and specific missionaries within the PCA
- The U.S.O.
- Various Catholic charities, including Ave Maria University, Florida
- Westminster Theological Seminary, Glenside, Pennsylvania
- Wounded Warrior Project
- Zion Choral Society, Allentown, Pennsylvania

An Entrepreneur Is...

"Bill was always technically curious, and he took risks. He was always coming up with new products. He was always—always—working on a new concept for something. Bill was the genius behind the designs. He was also very inventive. He was always thinking of ways to make the product better." —Ron Zorn

Innovation is a two-sided coin, a balance between vision and risk. As I said before, I've been privileged either to be the first to design something new or to head a team transforming our industry. But I had to always keep this fact in mind: When you're making so-called innovations, they come at a price. You're getting this new idea, this new thing, up and off the ground, and now you have to worry about making it work. If it fails, you're going to have to stand behind it somehow. This process is a balancing act. You say to yourself, "I could make this change, but if I do this, will it put the whole project in jeopardy? How much money could we potentially lose by initiating this innovation?"

It's a real balance. And this balancing act isn't just with me. It is the battle of every engineer—every entrepreneur.

When you're working on something, designing it, many times your mind is trying to figure out how to fix something, and you're torn three ways. On one hand, you've got to build this thing within a budget. Then, you're constrained by whether or not the thing you're innovating will work or cause the whole project to fail, so you don't want to be too radically different or make too many changes at one time—my philosophy for such moments is to innovate in iterations so you have a sense of whether your idea will work. Lastly, you don't want to go about designing so that you're always innovating and changing things just to make improvements. You'll end up with a final product that is too different. When you build something, a cup, for example, you may be excited about it and want to build that cup and build it and build it and build it. Maybe a couple of years from now, there's something you want to change to improve it, so you do, but you can't keep changing the cup forever. If you do, you'll innovate yourself right out of business. The cup may no longer be recognizable as a cup.

Now, some engineers never get over this drive for innovation. I mean, for instance, some engineers never can see the whole picture, and that is why they're not good business people. There has to be somebody around—maybe the chief engineer of the company—who's looking at the business end of things and can say "It's a wonderful idea, but we can't afford to do that," or who can simply ask "what if" questions and look ahead at potential problems. You have to have checks and balances so that you can keep innovating, but within reason. Losing this balance was the issue with Dr. Bergson, at MEECO. He was an innovator, too, and that was some of his problem; he was interested in innovation in his own way, and the company was not nearly as successful as it could have been. It could have been a far more successful company if he hadn't always had his head in a cloud.

I had to learn that lesson, too. The people at King Fifth Wheel accused me of being, as they put it, "Scientifically creative and much more interested in innovations than in making any money." And there is some truth in that. You can't become so carried away with innovations that you don't make any money, and you end up losing money instead. Engineers are like this; it's a common trait. It's part of being an engineer. It's part of being an innovator.

So, while it was exciting to make design changes that impacted and influenced our industry, I think part of our success was that our innovations had to balance with realism and practicality. I think we struck a good balance, with the right mix of people. There is a temptation when you're starting your own company to think, "I can now do anything I want and run a little bit amuck." But you wake up really quickly. Suddenly, you find out you have a payroll to meet, and you built this thing, and you're not getting paid for it because it doesn't work. You can't let yourself get too far off center unless you're already quite profitable and at a point where you can take those risks. Fortunately for me, I'm at that point.

Since I've been in business—from my ABAR days to Solar—there were very few things that we've had to take back, but there were a few. There were a couple of furnaces that didn't perform as they should and were returned to us. If the customer had paid any advanced monies on them, we provided refunds. Those things happen. But it's important not to become discouraged even if you have to scrap an innovation and stick with a model that works. That's the important part of being an owner: If you own a business and you make a mistake, you can decide to simply give up on the idea. You can throw something away and move on because, at the end of the day, it's your money. Just like a bad investment—if it's your money, you can say, "Okay, I lost it. There's nobody else to kick but myself, and I'm not going to go away and cry about it." When you're working for somebody else, that's a different story.

When we tested that first large furnace in Hermitage, we could have used scrap pieces we had and that would have worked out just fine. But why do that? If you believe in your product, show your confidence. I chose to test that furnace with $3 million dollars' worth of titanium coils. If the furnace had failed, I would have lost that money, certainly. But it didn't, because we designed with a team of engineers and built it well, and I knew that. I wanted everyone to stand behind that furnace and have confidence in what we'd designed. And when Bob Hill came to me, suggesting we build yet another furnace for Hermitage—at a cost of several more million dollars after we'd just built two—I listened to his proposal. Yes, it was a lot of money—it was $10 million. But in the half hour it took Bob to lay it all out for me, I bought into it. He was right. It was a risk, but I knew it would pay off, because I trusted Bob and my experience.

There are so many examples I could give of taking risks—from starting VFS to Solar, to buying companies that failed, to expanding in California and South Carolina, to taking risks with employees and customers. It's all part of starting and owning a business. No matter what your goals, you have to start by taking a leap. Some people are better suited to that than others. Some can start, but lack the fortitude and foresight to continue. True entrepreneurs see past obstacles to the opportunities.

And just as you should prepare for failures, you should also prepare for success. Say you've built something and introduced it to the market, and say it's doing well. Your competitors will start to come in, and—if you're already successful—you'll saturate the market with your product. So, what do you do? You build another new product and another one. You have to do that. In our world, you can't just keep making the same thing. If you do, you're going to go out of business for any number of reasons. So, any business is forced to innovate in some way. I don't care what the industry is: If you don't innovate, in time, you will be out.

What should innovation look like? First of all, there has to be an opportunity that presents itself in some way. Then, the question becomes whether you're going to take advantage of that opportunity and whether it's within your pale. I haven't seized every opportunity that's come my way. But I am a risk taker, I really am. If I see that there's enough meat under an idea and that there's a good chance that an idea will go forward, I'll take the risk. But there's something else about such risks that you must realize, too. The world will not end if the risk doesn't work. It's going to cost some money, but failure's not necessarily going to be a total disaster.

So, I've taken that attitude about all of our designs and our equipment and even all the heat treating business that we do. I like to take add-on steps to yield innovations. Let's say we have a piece of equipment, and we want to be able to make it do something else. Well, can we stretch? Can we make the idea a little bigger this way? Can we take it to this higher temperature that we need? Or, how do we handle this evaporate that's coming out of it? Those are relatively small steps, small innovations, small risks. Such risks are not like inventing a new mousetrap.

I remember one time, a fairly big company came to us, and they wanted to buy a vacuum furnace that would work with a binder. The company had these sort of chrome briquettes—a chrome powder that had been pressed into the form of briquettes—and in order to press the briquettes, the company had to use what the industry calls a binder, or a lubricant, so the powdered metal compound would stick together. There are several types of binders—like cornstarch or stearic acid or something as simple as alcohol. These people were using something like cornstarch. Well, when you put cornstarch into a vacuum furnace and heat it, that stuff all boils out and condenses all over the inside of the chamber. Because the outside walls of the furnace are cold, we call this arrangement a "cold wall furnace." After one or two runs, normally you'll have maybe as much as 2% or 3% by weight of this binder boil out. That doesn't sound like much, but just imagine you have 10,000 pounds in the furnace: all of a sudden, a couple hundred pounds of this goop is in there. So, I realized I had to develop some way of trapping the stuff.

I didn't have the money for a lot of fancy pieces of laboratory apparatus, so I used ordinary tools. I used a pressure cooker and a wok and some other ordinary kitchen things, and I set everything up on a workbench. People thought I was crazy because it was like a small chemical laboratory. And I remember people coming over and shaking their heads—they couldn't understand what I was doing. But I was able to duplicate the way my idea would work on a larger scale. Based on my experiments with kitchen tools, we built the furnace, and it worked. But the crux was to work out the chemistry of the thing before I actually built it. A first-step innovation. To me, that task wasn't a chore at all. It was rather fun, trying to figure out how to solve the equation. That's just one example of an add-on step I took to unearth an innovation. I've done a lot of things like that. Being innovative means figuring out a solution to a problem, but it doesn't always have to cost a lot of money.

I think the source of this innovative drive is what others— Bergson, Bentley, Willan—saw in me that I didn't recognize in myself until later, something not necessarily linked to an industry but a characteristic within my personality in general. I probably could have applied this characteristic to almost any industry—I have a passion to complete whatever I am pursuing, and I'm technically oriented. Such traits could have applied to building bridges just as easily as furnaces, and I am confident that should I have started down that path, I would have built bridges and built them well, Lord willing. But life happened to land me in this field, and a lot of people helped me along the way. Much has been providential, and much has spurred me on.

Each day, I get up in the morning, I put my feet on the floor and thank God that I've done it. And then I start thinking,

"Okay, what are the opportunities? What can I do? What am I going to do today? What problems are there, and what am I going to be about?" I've often said that if I was going to fail at something, I was going to fail with my guns on. You can just imagine an airplane in a fight, a bomber, a big bomber with guns all over it, and it's fighting other fighter planes. Every one of my guns is going to be on. I might go down, but I'm going to go down with my guns on. That's how I look at it.

In a way, this point also speaks to reputation, which I think must be part of entrepreneurship, too. I have been all about image, and I have been all about perception. I've never felt I'd built an image I couldn't sustain, because I've always stayed true to who I am. Also, I have not presented an image that was unrealistic. With each meeting, each proposal, each sale, I have been acutely aware of how I presented myself and my business to others. This has always been enormously important to me, going all the way back to my very first businesses mowing lawns and repairing radios and televisions. My reputation and how others perceive me has been carefully cultivated over the years—not in order to be false or deceptive, but to build on one accomplishment to the next until there's a true sense of authority and trust. It's something I've sought to instill in each employee, no matter their position. Each employee is the face of Solar and Bill Jones.

Myrt's been a decidedly big part of building that, too. She has set the tone of this whole thing. And I haven't interfered with her work. She has decorated all our plants. She has picked out all our paint colors, the drapes and the shades and the tables and the chairs. She's made mistakes at that, too, and she's learned from them. If you were to ask her if she could ever have done this when she was twenty-five years old, she would have said, "Oh, no! My gosh, I wouldn't know where to start." But the truth is, everything that you see reflects on Solar and reflects on both of us. So, we've taken care to make sure we maintain a true image.

So, yes, being an entrepreneur means taking risks, being innovative, being willing to spend money and take a leap of faith. But I'll tell you, you have to do what's right for you. Don't go trying to work in technology if you hate technology. Just because there's a market for something doesn't mean it's a good fit for you. How far would I have made it in this business if I didn't like working with electronics and vacuum technology? There is no one-size-fits-all in risk and innovation—some people are willing to get into a space rocket to fly one-way to Mars, some are not. If you want to take risks and innovate—if you want to be an entrepreneur—be sure you make the moves that will fit for you. The risk and innovation has to match your personality, otherwise you'll lose the drive before you succeed.

Let me end with this thought: Boeing built the 707 plane to put themselves ahead of the game. The company had made numerous innovations prior to this aircraft, but with this commercial jet plane, they were going to reset the industry. The problem: nobody wanted to buy the 707. Why? Because the industry didn't trust commercial jets. Too many people remembered the British-built Comet—it blew up.

So, Boeing had twenty-five of these 707s sitting on the tarmac, and nobody wanted to buy the planes. But the CEO of Boeing at that time was smart. He called all the airlines executives together—TWA, Pan Am, and so on—put in a set of bleachers, and held a demonstration run for the 707s. That way, all of the executives could see firsthand how sturdy and reliable the 707 was.

The pilot took off, took the plane up, and circled it around the bleachers. Unbeknownst to the CEO, though, the pilot decided to put on a show. As the plane came around—at maybe 1,000 feet—the pilot took the plane on a barrel roll right in front of the executives. Talk about risk—and confidence!

That demonstration flight was risky—and the CEO may have nearly had a heart attack from the experience—but it sold the plane. Boeing walked away from the show with a dozen orders.

Now, I don't recommend doing something foolish and dangerous to make a sale. But that pilot and CEO were confident in their product, and wanted to show their customers that confidence. I think such a blend of confidence, risk, and a willingness to innovate all must blend and balance to set a path toward success. As I have reflected on the traits that have influenced my experience as an entrepreneur—as I have reflected on the golden nuggets I found within every experience—I have spent a lot of time thinking about what makes me different from others. Why do I take risks others might not? Why was I—and why am I still—compelled to keep discovering?

I'm not sure I can explain the reasons why I kept stepping out of my comfort zone to try something new and push the boundaries. My father enjoyed his career but couldn't wait to retire. But that's not me. I couldn't—can't—understand how he could just stop at age 65. At 80, I'm still just as driven, still looking for opportunities and new discoveries. That may be what makes me different and what enabled me to be successful in my careers with MEECO, IDL, ABAR, VFS, and ultimately in Solar. I think my success has had a lot to do with my creative drive, my technical curiosity, my willingness to accept the challenge of "Well, there it is—we can use it to defeat us or we can somehow take advantage of it." There haven't been too many things that I have looked at as defeats—though there were a few risks I've taken that just didn't work out for one reason or another. But I'm not afraid to fail or make mistakes in the pursuit of uncovering another opportunity. I never was. Perhaps that's what makes me an entrepreneur.

TRIBUTE TO
WILLIAM R. JONES

WRJ inspects 120" diameter hot zone, Vac-Hyd Corp, Compton, CA.

Biography

William R. Jones, FASM, was born and raised in Bethayres, Pa., and graduated from Lower Moreland High School in Huntingdon Valley, Pa. He received a degree in Electrical Technology from The Pennsylvania State University in 1955 and has dedicated his entire career, since 1962, to the development and application of thermal processing and equipment.

Mr. Jones worked for ABAR Corp. for 18 years and served as its president for five years. He left ABAR and established his own vacuum furnace company, founding Vacuum Furnace Systems Corp. (VFS) in 1978.

After VFS was well established, Mr. Jones founded Solar Atmospheres, Inc. in 1982 as a commercial vacuum heat treating company. Before the decade was over, plans were made to expand the existing plant in Souderton, Pa., to more than double its size to accommodate the growth of both VFS and Solar Atmospheres. Then, in 1992, Solar Atmospheres opened the doors of its own new heat treating facility next to VFS.

By the mid-1990s, with the heat treating business expanding rapidly, there was a need again to open additional plant capacity, especially for vacuum brazing and other special projects. Thus, in 1996, Solar Atmospheres acquired another heat treating facility in nearby Hatfield, Pa.

At about the same time, another major change was about to occur that would shape the future of the business. Solar Atmospheres was rapidly expanding and required more of his attention, so Mr. Jones transferred the day-to-day responsibilities of operating VFS to the five top managers of the company. In 1995, VFS was eventually sold to those managers. Five years later, however, VFS was sold again, this time to the same holding company that also owned VFS' rival competitor Ipsen.

Further growth and expansion led to the bold decision to open a new commercial vacuum heat treating operation in 1999 to serve western Pennsylvania and eastern Ohio. Solar Atmospheres of Western Pennsylvania has grown from an 18,000-square-foot facility with three new furnaces to its current size of 58,000 square feet with 14 furnaces.

The year 2002 was very busy in terms of new start-up companies. Mr. Jones acquired Magnetic Specialties, Inc. (MSI), and it was relocated to nearby Telford, Pa. MSI manufactures specialty transformers, furnace power supplies and other electrical products. Solar Manufacturing was also founded that same year to design and build advanced vacuum furnaces and to develop new process technologies in cooperation with Solar Atmospheres.

Strategically, both Solar Atmospheres and Solar Manufacturing benefit each other; the heat treater becomes the proving ground for the furnace manufacturer and in return gains from the improvement in furnace designs and performance. The general heat treating industry also benefits from the natural outcomes created by this unique relationship between the companies.

The latest addition to the Solar family of companies came to fruition in the beginning of 2011 with the opening of a new heat treating plant in Fontana, Calif. The state-of-the-art facility is fully operational and satisfies a desire Mr. Jones has had for many years to establish an operation in California to serve the western U.S.

Mr. Jones has said that his entrepreneurial passions go beyond earning a living to support his family to enjoying the challenge of any worthwhile endeavor. As an engineer, he likens himself to a technical tinkerer gaining satisfaction out of making something and seeing it run.

Ground breaking Solar Atmospheres heat treating plant, circa 1985. Souderton, PA.

Mr. Jones holds 18 patents and is continuing to develop more. He has long been associated with ASM International, the American Vacuum Society (AVS) and the Metal Treating Institute (MTI). With a career spanning nearly 50 years in the industry, he has written numerous technical articles for ASM, Metal Heat Treating and Industrial Heating magazines, and he has authored papers for the ASM Heat Treating Conference and for MTI. He became a Fellow of ASM International in 1989.

Investors have often approached Mr. Jones about selling

the business, and he has always turned them away. He does not intend to sell the business because the development of the company is not driven by the accumulation of personal wealth.

He and his wife, Myrtle, have two grown children. There are a number of family members active in the Solar Companies, including son Roger Jones, who is corporate president. Outside of the office, Mr. Jones enjoys traveling. He also serves as an elder in the Presbyterian Church in America in Lansdale, Pa.

WRJ watches as Trevor Jones, then a Research Engineer, conducts early laboratory vacuum carburizing experiments at Solar Atmospheres, Inc. circa 2004.

Testimonials

ROGER A. JONES
Corporate President, Solar Atmospheres

On behalf of the entire Jones family, I am proud to congratulate my father, William R. Jones FASM, for being selected as the symposium honoree at the 2011 ASM Heat Treating Society Conference and Exposition. His contributions to ASM, the Heat Treating Society and the entire heat treating industry are numerous.

To some, it may be considered a challenge to work for family members, but to me it has been the best experience of my life. Due to my father's many personable character traits, I have enjoyed working for him since my high-school years. He is open and approachable, and with his extensive life experiences, he is able to impart wise counsel on a variety of business, technical and personal topics.

Apart from his down-to-earth nature, he is a respected businessman and an innovative engineer. He is an intelligent risk taker and I have seen a majority of his risks pay off in his favor. All of these aspects are reasons why he is not just my father and not just the CEO of three businesses, but why he is my life-long mentor as well.

Through his diligence and devotion to the industry, Solar Atmospheres now consists of three plants with preparations to establish a fourth. What he has accomplished with this company through honest, hard work is amazing.

It has been a pleasure to watch our business expand, during some difficult times, into a very successful family company employing three generations. I am excited to see him continue to grow this company because, for him, there are no limits. Again, congratulations, dad, from the entire Jones family on this prestigious honor and for your continued contributions to the heat treating industry.

JAMIE JONES
General Manager, Solar Atmospheres

I am proud to congratulate my grandfather as the distinguished recipient of ASM's honorary symposium at the 2011 ASM Heat Treating Society Conference & Exposition.

His ability to be a great husband, father and businessman is inspirational to many individuals, including myself. I am truly lucky to be a part of this family, and it is my hope that I can contribute to keeping the family businesses going as successfully as he has over the years.

His accomplishments throughout his career, his knowledge and his forward thinking in vacuum heat treating technology have directly given Solar Atmospheres the ability to be known as one of the top commercial heat treaters in the country. He has successfully developed new process technology and applications, which Solar Atmospheres performs regularly, that others would not think of trying in a vacuum furnace.

Also, under his leadership, we look forward to our sister company, Solar Manufacturing, to advance overall vacuum furnace technology to further improve our furnace designs and allow us to continue to lead the general heat treating industry.

Again, I am proud to say that Bill Jones is my grandfather, and I am proud to congratulate him on this recognition as an innovator in vacuum processing and vacuum technology. Our entire family is very proud of him.

TREVOR JONES
Principal Engineer, Solar Atmospheres

I am honored to congratulate my grandfather, William R. Jones, on receiving this notable award.

His accomplishments throughout his career in vacuum heat treating technology and his success as a true business entrepreneur are testaments to his hard work and dedication to continually advance the industry. His pioneering technical contributions, including 18 patents, countless technical presentations and service as CEO of several successful companies have distinguished him in the heat treat industry.

He has an enthusiastic interest to never stop learning in all areas of life. He has a unique ability to overcome technical issues with a combination of practical and intellectual solutions. This comes from his broad experiences as an innovative engineer using not only electrical and mechanical engineering but also all disciplines of the sciences to resolve technical issues. He is a highly respected engineer in the industry routinely being sought out from both friends and competitors alike requesting technical guidance on any number of topics.

Without a doubt, he is one of the most influential individuals in the heat treating industry.

A. BRUCE CRAVEN
President, Solar Atmospheres

Working for Bill Jones in various positions at his companies over the years has provided me with exposure and opportunities that are rarely available elsewhere. I have worked on the equipment side and the processing side, and I have worked with plant operations and maintenance. In all areas of business, Bill often travels a unique road that is not familiar to many, but he goes with purpose and determination. A history of business successes allows him to spare no resource in accomplishing the mission that he has envisioned, and there is always something new going on in every company that Bill has created.

Bill has never been afraid to push the envelope, whether it is in technology development or in business risk taking. He has been blessed in that even what seems like a failure is usually turned around into a success. He surrounds himself with good people, and he never loses touch of what is going on at the shop-floor level. Seeing him with an electrical multi-meter or wrench in his hand is not at all unusual. His connection to the core of the businesses has allowed him to make prudent decisions in the boardroom. Without question, Bill is one of the brightest technical minds in vacuum technology, and I have appreciated the education that he has given me.

SUNNIVA R. COLLINS, PH. D., FASM
Senior Research Fellow, Swagelok Company
ASM Board of Trustees 2008-2011

Ithink Bill Jones is one of the great men of modern metallurgy. He is an unusual combination of technologist, businessman and entrepreneur. As a leader in developing vacuum treatment equipment and technologies, he has made contributions that enabled improvements in other technologies. After all, the parts don't work if they're not heat treated correctly!

I have enjoyed getting to know Bill and the folks at Solar Atmospheres and Solar Manufacturing over the last several years. It's a real pleasure to work with multiple generations in a family business, and Bill and his associates are genuinely nice people. Bill's values really define Solar's company philosophy and culture: ethical, honest and straightforward, with a focus on problem solving for the customer.

On one of my first visits to Solar, I noticed that Bill had on the wall a copy of "The Man in the Arena," a quotation from a speech by Theodore Roosevelt. I think that this quote represents an informal guideline on how Bill, his family members and his employees perform and conduct business. Paraphrasing from the original, Bill "strives to do the deeds; knows great enthusiasms, the great devotions; spends himself in a worthy cause; and knows in the end the triumph of high achievement."

Congratulations to Bill Jones on being recognized by his peers with this honorary symposium.

ROGER J. FABIAN, FASM
Roger J. Fabian Consulting LLC
Director at Large—Center for Heat Treating
   Excellence at WPI
Metal Treating Institute President (1997-1998)
ASM International President (2008-2009)

The Bill Jones I know is a consummate engineer, innovator, risk taker and entrepreneur. As the founder and CEO of the Solar Atmospheres family of companies, he is a well-established leader in the heat treating industry.

Bill Jones, in my view, is an icon in our industry. He has almost single handedly led the movement to create eco-friendly commercial and in-house heat treating plants. He has done that with his leadership in the use of helium gas and high-pressure gas quenching to process parts with minimal distortion and also by designing and building 36-foot vacuum furnaces capable of processing titanium with minimal alpha case.

Most of all, what separates Bill from the rest of the crowd is that he tells it straight and tells you exactly what he thinks. Invariably, by the way, he is usually right.

I am fortunate and truly honored to call Bill Jones my friend and an esteemed colleague, and I add my congratulations to him on a career that has certainly benefitted our industry.

ROBERT F. GUNOW JR.
President, Vac-Met Inc.

My congratulations to Bill Jones, who is truly a pioneering leader concerning vacuum processing equipment and technology. He has led the way for many of us, and we have appreciated his advice and counsel these past several decades.

Bill has been admired for his abilities during a long career encompassing several furnace manufacturing companies and his own heat treating companies spanning the U.S. from eastern and western Pennsylvania all the way to California.

We wish Bill and his family great success in the future.

DAN HERRING
"The Heat Treat Doctor," The Herring Group, Inc.

Did you ever wonder whom the experts call when we need sound technical advice on heat treating problems? Who do we look to when we need answers? Who, in our industry, has that rare combination of practical experience and solid engineering/scientific knowledge?

Bill Jones is such a person. Bill is a unique individual, and I'm honored to say a special friend. He is both a mentor and a shining example of all that's right in the world of heat treating. What sets Bill apart is his generosity and his willingness to openly share what he knows as well as what he has learned and to bring the considerable resources of his organization to bear on solving any problem. He's unafraid to question, criticize or insist that you strive for perfection. Bill has an inquisitive mind. As such, it is no wonder he is an inventor, a tinkerer and someone who never bothers to look in the rear-view mirror. Bill's passion is for advancing the state-of-the-art in our industry and helping mentor the next generation of heat treaters, metallurgists, inventors and engineers.

Congratulations, Bill, for this recognition of your influential and successful career.

RONALD D. MARKLE, FASM
Past President, Aerobraze Corp.

My early contact with Bill Jones was when he was president of ABAR. We wanted a large vacuum furnace with an all-metal hot zone. In spite of its size, it had to fit into a restricted space yet had to be loaded by hand or with a loader. We wanted large pumps for speed, but they had to be easy to maintain. This was in 1978, and Bill put together what was needed.

Bill's contributions to vacuum furnace design were learned from experiences on the heat treat floor, and they found their way into the final product through keen insight and innovation.

My association with Bill Jones brings to mind many technical as well as business discussions that developed into a mutual friendship. I have found another side to Bill. He has a genuine concern for people; he is a humble person, a family man, down to earth, usually in the background, but always ready to help.

I have a tremendous regard for Bill and have seen his many contributions that have influenced the advancement of vacuum furnace technology.

JOHN REGER
President, Winston Heat Treating

Since my first encounter with Bill Jones at ABAR in the 1970s, and later at VFS and now at Solar, I have come to regard him as our industry's foremost vacuum innovator. I have always been struck by Bill's enthusiasm for and love of vacuum technologies. This observation was reinforced by a rumor that he had maintained a working furnace in the basement of his home for many years.

Bill perpetually develops cutting-edge designs, and I have never known him to balk at a new challenge or application. He is a man of great wisdom and convictions, so if you choose to debate him, it is best that you come well prepared.

Bill has always lent an expert helping hand to his customers and competitors alike, and he has passed down that same spirit of collaboration to his son, Roger Jones, and the rest of the Solar organization. His talents are not limited to the technical. He is also a well-accomplished businessman, salesman, manager and marketer.

Thank you, Bill, for your friendship and technical assistance throughout the years. The heat treating community has benefited from your tireless devotion and contributions. You are richly deserving of this tribute. I am honored to recognize Bill Jones the man and the innovator.

DALE J. WEIRES
Technical Fellow—Metallurgy—The Boeing Company

Many of Bill Jones' accomplishments are documented in the furnace designs and heat treating processes that we now accept as industry standards. Lesser known is the great influence that Bill has had within our industry through the sharing of his knowledge and his support for the betterment of our industry.

My personal development as a leader within the heat treating industry is strongly tied to my relationship with Bill. He has been extremely generous in sharing his time and knowledge in support of our projects. My conversations with Bill energized me to think more deeply, test concepts, mentor the new generation and share my time within our industry. His enthusiasm for heat treating, conquering technical obstacles and sharing his resources for problem solving are unmatched, with the exception of the dedication of the Jones family and their employees to their patriarch. This attribute of the Solar family illustrates that Bill Jones has succeeded at balancing both professional and personal success.

The Honorary Symposium at the 2011 ASM-HTS Technical Conference is a fitting acknowledgement of the wonderful career of Bill Jones from a grateful heat treating industry.

APPENDIX

Appendix

PATENTS

(Patents influenced/invented/owned by WRJ/ABAR/VFS/ Solar Atmospheres)

PATENT #	DATE	DESCRIPTION	INVENTOR(S)	OWNER
3,476,862	12/4/1969	Electric Resistance Heating Elements	Edward N, Cyrway, Jr. William J. Metalsky	ABAR
3,698,698	10/17/1972	Fixture for Heat Treating Furnaces	Benjamin A. Kreider Charles J. Schmidt Howard R. Martindell	ABAR
3,737,553	6/5/1973	Vacuum Electric Furnace	Benjamin A. Kreider William R. Jones William J. Metalsky Thomson B. Gibb	ABAR
3,847,539	11/12/1974	Driving Mechanism for Vacuum Electric Furnaces	Benjamin A. Kreider William J. Metalsky	ABAR

PATENT #	DATE	DESCRIPTION	INVENTOR(S)	OWNER
3,874,845	4/1/1975	Control Operator	William J. Metalsky William A. Reynolds	ABAR
3,879,165	4/22/1975	Vacuum Electric Furnaces	Benjamin A. Kreider William J. Metalsky Edward N. Cyrway, Jr.	ABAR
4,102,637	7/25/1978	Work Support for Vacuum Electric Furnaces	Benjamin A. Kreider William J. Metalsky	ABAR
4,124,199	11/7/1978	Process and Apparatus for Case Hardening of Metal Work Pieces	William R. Jones Prem C. Jindal	ABAR
4,212,633	7/15/1980	Vacuum Electric Furnace	Benjamin A. Kreider William J. Metalsky	ABAR
4,225,744	9/30/1980	Fixed Thermocouple for Vacuum Electric Furnaces	William R. Jones Prem C. Jindal	ABAR
4,227,032	10/7/1980	Power Feed Through for Vacuum Electric Furnaces	William R. Jones Rush B. Gunther	ABAR
4,245,943	1/20/1981	Unloading Apparatus for Vacuum Electric Furnaces	William J. Metalsky	ABAR
4,259,538	3/31/1981	Vacuum Furnace Arrangement Having an Improved Heating Element Mounting Means	William R. Jones	WRJ
4,395,832	8/2/1983	Gas Duct Arrangement for a Vacuum Furnace	William R. Jones Fred W. Ripley	VFS
4,425,660	1/10/1984	Shielding Arrangement for a Vacuum Furnace	William R. Jones	WRJ
4,489,920	12/25/1984	Hot Zone Chamber Wall Arrangement for Use in Vacuum Furnaces	William R. Jones	WRJ
4,490,110	12/25/1984	Plenum Arrangement	William R. Jones	WRJ

PATENT #	DATE	DESCRIPTION	INVENTOR(S)	OWNER
4,499,369	2/12/1985	Heating Element Arrangement for a Vacuum Furnace	Thomson B. Gibb	VFS
4,512,737	4/23/1985	Hot Zone Arrangement for Use in a Vacuum Furnace	Clifford R. Pierce	VFS
4,604,056	8/5/1986	Vacuum Furnace System Hearth	William R. Jones	WRJ
4,760,584	7/26/1988	Hearth Support Arrangement	William R. Jones	WRJ
4,765,068	8/23/1988	Hot Zone Arrangement for a Vacuum Furnace	Fred W. Ripley	VFS
4,813,554	3/21/1989	Reversible, Adjustable, Stackable Loading Grid Assembly	Clifford R. Pierce	VFS
4,850,863	7/25/1989	Sealed Insulating Wall for a Furnace	Clifford R. Pierce	VFS
4,856,022	8/8/1989	Graphite Hot Zone Assembly	William R. Jones	WRJ
4,860,306	8/22/1989	Hot Zone Employing Graphite Heating Elements	Thomson B. Gibb	VFS
5,109,917	5/5/1992	Maintenance Arrangement for a Furnace	Fred W. Ripley	VFS
5,121,903	6/16/1992	Quenching Arrangement for a Furnace	Fred W. Ripley David E. Felker	VFS
6,021,155	2/1/2000	Heat Treating Furnace Having Improved Hot Zone	William R. Jones	WRJ
6,023,487	2/8/2000	Process for Repairing Heat Treating Furnaces and Heating Elements Therefor	William R. Jones	WRJ

PATENT #	DATE	DESCRIPTION	INVENTOR(S)	OWNER
6,111,908	8/29/2000	A High Temperature Vacuum Heater Supporting Mechanism with Cup Shaped Shield	William R. Jones	WRJ
6,936,792	8/30/2005	Furnace Cart and Load Transfer System for High Temperature Vacuum Furnaces and Process Therefor	William R. Jones	WRJ
Turned down by US Patent Office		Process for Treating Steel Alloys	William R Jones Virginia M. Osterman Harry W. Antes Trevor M. Jones	WRJ
7,514,035	4/7/2009	Versatile High Velocity Integral Vacuum Furnace	William R. Jones	WRJ
8,088,328	1/3/2012	Vacuum Nitriding furnace	William R. Jones	WRJ
9,187,799	11/17/2015	20 Bar super Quench Vacuum Furnace	Robert J. Wilson Robert F. Daley	WRJ
9,702,627	7/11/2017	High Temperature Vacuum Furnace Heater Element Support Assembly	Robert J. Wilson Mark J. Hughes	WRJ
In Process	In Process	High Temperature Vacuum Furnace Hot Zone with Improved Thermal Efficiency	Réal Fradette Benjamin Isaak	WRJ
In Process	In Process	High Temperature Low Mass Vacuum Furnace Hot Zone	Réal Fradette Benjamin Isaak	WRJ

Note: 18 patents by William R. Jones with others, 27 patents either owned or controlled by William R. Jones

AWARDS

1953
- American Legion Outstanding Leadership Award, Lower Moreland High School

1988
- ASM Philadelphia "Liberty Bell" Chapter, Delaware Valley Metals Man of the Year

1989
- ASM Fellow
- ASM Philadelphia "Liberty Bell" Chapter, William Hunt Eisenman Award
- ASM International, William Hunt Eisenman Award
- Solar Atmospheres Inc. awarded Outstanding Company Support, ASM
- Philadelphia "Liberty Bell" Chapter
- Hope '96, with Evangelist John Guest
- Executive Director Recognition
- Solar Atmospheres Inc. "Commercial Heat Treater of the Year Master Craftsman" Award presented by Industrial Heating magazine and the Metal Treating Institute (MTI)
- Metal Treating Institute (MTI), Distinguished Service Award

2005
- George H. Bodeen Heat Treating Achievement Award (ASM)

2008
- Executive Leadership Radio Interview, Philadelphia, PA

2011
- ASM Honorary Symposium

2013
- Metal Treating Institute (MTI) Heritage Award

2016
- MS&T Lifetime Distinguished Service Award (ASM)

TECHNICAL ARTICLES

Solar continually offers helpful and informative technical papers, as well as podcasts and presentations, on our website. For a complete and up-to-date list of available titles and series, please visit www.solaratm.com.

SOLAR ATM & MFG PAPERS COMBINED BY DATE—NEWEST TO OLDEST
- *Using Vacuum Furnaces to Process 3d-Printed Parts (RH)*
- *Minimizing Titanium Alpha Case During Vacuum Furnace Heat Treating (DJ)*
- *Vacuum Furnaces Were Made for Additive Manufacturing (RH)*
- *Reducing Vacuum Furnace Losses by Changing Hot Zone Emissivity (New) (RJF & BS)*
- *New Advances in Vacuum Furnace Insulation (New) (RJF)*
- *Why the Batch Vacuum Furnace? (New) (RJF)*
- *Selecting the Right Vacuum Furnace Hot Zone for the Application (New) (TJ & RJF)*
- *Comparing Vacuum Furnace Hearth Power Losses (New) (RJF)*
- *Retiring Paper-based Maintenance Systems in Commercial Heat Treating Shops (RAJ)*
- *Designing a Vacuum Furnace Hot Zone for Optimum Thermal Efficiency and Vacuum Performance (New) (RJF,WRJ,TJ)*
- *Understanding Vacuum Furnace Temperature Measurement Issues (New) (RJF,GMO,WRJ)*

- *Enhancing Titanium Friction & wear Properties (2014) (DJ)*
- *Understanding Emissivity and the Use of Thermocouple Test Blocks in a Vacuum Furnace (2014) New (RJF & TJ)*
- *The Use of a Residual Gas Analyzer (2014) New (TJ & RJF)*
- *Critical Areas of Preventive Maintenance (2013) New (WRJ & RJF)*
- *Gear Market Offers Opportunities for Ingenuity and Innovation (2013) (Others)*
- *In Situ Oxidation of Steels as an Effective and Economical Pretreatment for Uniform and Consistent Vacuum Gas Nitriding Results (2013) (TJ)*
- *Leak Detection and Checking of Vacuum furnaces (2013) New (WRJ & RJF)*
- *Vacuum Gauge Correction Factors (2013) New (TJ & RJF)*
- *Explaining Vacuum and Vacuum Instrumentation (2012) New (RJF & WRJ)*
- *Operating a Vacuum Furnace Under Humid Conditions (2012) (RJF & WRJ)*
- *Understanding PID Control As Applied to Vacuum Furnace Performance (2012) (RJF & WRJ)*
- *Cryogenic Treatment Review (2012) (DJ)*
- *Maximizing Vacuum Furnace Gas Quenching Performance (2012) New (NC & RJF)*
- *Considerations When Selecting a Vacuum Furnace Water Cooling System (2011) (RJF)*
- *Understanding Power Losses in Vacuum Furnaces (2011) (RJF,WRJ,NC)*
- *Optimizing Procedures for Temperature Uniformity Surveying for Vacuum Furnaces (2011) (RJF & WRJ)*
- *Critical Melting Point Booklet (2010 Rev) (WRJ,VMO,RJF)*
- *Nature Nano: Ultrahigh-power Micrometer-sized Supercapacitors Based on Onion-like Carbon (2010) (Others)*
- *The Vacuum Heat Treatment of Titanium Alloys for Commercial Airframes (2010) (RH)*

- *Controlling Compound (White) Layer Formation During Vacuum Gas Nitriding (2010) (DJ)*
- *No Hydrogen Embrittlement with Low Pressure Gas Carburizing (2009) (DJ & TJ)*
- *Explosive Nature of Hydrogen in Partial-Pressure Vacuum (2009) (TJ)*
- *What the Medical industry Can Learn from the Aerospace Industry (2009) (RH)*
- *Vacuum Gas Nitriding Furnace Produces Precision Nitrided Parts (2009) (DJ)*
- *Utilization of Vacuum Technology in the Processing of Refractory Metal, Titanium and their Alloys for Powder Applications (2008) (VMO)*
- *Reconditioning Ceramic insulators (2008) (TJ)*
- *Raw Vs. Part Heat Treatments—What is the Difference? (2008) (RH)*
- *Low Torr-Range Vacuum Nitriding of 4140 Steel (2008) (DJ,TJ,VMO,HA)*
- *Airplanes Don't Fly Without Heat Treating (2007) (RH)*
- *Carburizing for Our Troops (2006) (VMO)*
- *High Pressure Gas Cooling: the Case for Hydrogen (2006) (RH)*
- *Heat Transfer and Insulation in Vacuum Furnaces (2006) (HA)*
- *Calculating the Gas Flow rate for Vacuum Carburizing (2005) (HA)*
- *Development Experience in Low-Torr Range Vacuum Carburizing (2005) (VMO)*
- *Austempering at Conventional Sintering Temperatures (2005) (WRJ)*
- *Adding High Velocity to High Pressure Gas Quenching (2005) (RH)*
- *High Gas Velocity: A new Frontier of Cooling Performance in Vacuum Furnaces (2004) (RH)*
- *Conserving Electric Power Part II (2003) (WRJ)*

- *Conserving Electric Power Part I (2002) (WRJ)*
- *Assessing Work-Basket Alloys for vacuum Furnaces (2002) (RAJ)*
- *High Pressure Gas Quenching Typical Oil Hardening Grades of Steel (2002) (RH)*
- *Vacuum Pressure Quenching of Oil-Hardenable Materials (2001) (RH)*
- *Power Factor Costs: How are They Affecting the Bottom Line? (1999) (OTHERS)*
- *Partial Pressure Vacuum Processing—Part II (1997) (RAJ)*
- *Partial Pressure Vacuum Processing—Part I (1996) (WRJ)*
- *Vacuum Heat Treating for M2 High Speed and D2 Tool Steels (1996) (WRJ)*
- *The Advantages of Ion Nitriding Gears (1996) (OTHERS)*
- *Vacuum Brazing: A Three in One Process that Provides Efficiency (1996) (CFB & RL)*
- *Energy Dominates in Job Costing (1996) (BC)*
- *Brazing of Electric Power Interrupters in Vacuum Furnace Specially Designed for the Process (1994) (WRJ & RJF)*
- *Product Quality Improvement with Correct Moisture Measurement in Thermal Processes Using Electrolytic Hygrometers (1993) (OTHERS)*
- *Vacuum Sintering—A Way to Improve Ductility and Toughness of Structural P/M Parts at the Right Price (1992) (WRJ)*
- *Operating Experience with a New Reactive Ion Plating Unit for TiN Coating (1990) (BC)*
- *Vacuum Furnace Brazing Large Segments of Heat Exchanger for Nuclear Fusion Reactor (1990) (CFB)*
- *Ion Nitriding Principles and Applications (1989) (BC)*
- *Hot Zone Contamination (1989) (WRJ)*
- *Pumping and the Vacuum Furnace (1986) (WRJ)*

- *Vacuum—Another Atmosphere (1986) (WRJ)*
- *Why Vacuum? (1986) (WRJ)*
- *High-Velocity Gas Flow Seen as Key to Rapid Quench (1985) (WRJ)*

AUTHOR LIST ON ABOVE PAPERS

WRJ—William R. Jones
RH—Robert Hill Jr
RJF—Real J. Fradette
BS—Bryan Stern
TJ—Trevor Jones
RAJ—Roger A. Jones
VMO—Virginia M. Osterman
DJ—Don Jordan
NC—Nick Cordisco
HA—Harry Antes
CFB—Charles F. Burns
BC—Bruce Craven

PODCASTS & WEBINARS

SOLAR PODCAST LIST

February 2013:	The Advantage of Processing Titanium in Vacuum Furnaces
April 2013:	Responding Effectively To Utility Loss—Power/Gas/Water
June 2013:	Cost-Reduction Considerations in Operation, Maintenance of Vacuum Furnaces
August 2013:	Tips for Operating a Vacuum Furnace Under Humid Conditions
October 2013:	Temperature Uniformity Surveys—Part 1
December 2013:	Temperature Uniformity Surveys—Part 2
February 2014:	The Helium Shortage
April 2014:	Graphite Materials for Hot-Zone Components—Part 1

June 2014:	Graphite Materials for Hot-Zone Components—Part 2
August 2014:	Preventive Maintenance—Part 1
October 2014:	Preventive Maintenance—Part 2
December 2014:	Preventive Maintenance—Part 3
February 2015:	Preventive Maintenance—Part 4
April 2015:	Measuring and Monitoring Trace Levels of Dew Point and Oxygen in Quench Gases—Part 1
June 2015:	Measuring and Monitoring Trace Levels of Dew Point and Oxygen in Quench Gases—Part 2
August 2015:	The Problem of Contaminated Ceramic Electrical Insulators in a Vacuum Furnace
October 2015:	Preventing Distortion and Cracking in a Vacuum Furnace
December 2015:	The Advantages of Vacuum Furnace Brazing
February 2016:	Vacuum Furnace Brazing of Stainless Steels
April 2016:	Active Brazing of Titanium in a Vacuum Furnace
June 2016:	Hot Zone Designs—Past, Present and Future (Part 1)
August 2016:	Hot Zone Designs—Past, Present and Future (Part 2)
October 2016:	Hot Zone Designs—Past, Present and Future (Part 3)

BILL JONES ASM WEBINARS

Oct. 17, 2013:	Operating and Maintaining Vacuum Furnaces: "Up-Time" Considerations (Pt. I)
Nov. 7, 2013:	Operating and Maintaining Vacuum Furnaces: "Up-Time" Considerations (Pt. II)
Dec. 4, 2014:	Vacuum Furnace Pumping Systems
Feb. 9, 2014:	Vacuum Furnace Temperature Measurement

TECHNICAL BOOKLETS
Available in Print or by Download.

RELEASE 1: Critical Melting Points for Metals and Alloys

This handy reference guide provides valuable information regarding critical melting points for Metals and Alloys.

This work is an update of the original reference compilation by Charles F. Burns, Jr., Copyright 1997. The current booklet contains revisions to the original work as well as numerous additions. This booklet should serve as a handy reference for people that work in the metals industry.

RELEASE 2: Temperature Uniformity Surveying For Vacuum Furnaces

A Temperature Uniformity Survey (TUS) for a vacuum furnace to satisfy AMS 2750D must be performed using established procedures and methods that fully meet the requirements of the specification and allows for consistent and more accurate results of actual furnace capabilities.

RELEASE 3: Operating a Vacuum Furnace Under Humid Conditions

A specific concern to a vacuum furnace user is processing critical work during summer months with high temperatures and high humidity. This same concern could also be a problem on rainy winter months.

RELEASE 4: Understanding PID Temperature Control as Applied to Vacuum Furnace Performance

Proportional-Integral-Derivative (PID) control is the most common control type algorithm used and accepted in the furnace industry. These popular controllers are used because of their robust performance in a wide range of operating conditions and because of their simplicity of function once understood by the processing operator.

RELEASE 5: Understanding Power Losses in Vacuum Furnaces

Since the early development of the vacuum furnace, engineers and thermal experts have continually tried to improve the insulating characteristics of the furnace hot zone. Several materials have been used for different applications with varying success.

RELEASE 6: Important Considerations When Purchasing a Vacuum Furnace

There are many factors that should be considered when investing in a new vacuum furnace. Although price is obviously important, there are many detailed design and other technical considerations buyers should evaluate to ensure that they select the best equipment for their requirements.

RELEASE 7: Important Considerations in Selecting a Vacuum Furnace Water Cooling System

The proper selection of a water cooling system to support all aspects of vacuum furnace operation is a critical decision. This booklet highlights the advantages and disadvantages of various systems to help you determine which one will best suit your specific requirements.

(Release 8 was delayed indefinitely)

RELEASE 9: Understanding Vacuum and Vacuum Measurement

The purpose of this paper is to provide a better understanding of vacuum, including an explanation of vacuum, a definition and description of vacuum measuring instrumentation and an explanation of their application to vacuum furnace operation.

FURTHER THOUGHTS ON THE SUCCESS OF SOLAR ATMOSPHERES

A few bulleted points of information I've learned on my journey. I hope you find these helpful, and a practical starting point for your ventures.

INNOVATION

• Wherever possible, we invest in engineering projects that will repeat. We try to avoid one-time projects.

• We do file for patents, but this has become a very expensive process, and there is a doubtful return on the investment. There had better be a sound basis for investing in the patent process.

• Compare your business ratios monthly and—wherever possible—against industry standards.

EMPLOYEES

• All of our employees are on a sales incentive program paid as a ratio of sales to their pay rate, paid monthly. Our sales personnel and our executives are paid as much as 40% of their base salary as an incentive. This means all employees buy into company objectives.

• If we make a mistake, I try not to search for the guilty party or punish someone. I rather expect mistakes as tuition: learn and go on. Willful carelessness is another matter, though. We will not tolerate stealing, dishonesty, misuse of company computers, or falsification of data or expense accounts and the like.

ETHICS

• You need to set the example of work ethic. You need to be ever about "work" and thinking about how to develop the company and products. If need be, you work in the plant with the workers.

- The best work ethics are found in the Ten Commandments (Exodus 20)
- Final thoughts on business ethics: The following is a business ethics statement developed by our Solar management team a number of years ago. This type of statement is highly recommended to any operating or startup company: *Our mission is to add significant value to our customer's operations by thermally treating parts, principally in a vacuum environment, with an unwavering commitment to honesty in all relationships.*

MARKETING

- Lobby and housekeeping, office and plant are all part of your image and are important for visitors.
- A good informative, and *up to date* website is highly important in today's society. The Boeing Company issues a minimum of ten news releases per day, and lists them daily on their website. This cannot be overstated.
- We try to issue a news release each month to build our individual images and the image of the company.
- For the last ten years, we have sent a quarterly newsletter to each employee, customer, and supplier.
- We spend money on space advertising and compete on a dollar basis with the leaders in our industry.
- We attend trade shows as often as possible to meet old and new customers. In fact, we may attend as many as one trade show per month.
- We try to project the image that we are the authority in our field.

GENERAL

- We are active in both local and national technical societies, particularly ASM and MTI—much more so than our competition.

- I expect our key people to present a technical paper once each year before our technical societies. I do so myself, whenever possible.
- We are open and share our technology with customers and even competition. It does not really bother me to have someone copy some of our technology. After all, we will always be one step ahead. I particularly like the Biblical expression from Jesus, "Nor do people light a lamp and put it under a basket, but on a stand, and it gives light to all in the house. (Matthew 5:15 ESV)"
- I believe it is important for all management to be directly involved in production and sales wherever possible.

About the Authors

WILLIAM R. JONES is the founder and owner of several industry-leading companies in vacuum furnace technology and commercial heat treating: Vacuum Furnace Systems Corporation (1978); commercial heat-treating company Solar Atmospheres, with plants in Southeast Pennsylvania, Western Pennsylvania, Southern California, and Greenville South Carolina; a vacuum furnace manufacturing company Solar Atmospheres Manufacturing; and owner of Magnetic Specialties, a manufacturer of power supplies for vacuum furnaces as well as other special transformers, located in Southeastern Pennsylvania. Mr. Jones's entire career has been associated with the development and application of electromechanical products and, since 1962, with the vacuum heat treating furnace. He holds numerous patents in this field and has long been associated with the American Society for Materials (ASM), Metal Treating Institute, and related technical organizations. Mr. Jones is a Fellow of ASM International (1989), is the recipient of many awards, including the ASM International William Hunt

Eisenman Award (1995), the George H. Bodeen Heat Treating Achievement Award (2005), and the Metal Treating Institute Heritage Award (2013). He has contributed numerous articles for ASM, Metal Heat Treating and Industrial Heating magazines, and authored papers for the ASM Heat Treating Conference, as well as other technical organizations, including the Metal Treating Institute. He is also a member of the American Vacuum Society. Mr. Jones is an elder emeritus in the Presbyterian Church in America, and has served as a member of the Biblical Theological Seminary Board of Directors, in Hatfield, Pennsylvania. He and his wife, Myrt, have grown children and grandchildren who are also active in the Solar family of companies, now into the third generation.

HEATHER L. IDELL is currently a full-time writer, after a 20 year career in publishing, marketing, and communications in various industries. She was educated at the University of Pennsylvania, and spent a summer abroad at Oxford University studying playwriting. Ms. Idell makes her home in Bucks County, Pennsylvania with her partner and two children. This is her first book.

To order additional copies of this book, please contact Solar Atmospheres at info@solaratm.com.